COUNTRY HOUSE

LIGHTING

1660 · 1890

Financial assistance received from:

The Museums and Galleries Commission

The Marc Fitch Fund

The Sir George Martin Trust

The Paul Mellon Centre for Studies
in British Art (London) Ltd.

British Gas

Sugg Lighting Ltd.

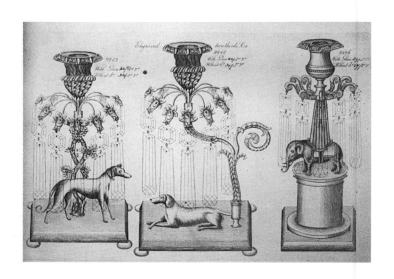

Page from a manufacturer's catalogue, early 19th century,
possibly Smith and Chamberlain of Birmingham

Contents

Foreword

The present exhibition is the fourth in a series devoted to neglected aspects of historic interiors which started in 1983 with *Historic Paper Hangings from Temple Newsam and other English houses*, which was followed by *The Fashionable Fireplace*, 1985 and *Country House Floors*, 1987. We are very happy that the present show will travel to a second venue at Brighton Museum and Art Gallery and are delighted to include in the catalogue an essay by Jessica Rutherford on the introduction of gas and electric lighting in the Royal Pavilion. Our survey ends just after the point when electricity first came to country houses.

Five members of Leeds City Art Galleries' staff, the Director, Anthony Wells-Cole, James Lomax, Daru Rooke and Adam White, have collaborated on investigating different aspects of this under-researched topic. At Brighton, the exhibition has been curated, designed and organised by David Beevers, together with Michael Jones and Shelley Tobin. An attempt has been made to break genuinely fresh ground, include as much original source material as possible and illustrate in the catalogue various objects which were not available for loan.

We are infinitely grateful to the Museums and Galleries Commission for making a generous grant from their Travelling Exhibition Fund towards the cost of the project at both venues. The Paul Mellon Centre for Studies in British Art (London) Ltd once again provided vital help with the cost of fieldwork, research and photography, while the Marc Fitch Fund enabled us, with a grant and an interest free loan, to produce a catalogue which is at least equally substantial as its predecessors. The Sir George Martin Trust made a handsome contribution and British Gas furnished extremely welcome sponsorship.

Everyone who needs to be thanked is hopefully named somewhere in this publication. However we wish to express special gratitude to Richard Littlewood, who took many of the photographs; to John Cornforth, Ian Gow, Martin Mortimer and Timothy Clifford, each of whom kindly allowed access to material in their personal files; to John Lord, who transcribed numerous documents in the Lincolnshire Record Office. Samantha Flavin typed much of the catalogue while countless librarians, archivists, administrators and others provided the essential assistance which is inseparable from a project of this nature. Finally, we wish to express our appreciation to the lenders without whom this exhibition would have remained a curator's dream.

Councillor Bernard Atha OBE
Chairman, Leeds Cultural Services Committee

Christopher Gilbert
Director of Leeds City Art Galleries

Bibliography

Accum Fredrick Accum, *A Practical Treatise on Gas-Light*, 1815

Accum 1820 Fredrick Accum, *Description of the Process of Manufacturing Coal Gas*, 1820

Adams Samuel and Sarah Adams, *The Complete Servant*, London 1825

Army and Navy 1907 *Yesterday's Shopping: The Army and Navy Stores 1907 catalogue*

Balston Thomas Balston (ed.), *The Housekeeping Book of Susanna Whatman 1776–1800*, 1956

Bourne and Brett Jonathan Bourne and Vanessa Brett, *Lighting in the Domestic Interior*, 1991

Burks Jean M.Burks, *Birmingham Brass Candlesticks*, 1986 (Charlottesville)

Campbell Robert Campbell, *The London Tradesman*, 1747

Cassell *Cassell's Book of the Household*, c.1890

Caspall John Caspall, *Making Fire and Light in the Home pre 1820*, 1987

Cecil Gwendolen Cecil, *Life of Robert, Marquis of Salisbury*, 1931

Chandler Dean Chandler, *Outline of the History of Lighting by Gas*, 1936

Chapman Martin Chapman, 'Flame and Fashion', *Traditional Interior Decoration*, Vol II, No.1, Summer 1987

Colvin C. Colvin (ed.), *Maria Edgeworth — Letters from England 1813–1844*

Cooper Diana Cooper, *The Rainbow Comes and Goes*, 1958

Cosnett Thomas Cosnett, *The Footman's Directory and Butler's Remembrancer...*, London 1825

DEF *Dictionary of English Furniture*, Ralph Edwards (ed.), 1954

Davidson Caroline Davidson, *A Woman's Work is Never Done*, 1982

Davis John D.Davis, *English Silver at Williamsburg*, 1976

Dower Pauline Dower, *Living at Wallington*, 1984 (Ashington, Northumberland)

Eller Irvin Eller, *The History of Belvoir Castle*, 1841

Fitzgerald Brian Fitzgerald, *Emily, Duchess of Leinster*, 1949

Fowler and Cornforth John Fowler and John Cornforth, *English Decoration in the 18th Century*, 1974

Gere Charlotte Gere, *Nineteenth Century Decoration: the art of the Interior*, 1989

Gilbert Christopher Gilbert, *Furniture at Temple Newsam and Lotherton Hall*, 1978 (Leeds)

Girouard Mark Girouard, *Life in the English Country House*, 1978

Girouard 1985 Mark Girouard, *The Victorian Country House*, 1985

Girouard 1987 Mark Girouard, *The Country House Companion*, 1987

Gore, John Gore (ed.), *Creevey's Life and Times*, 1934

Grierson H.J.C.Grierson (ed.), *The Letters of Sir Walter Scott*, 1932

Grimwade Arthur G.Grimwade, 'Silver at Althorp — The Candlestick and Candelabra', *Connoisseur* 152 (March 1963), pp.159–65

Hall Elisabeth Hall (ed.), *Michael Warton of North Bar House Beverley: An Inventory of his Possessions*, 1986 (Hull)

Harrison Rosina Harrison, *Gentlemen's Gentlemen*, 1976

Harrods 1895 *Victorian Shopping: Harrods 1895 Catalogue*

Hartcup Adeline Hartcup, *Below Stairs in the Great Country Houses*, 1980

Ilchester The Earl of Ilchester (ed.), *Elizabeth, Lady Holland to her Son, 1821–1845*, 1946

Kerr Robert Kerr, *The Gentleman's House*, 1871

Laing Alastair Laing, *Lighting*, 1982

Lomax 1986 James Lomax, 'Piranesi, Mr Messenger and the Duke of Newcastle', *Leeds Arts Calendar*, 98 (1986), pp.26–32

Lomax James Lomax, *British Silver at Temple Newsam and Lotherton Hall*, 1992 (Leeds)

Lutyens Emily Lutyens, *A Blessed Girl*, 1953

Mortimer Martin C.F.Mortimer, 'The English Glass Chandelier', *Handbook of International Ceramics Fair and Seminar*, 1987

O'Dea W.T.O'Dea, *The Social History of Lighting*, 1958

Orrinsmith Mrs Orrinsmith, *The Drawing Room*, 1878

Pinto Edward H.Pinto, *Treen and other Wooden Bygones*, 1969

Ridley *The Letters of Cecilia Ridley, 1819–1845*, 1958

Robins F.W.Robins, *The Story of The Lamp*

SG & FM, *The Servant's Guide and Family Manual*, 1830

Smith John P.Smith, *Osler's Crystal for Royalty and Rajahs*, 1991

Swift Jonathan Swift, *Directions to Servants and Miscellaneous Pieces 1733–42*, 1959 (Oxford)

TN 1666 etc *Temple Newsam Inventory*, with year, Leeds Archives Department

TN 1902 *Temple Newsam Inventory*, property of the Earl of Halifax

TN EA *Temple Newsam Papers*, Leeds Archives Department

Thornton 1978 Peter Thornton, *Seventeenth Century Interior Decoration in England, France and Holland*, 1978

Thornton 1984 Peter Thornton, *Authentic Decor: the Domestic Interior 1620–1920*, 1984

Timmins Samuel Timmins, *Birmingham and Midland Hardware District*, 1866

Wainwright Clive Wainwright, *The Romantic Interior*, 1989

Walton Peter Walton, *Creamware and other English Pottery at Temple Newsam House*, 1976 (Leeds)

Watkin David Watkin (ed.), *The Royal Interiors of Regency England, from watercolours first published by W.H.Pyne in 1817–20*, 1984

Williams *Footman and Butler*, c.1860

Wills Geoffrey Wills, *Candlesticks*, 1974 (Newton Abbot)

Lighting the Country House

The period with which we are concerned falls towards the end of the thousand year span in which candles of one sort or another provided the essential form of artificial lighting in northern Europe. It begins in the later 17th century, when the property-owning classes began to accumulate surplus wealth and use it to buy for themselves more luxurious ways of life, not dependent as hitherto on the hours of daylight; and it ends two hundred years later, with technical innovation and the wider spread of wealth combining to make artificial lighting generally available. During this time, numerous kinds of fittings — whether for candles, oil, gas or electricity — evolved to suit the particular needs of different types of rooms in country houses.

Candles of wax or tallow?

Although rush-lights or tapers of rush dipped in tallow were occasionally used in country houses during the 18th century (Sir Solomon Simon and his bride went to bed on their wedding night by rush-light) their light was feeble and candles were usually preferred. All candles were expensive whether made of tallow (animal fat, the best being a mixture of mutton and beef) or beeswax, the latter — costing three times as much as tallow and taxable, at 4d. a lb. in 1710, at eight times the rate — being preferred. During the course of the 18th century, however, candles of spermaceti (a wax refined from oil recovered from the head-cavities of sperm-whales) were introduced, but proved hardly less expensive, while stearine (from the fatty acids present in oils) and paraffin wax were employed during the 19th century.

Candles were generally made by the tallow and wax chandlers, incorporated as Companies in 1462 and 1484 respectively, although candles were also made on site by the Housekeeper. Robert Campbell, *The London Tradesman*, 1747, describes the commercial manufacturing techniques (pp.270–71):

Tallow Candles are made two Ways; in order to make the common store Candles the Tallow is first rendered and strained from the Skin and all Impurities in the Fat. The Wicks are made of Cotton spun for that Use; the Workmen cut them into the proper Lengths; the Tallow is melted and put into a Fat [vat] of boiling Water, which keeps it in constant Flow; the Wicks are ranged five or six upon a long small Stick, and placed upon Stands near the Fat; the Candle-Maker takes one of these Sticks by both Ends, plunges it into the Fat and takes it out again; this he lays down upon the Stands, and takes up another, until he has dipped them all; then he begins with the first and dips it again, and continues dipping them one after another till they are of the Thickness wanted.

Mould Candles are made thus; they have Moulds made of Lead, Tin, or Glass, of different Sizes, according as they intend to make Candles; the Wick is prepared of Cotton, the same as for Store-Candles, and fixed in the middle of the Mould. When all the Moulds are wick'd, the Tallow already rendered, is melted and poured into the Moulds, and is allowed to stand some time until the Tallow is perfectly congealed and cold, and then the Candle is drawn out...

Wax candles are made after a different Manner, they are neither cast in Moulds nor dipped, but rolled and drawn. They make Sealing Wax and Wafers, and Flambeaus, Links, &c...

The disadvantages of tallow had been characterised in Shakespeare's words, 'Base and unlustrous as the smokey light/That's fed with stinking tallow'; tallow melted at less than half the temperature of beeswax and tended to burn more quickly than the cotton wick, which consequently needed snuffing or trimming at very regular intervals. Attempts were made throughout the period to get candles to burn without guttering, but it was not until nearly the end of our period that this object was actually achieved. Both tallow and beeswax candles (whether English-made or imported) were liable to tax, first imposed in 1709 at the rates of a halfpenny a pound for tallow and fourpence a pound for wax, rates doubled in 1711 and made permanent six years after that. Like all taxes, they were constantly evaded necessitating still closer supervision, registration of candle-making premises and so on. The duties were repealed on 1 January 1832, although the manufacture of candles had already been suspended in anticipation of the measure. The loss of income to the government was considerable; figures for the last five years of the tax not only show the net product of the duty but the relative amounts of tallow to wax and spermaceti candles made (*The Penny Cyclopaedia*, VI, London 1836, p.236):

	Tallow lbs.	Wax/spermaceti lbs.	Net product of duty £
1826	110,102,643	907,405	467,101
1827	114,939,578	932,932	437,308
1828	117,342,157	1,018,556	497,953
1829	115,556,802	1,049,735	490,750
1830	115,586,192	1,265,113	482,413

From this it is clear that more than a hundred times the weight of tallow candles were made than of wax or spermaceti.

That candles were accepted indicators of a person's social position could not be better illustrated than by an incident that occurred in the 1770s (Fitzgerald, p.128):

Emily was at Leinster House, entertaining Lady Leitrim, when the 'Groom of the Chamber' came in and announced that the new tutor, Mr. Ogilvie, was come. 'Show him to his room,' said the Duchess. 'Please, your Grace, is he to have wax candles or tallow?' the butler asked. Upon which Emily turned to Lady Leitrim and said in French: 'Que pensez-vous?' 'Oh, moulds will do, till we see a little!' Such was the introduction of Mr William Ogilvie into the FitzGerald family.

Ironically, Mr Ogilvie, who had thus been denied the courtesy (or luxury) of a wax candle, later became Emily's husband.

Wax candles were mostly white but they were also available in colours, natural green wax from America or Barbados, or dyed with red lead or vermilion, green verdigris, yellow gamboge, lamp-black or ivory-black (Fowler and Cornforth, p.222; Wills, p.114).

They also came in standard sizes. Matteo Bianchi (agent to Rich, fifth Viscount Irwin, of Temple Newsam) reported that he had sent off from London, in the body of a coach for safe-keeping, '...ten Doz of Waxcandles. 5 Doz are 6 in ye pound & 5 Doz. are 4 in ye pound...' (Even in the 1890s Harrods were supplying candles in 4's, 6's, 8's and 12's.) The appropriate size of candles would have been selected according to the length of the evenings for which they were intended, the larger-sized, four-to-the-pound candles, costing 2s. 10d., being chosen for the entertainment for the King of Denmark at the Mansion House in London in 1768; the Lord Mayor was authorised to distribute the remainder of the wax candles to the servants after the entertainment.

The price was almost the same as candles supplied to Lord Monson a few years earlier in 1760 by John Coggs, 17/- for 6lb of Wax Candles and the same amount for the same weight of 'mortars' (thick wax night-lights). Spermaceti candles were almost as expensive: Sir John Filmer recorded, on 14 April 1758, 'Paid John Lorum in Naked Boy Court in the Strand, for 1 dozen [pounds] of spermaceti candles, no 3 to the pound, £1.7.0.' (Pinto, p.114). Tallow, on the other hand, were relatively inexpensive, Parson Woodforde recording in 1795 '...To Yollop, Haberdasher, for half a dozen pound of Kensington or London Mould candles, 4 to the lb. paid him 5/-...'

The choice of one size rather than another was made on the basis of how long it burnt, as the anonymous *Servants Guide and Family Manual* published in 1830 shows (p.67):

> ...wax candles, four in the pound, will last about eleven hours and should be used when the evening is expected to be five hours, as, in that case, each candle will serve two nights. Shorter candles, of six to the pound, are preferable when required to burn six or seven hours.

In late-Victorian times, at Naworth Castle in Cumberland, 'balls began at 8 or 8.30, and went on till 4.30 or 5. My mother said they used to go on longer — but I don't know how the candles could have lasted much more than ten hours. She said they had once gone on till 7.' (Dorothy Henley, *Rosalind Howard, Countess of Carlisle*, quoted in Girouard 1987, p.104.)

If only half-consumed, candles could be re-lit once, but it is unlikely that they would have been left in their candlesticks or sconces during the intervening hours of daylight; indeed, there are very few illustrations of unlit candles in

contemporary art. Refined notions of decorum, but more particularly the cost of candles ensured that the unburnt ends would have been removed to the store and replaced in the evening. Perhaps these factors also account for the provision at Burton Constable of false candles of marble with cotton wicks (Cat.52) which could be left in place without risk, to give the appearance of conspicuous well-being.

Lighting for families on their own

In country houses the cost of wax candles ensured that few were burnt when the family were on their own. It is said, for instance, that during the winter of 1765 at Audley End, only about twelve candles were burnt each night, and when Mrs Delany went to Holkham in 1774 she found that 'my Lady Leicester works at a tent-stitch frame every night by *one candle* that she sets upon it, and *no spectacles*.' Nor did the royal family behave very differently, as the Duchess of Northumberland found when she visited Queen Charlotte in her dressing room in 1772: the room

> being very large and hung with crimson damask, was very dark, there being only 4 candles on the Toilet [dressing table] & these being in Branches, and the King, wanting to shew us some improvement he had made in the stove, was obliged to carry one of them about in the nossell of the candlestick in his fingers.

Isaac Ware had noted, in his *Complete Body or Architecture* of 1746, that a room 'which if wainscoted will take six candles to light it, will in stucco require eight or if hung ten', and the cost of lighting was clearly a consideration when selecting wall finishes. At Wimpole, Philip Yorke, first Earl of Hardwicke, who died in 1764, reportedly sat with his wife 'discussing the painting of the room they usually sit in...my Lord was for having it an ash or olive colour as being the cheaper and more durable. But my Lady objected that, though more expensive, the fashionable French white would be cheaper in the end' since it enabled the room to be lit with two instead of four candles (The National Trust, *Wimpole Hall*, 1982, pp.56–57).

Even in the first decade of the 19th century, the relatively well-to-do Harden family of Brathay Hall in Westmorland huddled round a table illuminated by a one or two candles at most, as we know from the well-known drawings at Abbot Hall, Kendal. Similarly, Maria Edgeworth, writing in 1813 (Colvin, pp.15 & 35): 'I finish this my dearest aunt in the dark at Mr.Holland's at Knutsford...' and later she went on 'I have got a candle at last...' To Honora Edgeworth on 26 April 1813 she wrote 'I snatched it [the 'bit of wax candle Kitty gave me'] up from

Fig.1. Thomas Rowlandson, 'The Antiquarian and Death' from The English Dance of Death, 1815

the chimney piece and said I would put it in my box for that it might be of vast use to us at some place or other.'

When rooms were unoccupied and unlit because of the cost involved, other sources of light were relied upon, as Cecilia Ridley describes (Ridley, pp.47–48):

> As to lights — that is really one of the great difficulties in all houses and greatest expense. But I think it is not necessary to use all rooms at night. All being used in the daytime keeps all aired and comfortable, and fortunately having coals on the spot makes all the difference, for good fires you must always have, and in all the rooms, or you get cold smoke and it looks wretched and the said fires light for passing through to a certain extent.

Lighting for entertainments

By contrast with everyday illumination, little expense was spared when lighting a house for an entertainment, the unaccustomed effect and enormous cost usually calling for special comment, as when the Queen and the royal family dined at Claremont in 1729 (described by Peter Wentworth in a letter to Lord Strafford on 29 August, Girouard 1987, p.112):

> We walked till candle-light, being entertained with very fine french horns, then returned into his Great Hall, and everybody agreed that never was any thing finer lit.

In Hogarth's depiction of a wedding entertainment at a country house in the middle of the 18th century (illustrated on the Front Cover), the room is lit not only by the twelve-branch chandelier but from two-light sconces along the walls, while the casement of the bow window is thrown open to allow the moonlight to contribute. Many-branched chandeliers were extremely luxurious and might only have been lit very occasionally. Mrs Delany commented on measures taken by the Dowager Duchess of Portland at Bulstrode to welcome George III in 1779: 'Her Grace had the house lighted up in a most magnificent manner; the chandelier in the great hall was not lighted before for *twenty years*.' Far more lavish provision had been made half a century earlier at Houghton when Sir Robert Walpole entertained the Duke of Lorraine in 1731: Sir Thomas Robinson described how they 'dined in the hall which was lighted by 130 wax candles, and the saloon with 50; the whole expense in that article being computed at fifteen pounds a night' (Fowler and Cornforth, p.222). Special efforts were also made at Fawley Park in 1777 when ninety-two guests sat down to dinner in the hall, as Caroline Powys described in a letter on 17 January (Girouard 1987, pp.98–99):

> At half an hour after twelve the supper was announced, and the hall doors thrown open, on entering which nothing could be more striking, as you know 'tis do fine a one, and was then illuminated by three hundred colour'd lamps round the six doors, over the chimney, and over the statue at the other end.

When Lord Nelson and Emma Hamilton visited Fonthill in 1801, they were particularly impressed by the lighting, not only of the park and the exterior of the house but also of the interiors; in the Dining Room, for instance, the 'tables and side-boards glittered with piles of plate and a profusion of candle-lights'.

But no country house owner could compete with the lighting of the Lord Mayors' Banquet at Guildhall: in 1761, 1,200 guests were entertained and the room lighted by 'near 3000 wax tapers', reportedly at a cost of £92 4s. The sum included a payment of £20 to 'Denny for lighting them'. Incidentally, candles could be lit almost simultaneously by connecting them together with a long thread of cotton dipped in sulphur, as at the coronation of George II in 1727 when the 1,800 candles at Westminster Hall (apart from those on the tables) were 'all lighted in less than three minutes' (Wills, pp.117–18).

Wax candles remained a symbol of luxurious living in the 19th century, as Thackeray makes clear in *Vanity Fair* (1848, chapter XI):

> When she [Miss Crawley] is come into the country our Hall is thrown open, and for a month, at least, you would fancy old Sir Walpole was come to life again. We have dinner parties and drive out in the coach and four...We have wax candles in the schoolroom and fires to warm ourselves with.

The Duke of Rutland certainly did not skimp on candles at Belvoir (Eller, p.329, note):

> Consumption of Ale, Wax-lights, &c. from December, 1839, to April, 1840, or about eighteen weeks...Wax-lights, 2330; sperm oil, 630 gallons. Dined at his Grace's table, 1997 persons; in the steward's room, 2421; in the servants' hall, nursery and kitchen departments, including comers and goers, 11,312 persons.

Because of the cost, rooms were usually illuminated only when they were occupied. Under exceptional circumstances lights were left burning all night as at Windsor, where George III was confined in his madness, and at lesser houses: a set of instructions perhaps dating from 1811 urges the Butler to enable the Laundry-maids to make an early start by ensuring that 'The night preceding a light must be left burning all night for the maids to get up by. To take care that it is put in a safe place and without risk of fire.' At the Mansion House in London, the specification for a contract drafted around 1798 specifies which lights were to be kept burning in this way (City Lands Contracts, vol.2 (131B), p.216):

> Particular of the Lamps at the Mansion House and Description of the manner of finding and providing the same with Cotton and Oil and for properly trimming and keeping the same in good repair for one year.
>
> The Lamps hereinafter mentioned are to be from time to time duly supplied with a sufficient quantity of good Cotton and such good and proper oil as will burn dry except the Patent Lamp over the kitchen steps which must be furnished with the best Spermaceti Oil, The Twelve lamps at present with double Lens burners are to provided instead thereof with common four spout burners...These together with the six

common two spout burners and the two spout lanthorn at the back staircase in the inside are to be lighted and constantly kept burning from Sun setting until Sunrising and once or oftener in every Night properly snuffed and trimmed and once at least in every week well and properly cleansed...The Patent Lamp over the Kitchen steps and the four two spout lanthorns there are to be trim'd and lighted by sun rise and to be kept burning and properly snuffed and trimmed and supplied with oil during the whole of the day and till one oclock of the morning following...

A contract was eventually signed with Thomas Patrick (described as 'Citizen and Tin Plate Worker') for this work.

Candles were not always discarded after being burnt for one evening for at Longleat the candle boy had to break the hardened wax off the sides of the hundred and forty candles in the chapel and 're-point them into shape so that they looked as if they had not been used. This was a daily drill and the candles were relit until they were down to their last two inches. Then they were allowed as perks to the candle boy, who made an extra few shillings each year by selling them to the local grocer.' (Hartcup, p.61).

Lighting and the servants

By contrast with the family, particularly at formal entertainments, their servants fared badly. Much of their life in winter must have passed in darkness: at Woburn Abbey — a house which would not have been exceptional — 'Stores were given out to the servants at the Abbey every month, and quantities varied according to the time of year. In the two summer quarters (25 March to 29 September) fourteen candles a month were dealt out to the housemaids, still-room maid, and office maids, and they had twice as many during the winter...The kitchen-maids had to make do with only fourteen candles between the lot of them each month, as it was reckoned that they used oil to light the kitchen, and during the summer they did not need more than six to eight candles a month.' (Hartcup, p.167.)

Unconsumed candle-ends from the houses were generally considered to be legitimate perks for servants, as Swift suggested in his *Advice to Servants* in 1729:

> Snuff the candles with your fingers then throw the snuff on the floor, then tread it out to prevent stinking: this method will make them run and so increase the perquisite of the cook's kitchen stuff, for she is the person you ought in prudence to be well with.

However, rather than using them themselves, servants sold them to grocers to enhance their wages and income from the sale of unburnt candle-ends from St.James's Palace is said to have provided the original Messrs. Fortnum and Mason, two footmen at the Court of Queen Anne, with sufficient capital to set up in business (Pinto, p.114). The system was clearly open to abuse. A set of instructions to servants published about 1811, urges the Butler 'To receive candles from the Housekeeper, and not to allow the Footmen to ask for them', and evidence that the cost of allowing servants in the royal households to appropriate unburnt portions of candles as perks had become unacceptable is provided by a memorandum dated 23 January 1813, which gives a fascinating insight into contemporary practices (Taylor Papers, Royal Archives 50267-9, quoted here by gracious permission of Her Majesty The Queen):

It having occurred that the only effectual check to the excessive expenditure in the Article of Wax Candles would be the total Extinction of the Purquisites, or nearly that, Colonel Taylor [Lt. General Sir Herbert Taylor, Private Secretary to George III, Queen Charlotte and William IV] submitted to the Queen the following Regulations which were approved and accordingly conveyed to Lord Winchelsea and Mr Stephenson.

That *whole* Candles should be issued every Evening for the Queen's Private Apartments and those in which Her Majesty receives Her Company, but that the Remains should, on the following morning, be returned into the store, to be applied to the Inferior Apartments, or to light the Passages leading to the Queen and the Princess's Rooms.

That the Princesses having stated that they had occasion for only four Candles (instead of six actually issued for their Rooms) and that even these are only in small part consumed, it is proposed that four Candles only should be issued for each of their Apartments and should be considered as issued for two or three Evenings use according to the Season.

N.B. It has frequently been the practice of the Princesses Pages to receive [reserve] the whole Candles issued for one Evening's use and to place only the Ends of others in the Royal Highness's Rooms and very often not to supply any for the outer Rooms. Those for the Passages (altho' issued *whole*) have been either so short or so soon extinguished as to leave the Passages dark at an early Hour.

That the Candles for the Royal Duke's Apartments should be issued under the same Regulation, but if they staid only one Night, the Remains should be returned on the following morning to the Store.

That Candles should be issued to the Ladies and Visitors, in the Proportion of two *to each Individual*, not two to each Room as at present and should serve for two or three Evening's use.

That the Passages (those leading to the Queen's and Princesses's Rooms excepted) should be lighted with Spermacite Oil from which there is no smell, instead of Wax.

That the Regulations which apply to the Apartments of the Royal Family should be subject to such occasional infraction as they should deem proper or necessary.

That the Candles in the Upper Lodge for the Dining and Sitting Rooms should be issued *whole* and the Remains returned to Store on the following morning. Those for the Gentlemen's and the Visitors' Rooms on the same Principle which is applied to the Apartments of the Ladies in the Castle, and that Spermaceti Oil should be burnt in the Passages throughout the building.

As Candles are necessarily burnt in three of the King's Rooms throughout the Night, the only regulation which appears applicable to His Majesty's Apartment is that they shall be issued for such Rooms only as are actually occupied.

For their own use, servants generally had pewter or tin versions of the family's silver fittings and they naturally came in for hard usage, as Jonathan Swift's facetious advice indicates:

The servants' candlesticks are generally broken, for nothing can last for ever. But you may find out many expedients: you may conveniently stick your candle in a bottle, or with a lump of butter against the wainscot, in a powder-horn, or in an old shoe, or in a cleft stick, or in the barrel of a pistol, or upon its own grease on a table, in a coffee-cup, or a drinking glass, a horn-can, a tea-pot, a twisted napkin, a mustard-pot, and ink-horn, a marrow-bone, a piece of dough, or you may cut a hole in the loaf, and stick it there...

Some unusual expedients were indeed devised to allow servants to carry on their work in poor light, as at Longleat where the dustpans were provided with thumb-holes to enable the housemaid to dust with one hand and hold the pan and a candle with the other (Hartcup, p.69), oddly prefiguring the headlight on some modern vacuum cleaners.

The duties of servants in providing light

The family rarely had to worry about the practicalities of artificial lighting beyond controlling the expenditure: most of the hard work was left to servants. In the 18th century responsibility for buying and, sometimes, making candles seems to have rested on the Housekeeper, as at Cannons, the Duke of Chandos's house in Middlesex, where she was expected to have 2,400 lb. of wax always in stock, sufficient for two candlemaking sessions in the house. At five candles to the pound, 140 lbs. of wax would have made 700 candles, each candle using less than 1d. worth of wax (Fowler and Cornforth, p.222). Her 19th century equivalent's duties were spelled out by Samuel and Sarah Adams, in *The Complete Servant*, 1825:

CANDLES and SOAP made in cold weather, are best; and when the price of these articles are likely to be high, a reasonable stock of both should be laid in. — Candles, if kept packed in a chest, will be the better for keeping eight or ten months, and may be kept well, if necessary, for two years.

The Housekeeper also presided over the store room (sometimes associated with the kitchen), issuing candles and ensuring that the candlesticks were cleaned by the scullion or under-cook. The silver light-fittings, on the other hand, were under the control of the Butler who guarded them in the Butler's Pantry or Plate Closet overnight and ensured that they were cleaned next morning and ready for use. The distinction is discernible at

Fig.2.   The Lamp-room at Port Eliot in Cornwall

a middle-class level in an inventory of the belongings of Michael Warton at North Bar House in Beverley in 1688: he was MP for Beverley for twenty-eight years and had married Susanna Powlett, the daughter of Lord Powlett of Hinton St. George in Somerset. The base metal fittings were stored in 'the garrett over best Chamber...In a Large press (vizt) 1 pare of Candlesticks 1 Tinn Sconce 1 pare of brass candlesticks'; these were made of pewter. The Pantry contained, on the other hand:

1 pare Large candlesticks wth socketts
1 pr. of Lesser Candlesticks wth socketts } brass
1 sconce Dyningerome Stairs head
1 Candlestick & tinderbox all in one } Tinn
1 extinguisher & Savall

and fifteen candlesticks, '1 pr of them wth scrues to make Fruit Dishes 13 sockets [for Candlesticks] 4 snuffers & plates for (the)m and 4 Extinguishers' were included in a list of Plate (Hall, pp.31, 36, 38).

In grander circumstances, at the Blathwayt's house, Dyrham Park near Bath, in 1710 the Pantry contained '11 : high Brass & 11 hand Candlesticks 7 Pr: of Snuffers 4 Extinguishers' while outmoded fittings were relegated to the 'Garret over ye: Brewhouse Lumber Room' which contained '1: Trunk wth: old Brass Sconces, Hand Irons, Candlestick etc.' (*Furniture History* XXII (1986), p.66.) At Kiveton Hall, the Duke of Leeds's grand country house near Sheffield, the lights were stored in 1727 in a room called the Wardrobe:

5 Pr. of Brass Sconces Silver'd
20 Pr. of Brass Candlesticks
10 Snuff pans, & 2 pr. of Snuffers Do.
3 Tinder Box Candlesticks
1 Hand Candlestick...

In the catalogue of the sale of the Duke of Chandos's house at Cannons in 1747 the lights were clearly kept in 'The Kitchen and Offices adjoining Four high brass candlesticks, and 19 hand ditto 0-10-6'.

After the introduction of more convenient forms of lighting candlesticks were kept under the eye of the housemaid, as Robert Kerr, writing in 1871, makes clear (Kerr, p.322):

HOUSEMAID'S CLOSET...This is generally a small apartment, with proper light and ventilation, in which the housemaid keeps pails, dusters, candlesticks, a coalbox, &c, for the service of the Bedrooms...

The servants were also responsible for lighting candles, either from the fire by using a taper, or from a tinder-box containing a fire-steel and flint, tinder (or charred rag) to catch the spark and sometimes a sulphur match to help this burst into flame. This cannot always have been easy, particularly when the fittings were attached out of reach on walls, or suspended from the ceiling as with chandeliers, although these were often provided with counter-balances — or, if Hogarth's painting of an Assembly at Wanstead is to be believed, the <u>line</u> might be looped over the hook in the ceiling and fastened back to the wall, allowing the chandelier to be lowered to within reach. Thomas Cosnett recommended in 1825 using 'a small cane or stick with a wax-taper tied at the end, and an extinguisher'.

Once alight, the wicks, particularly of tallow candles, needed their 'cottons' or wicks trimming or snuffing every few minutes otherwise their wicks would burn too slowly and topple over, melting the tallow at one side. Snuffers, in the form of scissors with a box attached to the blades to catch the bits of wick removed, were the answer and these were often integral with 'flat' or chamber candlesticks. Douters, of similar form, or conical extinguishers of the kind we mistakenly call snuffers today were used to put out the flame. Swift lists a number of other means servants could use instead:

...there are several ways of putting out candles, and you ought to be instructed in them all: you may run the candle-end against the wainscot, which puts the snuff out immediately; you may lay it on the ground, and tread the snuff out with your foot: you may hold it upside down, until it is choked with its own grease; or cram it into the socket of the candlestick: you may whirl it round in your hand until it goes out: you may spit on your finger and thumb, and pinch the snuff until it goes out. The cook may run the candle's nose into the meal-tub, or the groom into a vessel of oats, or a lock of hay, or a heap of litter: the house-maid may put her candle out by running it against a looking-glass, which nothing cleans so well as candle-snuff: but the quickest and best of all methods is, to blow it out with your breath, which leaves the candle clear, and readier to be lighted.

He also had some suggestions for ways in which servants could save themselves trouble, by encouraging their employers to economise on candles:

Let your sockets be full of grease to the brim, with the old snuff at the top, and then stick on fresh candles. It is true, this may endanger their falling, but the candles will appear so much the longer and handsomer before company. When your candle is too big for the socket, melt it to a right size in the fire, and to hide the smoke, wrap in a paper half-way up. Sconces are great wasters of candles, therefore your business must be to press the candle with both your hands into the socket, so as to make it lean in such a manner that the grease may drop all upon the floor, if some lady's head-dress or gentleman's periwig be not ready to intercept it; you may likewise stick the candle so loose that it will fall upon the glass of the sconce and break into shatters; this will save yourself much labour, for the sconces spoiled cannot be used.

The servants' responsibilities lasted until night-time, as Susannah Whatman indicates, in sensible instructions compiled after 1778 (Thomas Balston (ed.), *The Housekeeping Book of Susanna Whatman 1776–1800*, 1956, pp.34, 43–44):

The Housekeeper and Butler should see all fires and candles out before they go to bed.

The Servants' Guide and Family Manual (1830, p.252) describes the main division of responsibility in the first half of the 19th century: 'The lighting of rooms is generally attended to by the Butler, the lights or lamps having previously been prepared by the Footman...'

The proliferation of lamps necessitated specialised Lamp Men, as at Osborne on the Isle of White: in the Census

Returns for 1861, John Cocking, William Johnson and George Grinell were given the occupation of 'lamplighter'; as their addresses were noted as Middlesex, London, and Berks, Windsor they were presumably employed primarily in other palaces and moved to Osborne when required there. The introduction of gas for lighting also brought the need for special skills. At Culzean in Ayrshire the gas house was built in 1840 and equipment installed somewhat later; this was superintended by the Gas Manager who was clearly an important member of staff and had a cottage on the estate where he lived with his family.

The Servants' Guide and Family Manual continues, 'Among the other regular in-door duties of the Footman are taking up the supper-tray, and the night-candlesticks.' The chamber candlesticks had sometimes been left to the chambermaid, as in Molly Philipps's poem describing an evening with Sir John Philipps at Picton Castle in Pembrokeshire in 1754 (Girouard 1987, p.34):

> Now Sir John shuts his book, and my Lady's awake,
> The chambermaid's called for the candles to take.

On the other hand, Prince Puckler-Muskau found that, at Cobham Hall in 1829,

> A light supper of cold meats and fruits is brought, at which everyone helps himself, and shortly after midnight all retire. A number of small candlesticks stand ready on a side-table; every man takes his own, and lights himself up to bed; for the greater part of the servants, who have to rise early, are, as is fair and reasonable, gone to bed.' (*Tour in Germany, Holland and England*, 1832, Girouard 1987, p.54.)

In these circumstances the family and guests had to look after themselves. They would have had to when staying in a hotel — Thackeray describes, in the seedy Elephant Hotel in Pumpernickel whither Becky Sharp fled after her disgrace,

> ...the great room common to all frequenters of the Elephant, out of which the stair led. This apartment is always in a fume of smoke, and liberally sprinkled with beer. On a dirty table stand scores of corresponding brass candlesticks with tallow candles for the lodgers, whose keys hang up in rows over the candles.

Much the same system applied in the very different circumstances of Wallington in Northumberland within living memory. Pauline Dower, the eldest of six children of Sir Charles and Lady Trevelyan, recalled (in *Living at Wallington*, Ashington, Northumberland, 1984, pp.12–13):

> The bedroom lamps would be in charge of the head housemaid and would be filled and trimmed in the housemaid's pantry at the top of the back stairs. Every evening a row of silver candlesticks were set out on a table at the foot of the big staircase, and we each went upstairs to bed with our own one candle.

After the servants had retired, lighting a candle (or a lamp) in the middle of the night was left to each individual. Some took precautions against being left in the dark, as John

Aubrey says of William Oughtred (*Brief Lives*, Penguin edition, p.383):

> Stayed late at night; went not to bed till eleaven a clock; had his tinder box by him; and on top of his Bed-Staffe, he had his inke horne fix't.

Michael Warton of North Bar House, Beverley, had '1 Candlestick & tinderbox all in one' in 1688, perhaps for the same purpose. The universal problem of telling the time during the night could be solved, for those not wealthy enough to own a repeater watch, by a clock-lamp of the kind advertised in *The Daily Post* on 6 January 1731:

> WALKER'S Original new invented CLOCK-LAMP, BEING a most complete Machine, and so artfully contriv'd that it shews the Hours of the Night, supplying at once the Use of a Clock and Candle, and has been approved of by the most ingenious. 'Tis managed with so little Trouble, and so very neat, that it neither daubs the Fingers nor the Place where it stands, as others do; especially the counterfeit Lamp sold in Paternoster-Row, where you are oblig'd to take out the Oiley Cotton, and thrust your Thumb into the Oil every time 'tis lighted. In short, hardly a person that has Occasion to keep a Light in the Night, if they knew the Conveniency of them, would be without one.

Walker's clock-lamp was an inexpensive and simple device compared with those like Schmalcalder's of the Strand in London, a hundred years later, which projected an image of the polished silver concave dial onto the wall (R.W.Symonds, 'The Night Clock from Mediaeval Times — II', *Country Life*, 15 October 1948, Fig.6).

Boswell experienced difficulties when staying in a lodging house — it might equally well have been a country house after the servants had gone to bed (Laing, pp.38–39):

> I determined to sit up all night...about two o'clock in the morning I inadvertently snuffed out my candle, and as my fire before that was long before black and cold, I was in a great dilemma how to proceed. Downstairs did I softly and silently step to the kitchen. But, alas, there was as little fire there as upon the icy mountains of Greenland. With a tinder box is a light struck every morning to kindle the fire, which is put out at night. But this tinder box I could not see, nor knew where to find. I was also apprehensive that my landlord, who always keeps a pair of loaded pistols by him, might fire at me as a thief. I went up to my room, sat quietly until I heard a watchman calling 'past three o'clock'. I then called out to him to knock at the door of the house where I lodged. He did so, and I opened to him and got my candle relumed without danger.

Some people were careless. Becky Sharp had in her hotel room 'a French novel...on the table by the bedside, with a candle not of wax' and 'a little paper nightcap with which she had put the candle out on going to sleep'. Rowlandson graphically illustrated the dangers of reading in bed in 'The Antiquarian and Death' from *The English Dance of Death* published in 1815 (Fig.1) and, of the 110 fires caused by candles in London in 1835, fifty-two were occasioned by bed-curtains catching alight. Country houses were not exempt from such calamity. Emily Mary, Dowager Marchioness of Salisbury, lost her life in just such circumstances, as described by Elizabeth, Lady Holland, in a letter to her son on 1 December 1835 (Ilchester, pp.158–59):

> This dreadful catastrophe at Hatfield drives everything out of one's mind. The poor old lady fell a victim to her wilfulness. She never allowed any of her attendants to be with her. She had the habit of perpetually dropping asleep, & had been on fire frequently. No vestige of her, nor her diamonds have been found...Fortunately the magnificent old structure is not destroyed. MSS., Library & State rooms are all safe; offices and bedrooms are burnt. But the injury is not so great as we dreaded, except in the loss of the poor old lady, which is very horrible.

Even when lamps had been introduced, the lack of instantaneous illumination at night gave problems (Girouard 1987, p.92):

> Lord Charles Beresford told my grandfather that on one occasion he tiptoed into a dark room and jumped into the vast bed shouting 'Cock-a-doodle-doo', to find himself, when trembling hands had lit a paraffin lamp, between the Bishop of Chester and his wife. The situation seemed very difficult to explain and he left the house before breakfast next morning.

There were other circumstances in which servants were not expected to be on hand to provide illumination, William Wyndham requiring that there 'must be a good broad place to set a candle on...' in his earth-closet at Felbrigg in 1751 (Girouard 1987, p.172).

Simple spout lamps had been used during the 18th century and P.Montague's *The Family Pocket Book* (?1768, p.55) outlines a tip '*To prevent the smoaking of lamp-oil*. Steep your Match, or Cotton, in Vinegar, and dry it well before you use it. Many families have spoke much in Praise of this.' By the early 19th century, however, relatively complex Argand-type lamps had become the standard way to light a country house and their numbers meant that maintaining artificial light was a soul-destroying chore, which was avoided if possible. Thomas Cosnett vividly describes in *The Footman's Directory and Butler's Remembrancer...*, 1825, the inconvenience and unpleasantness of the tasks and affords incidentally an comprehensive picture of how lighting was provided and used:

> TRIMMING AND CLEANING OF LAMPS. Lamps are now so much used in dining and drawing rooms, as well as in halls and in staircases, that it is a very important part of a butler's or footman's work to keep them clean, and enable each to give a good light. I have seen houses almost filled with the smoke from lamps, and the stench of the oil; and all the glass parts clouded with dust and soot, through the cottons being left too long, or put too high up. This is a most disagreeable thing, enough to make the company cross or melancholy. It is not always a servant's fault, however, that lamps do not burn well; for unless good oil, and plenty of it, is allowed, no one can make them do so: but it is a servant's fault if they are dirty, or out of order. Where ladies or gentlemen are frequently changing their servants, the lamps are sure to be neglected.

Fig.3. The range of cupboards in the Port Eliot Lamp-room

> Every one who comes thinks they will last his time, and they are thus left month after month with the oil standing in them, till they are quite gummed up, and all the trimming in the world will not make them burn clear, when they are in such a state... [p.24; then follow detailed instructions for cleaning lamps.]
>
> Lamps for drawing-rooms and dining-rooms often have from two to six burners; you must be careful, after taking them to pieces, not to mismatch them, as that may cause you a great deal of confusion, when you are in a hurry. [p.26.]
>
> Use wax tapers, or matches without brimstone for lighting them [the lamps]; but not paper; as it not only flies about and makes dirt, but likewise the burnt part of it will stick to the cotton, and make it burn uneven. If you have any doubt as to your lamps burning well, light them a little before they are wanted, or even the night before; for, if any disaster should occur, and you should not find it out till the company are on the point of making their appearance, it will cause you great confusion and perhaps the breaking of some parts of the lamps in your bustle; besides, as they are often hung over the dining table, and cannot be reached without steps, consider how disagreeable it would be to have to trim them afresh, at a moment above all others when you have the least time to spare. [p.28.]

Cosnett continues:

> If you should be puzzled how to manage any of the lamps, always ask, rather than run any risk by guessing about them; and if no one in the house can tell you, go to some place where lamps are sold, and there you can get proper instructions on the subject.

It sometimes happens that the links of the chain from which the different lamps may be suspended, come open, or the cords wear out, thus causing the lamps to fall: this you must guard against, by often inspecting them, and getting them repaired or replaced as occasion may require; which will be a mere trifle in point of expense; whilst, on the contrary, a handsome lamp falling on the ground, and perhaps hitting somebody on the head in its way, is a matter of no little cost, and may involve a serious degree of danger.

Always leave the candles set up in the morning ready, particularly the hand candlesticks, as they may be wanted to seal a letter with in the course of the day; the others ought also to be ready, for, if they should be wanted in a hurry, you will most likely break the candles in putting them in; besides the disagreeableness of keeping your master or mistress waiting, and throwing yourself into confusion. [p.35.]

Always light the candles to burn off the cotton, before you set them up, but leave the ends long enough to be lighted with ease again, when they are wanted. If you have any candlesticks with several branches, you must be very particular in having the candles firm and upright in them, and, if they be too big for the sockets, scrape them carefully, so that you can put them far enough in, not to endanger their falling out when you move the candlestick...Be careful to keep your candles clean; for this you should have a drawer or box with a partition, so that the snuffs and scrapings may be in one part and the candles in the other. Always scrape the pieces before you put them into the drawer or box, then they will be ready for use. If the candles should have guttered down, you should take off the wax or tallow with a smooth-edged knife, but never use one with a notched edge, as it will scratch them. If the wax candles should get dirty at any time, or turn yellow, rub them with a piece of flannel, dried in spirit of wine, which will clean them, and make them look well. Always keep the whole candles by themselves, and let the pieces be scraped, and put into a drawer or box wrapped in paper, which will keep them from getting dirty, likewise the snuffs from being broken off too short, which makes them difficult to light, and causes them to gutter as soon as they are lighted. [p.36.]

In those small parties the company in general play at cards, and therefore observe to have all the lamps and candles lighted up in the drawing-room, before they come. If there be glass chandeliers or sconces, and if they be so high that you cannot reach them without steps, you had better have a small cane or stick with a wax-taper tied at the end, and an extinguisher; if you have this, you will be enabled to light them, and put them out, without having to bring the steps into the room, which is very inconvenient at such times: always prepare your candles before you set them up, that they may be ready to light without much trouble. I hope you will never attempt to blow them out, when the company are gone, with your *mouth*, or even a pair of *bellows*, as this is both dirty and very dangerous. [p.146.]

Let the lights in the drawing room and parlour be put out with the extinguisher, as before directed; and the lamps will be turned down, not blown out; let the thing which is to keep the oil in the lamp be put up, when you put it out, which will prevent the oil from overflowing, as it is apt to do when it is warm. [p.151.]

By the middle of the nineteenth century artificial lighting was provided by the traditional candles, together with candle-lamps, oil-lamps, spirit-lamps and gas. Most of these forms of lighting had been the subject of inventions

to improve their performance. Candles of stearine and of margerine mixed with tallow were introduced, while Palmer's candles, in which the wick bent out of the flame ensuring complete combustion of the cotton, were patented in 1842; this was achieved, as *The National Cyclopaedia* described,

by twisting the wick with one thread shorter than the rest, by coating one of the wicks with bismuth or by adding a mixture of borax, bismuth, flour, and charcoal, in the form of a paste, to one side of the wick. Wicks of the two latter descriptions are termed *metallic* wicks.

Candle-lamps for burning these and ordinary candles were developed by firms like Dibben's (Cat.50): as the *Supplement* to *The Penny Cyclopaedia* recorded in 1845 (II, pp.203–05), they have

...a conical cap to keep the candle within the tube, and a spiral spring in the lower part of the tube to press the candle upwards as it burns...These candlesticks, and the candles belonging to them, offer the two conveniences of maintaining the light always at an equal height, and of dispensing with the aid of the snuffers. Some sort of shade or globe is necessary for realising the latter of these two benefits fully...

Oil lamps also needed development because of the tendency of the oil to thicken in cold weather. Mechanical methods were employed to raise the oil to the wick, clockwork in the French sperm-oil Carcel lamp, a reservoir with an internal piston, activated by an external screw and nut, in the English colza oil Meteor lamp. Thinner oils distilled from shale and coal, such as kerosene (first sold as a lamp oil in America in 1846), paraffin (introduced in England during the same decade but patented in its present form by James Young in 1850) and camphine (from turpentine) were perfected; these fed the wick by capillary action rather than by gravity, from a reservoir 'generally of glass, placed between the supporting column and the burner; the spirit is contained in this reservoir, and a cotton wick is seen to dip down into it.'

Experiments showed the relative costs of the various fuels in producing the same level of lighting: using an Argand gas flame as standard, an Argand oil lamp proved nearly four times as expensive, or with sperm oil eight times; a tallow candle with a single wick was nearly fourteen times as costly, a wax candle almost twenty-six times as expensive and a spermaceti candle all but thirty. But the chief drawback of any lamp was its emissions. Heat could be countered by providing glass shades (called *calottes*) or Talc Smoke Consumers above the lamp (Cat.101) but the pollution was a different matter. The eminent scientist Dr. Michael Faraday was consulted, following

...a complaint, on the part of the members of the Athenaeum Club, that the air of their library was vitiated and the binding of the books injured by the lamps then used...Oil and gas each contains carbon and hydrogen, and each requires the addition of oxygen to bring about combustion...the substances which result from it are mainly two — water, by the combination of some of the oxygen with the hydrogen; and carbonic acid, by

Fig.4. Zinc-topped table with lamps in the Port Eliot Lamp-room

the combination of more of the oxygen with the carbon...'A pint of oil, when burned, produces a pint and a quarter of water, and a pound of gas more than two and a half pounds of water; the increase of weight being due to the absorption of oxygen from the atmosphere, one part of hydrogen taking eight parts (by weight) of oxygen to form water. A London Argand gas-lamp, in a closed shop window, will produce in four hours two pints and a half of water; a pound of oil also produces nearly three pounds of carbonic acid, and a pound of gas two and a half pounds of carbonic acid. For every cubic foot of gas burned, rather more than a cubic foot of carbonic acid is produced.'

The invention in 1884 of the very much more efficient in-candescent gas mantle, which consumed 70% less gas than other burners, reduced the emissions, but the effect of oil and gas lighting on the decoration and furnishings of rooms was catastrophic. Nonetheless, country houses continued to be lit by oil or gas as late as the 1950s. By then electricity had been introduced into most although, despite its cleanliness and convenience, even this technology met with some resistance — as Catherine Cumfrit found when she went to stay with her daughter and middle-aged clergyman son-in-law (in Elizabeth von Arnim's *Love*, 1925):

Virginia looked at her mother for a moment, and then fetched the bedroom candles from the table they had been put ready on,

the electric light now being cut off by Stephen's wish at half-past ten each night...Catherine, not used to bedroom candles, held hers crooked and dropped some grease on the carpet, and Virginia had the utmost difficulty in strangling an exclamation. Stephen did so much dislike grease on the carpets.

Lamp-rooms

Cleaning and refilling oil lamps and trimming their 'cottons' were unpleasant jobs relegated to a special room. The Lamp Closet at Hornby Castle in 1834 (Yorkshire Archaeological Society, DD5, Box 12, item 4) contained:

2 Lamp fillers, 2 Do Trays, 2 Funnels
8 Brass pedestal Lamps on Bronze stands
12 Japan & hanging Lamps
5 Do Reflecting Do
3 Hand Lamps
5 Wire Lanterns
9 Brass Lamps one burner each
2 Do 2 burners each
4 Do 3 Do Do
5 Globes 24 Chimnies
3 Lamp Cans

The four hundred lamps used at Longleat were 'brought by housemaids, footmen, and other servants to the lamp room every day. They were cleaned, trimmed, and filled by the candle boy, who was helped by the hall boy, the steward's room boy, and the odd men. They did them in batches of twenty at a time, bringing in others as each lot was finished. The great lamps which hung from the ceilings on chains were too heavy to move, so they had to be groomed and filled where they were.' (Hartcup, pp.61–61.)

By all accounts the Lamp-Rooms at Belvoir Castle were the best-appointed in England, as Irvin Eller writing in 1841 makes clear (Eller, pp.328 & 334):

> ...when with difficulty she had been persuaded to visit the Lamp-rooms — a not very attractive region by anticipation to a courtly lady — [she] was beyond measure astonished and gratified at the excellence of the arrangements, and their entire freedom from any thing that could disgust or annoy...The Lamp-Rooms are considered to be the most complete in their arrangements in the kingdom. The lamps are filled over cisterns, which receive the unavoidable waste of oil in the operation. The waste thus collected is afterwards used in the offices, &c. In the season of his Grace's residence, about sixteen or seventeen weeks, 400 burners are required, and about 600 gallons of oil consumed. The roofs are vaulted and groined, and every part fire-proof.

Kerr enlarges on the furniture of lamp-rooms:

> In Country-Houses where oil-lamps have to be used, it becomes necessary to provide, near the Kitchen, Servants'-Hall, or Butler's-Pantry, according to the scale of the house, a small LAMP-ROOM for trimming these, and indeed for depositing them during the day. It must contain a *table, shelves* around the walls, and perhaps a locked *cupboard*, or an inner closet, to receive the oil-cans and some of the valuable lamps. In smaller houses, candlesticks pertain to the Housemaid's Closet; and it is not uncommon to combine that apartment with the Lamp-room, or to make the latter and inner closet to the former. All silver of this department goes to the Butler's-Pantry for safety. [p.234.]

The lamp-room at Speke Hall near Liverpool (a house which was lit by lamps until 1935) contained in 1917:

Painted deal Lamp Cupboard.
Oil drum & Tin.
2 oil Stoves.
Pair of Bronze Lamps (for Standards in Great Hall).
6 Lamps (for Billiard Room Chandelier).
Pair of Brass & Bronzed Corinthian Column Table Lamps.

Pair of smaller	Do	Do.
3 White Metal	Do	Do.
4 Coppered Brass	Do	Do.
1 Brass twisted Column	Do	Do.

4 Wall Lamps.

3 Brass Hand Do.
2 old Carriage Lamps

Brass Table Lamp,	fluted Column.
Do Do	nulled pattern.
Do Do	circular base.

Some of these lamps had clearly been removed to the lamp-room for refilling. Another important utensil in a lamp-closet was a 'Stained Tray with zinc liner for lamps.' (TN 1902.) Unfortunately neither the immensely detailed 1848 Stowe sale catalogue nor the equally informative 1928 catalogue lists the equipment used in the lamp-room, although the latter itemises the lamps stored there. The same is true of one of Lord Halifax's country houses, Hickleton Hall near Doncaster, where lamps were used right up to the time of the sale in 1947, supplemented by electric light fittings which were brought out by the footman when required, exactly as oil lamps would have been. The basement lamp-room is still used by the electrician for servicing the lighting.

Osbert Sitwell describes the atmosphere of the lamp-room at Renishaw Hall in Derbyshire in the first volume of his memoirs, *Left Hand, Right Hand!*, 1945 (pp.110–11):

> In the lamp-room, under the heavy fumes of paraffin, the sightless Stephen Pare — with his vast and hollow eyes, that now I understand resembled the gaping eyes of an antique mask of tragedy — was already lighting the wicks, which, by an unhappy irony, were to make clear for everyone else the exterior world, to him so dim, and indicate the shape and corners of chair and table, blurred to him and fading...Many of the rooms were now beginning to glow with a light forgotten today, for we were the last generation of children brought up by candlelight, and the smell of snuffed wax lay heavy on our nostrils as we went to sleep.

An unaltered example survives at Port Eliot in Cornwall (Fig.2), simply abandoned when electricity came in 1922 with all its fittings. These included a range of cupboards (Fig.3), two vast zinc-topped tables (Fig.4), a stand with integral drip-tray for the oil drums (Cat.80), and a lamp-box used to take the oil reservoirs from hanging lamps for refilling (Cat.79): some of these are still half-full of paraffin. Romantic today, the lamp-room would have been a place of drudgery in use, as Lady Diana Cooper (writing of the lamp-room at Belvoir Castle in 1905) knew well enough:

> Then there were the lamp-and-candle men, at least three of them, for there was no other form of lighting...They polished and scraped the wax off the candelabra, cut wicks, poured paraffin oil and unblackened glass chimneys all day long. After dark they were busy turning wicks up or down, snuffing candles, and de-waxing extinguishers. It was not an apartment we liked much to visit. It smelt disgusting and the lamp-men were too busy.

Four Centuries of Lighting at Temple Newsam

Even in the first inventory of the contents of Temple Newsam, compiled in 1565 — half a century after the house was finished — there is evidence of how the house was lit. The *Inventorie of the goodes and chatelles of Therle of Lenoxe remaynynge at Temple Newsome...* mentions:

THENTRE TO YE GREATE CHAMBR...eighte olde pewdre candlestickes viijd [8d]

From this date until late in the eighteenth century, lighting was by candles. Some variety of light fittings is demonstrated in the *Inventory of the goods and Chattells of the right honoble: Henry [first] Viscount Erwyn of Temple Newsam...1666* (TN EA 3/10):

In the withdrawing Room to the great chamber...one branch for a candle
Upon the stare case Twenty pictures & two guilded candlestickes
In the great parlour...6 guilded candlestickes...

In the great Hall...a brass hanging candlestick wth twelve branches...
In the wyne sellar...a candle chest...
In the pantry...two pewter candlestickes...24 pewter candlestickes...
In the Kitching...three candlestickes...
In my Lords Study...a little silver candlesticke and Iron snuffers

The 1680s and 1690s are decades which are particularly well documented, so it is no surprise to find frequent references to lighting. The *Inventory of my Lady Irwins Goods att Templenewsu Decembr 4th 1688* lists:

In the Kitchin...two small candlesticks iron, one of brass
Best Lodginge Roome...one walnut Tree Table & stands   01-06-00

The latter may well be part of what is known today as a triad, consisting of a looking-glass (not present here, but usually hung on the pier between two windows), a side

Fig.5. Temple Newsam, Hanging Sinumbra lamp in the Great Hall, before 1894

Fig.6. Temple Newsam, wall-mounted colza lamps in the Blue Drawing Room, October 1894

table and pair of torcheres. Many of the references are to mending light fittings and the work seems to have been given to men who were primarily locksmiths and gunsmiths. Nehemiah Cloudsley also invoiced for work done during these years including:

> for 1 Large plate hand brass candlestick De: the 26 of Septr.
> 1692   Novr the 8 for a brass hand candle stick Desr the 24 for a hand candle stick
> 1693   Octr the 24 for 2 brass hand candle stickes mending...
> 1694   Desr. the 16 for a candle stick mending...

He was paid on 10 May 1697 & 12 July 1698.

Even greater variety of fittings is evident in the 1702 inventory taken after the death of Arthur, third Viscount Irwin:

In the Mohaire Chamber...2 Sconses...
In the Clossett [next to the Damask Chamber]...2 sconses
In the Pantry...1 wax candlestick
In the Dyneing Roome...4 Sconses
In the Still Roome undr: ye Stairs...2 glasse Lantherns...
In the Kitchen & belonging it...1 candlestick wth.
2 stone & 1/2...Brass candlesticks weighing one
stone 6lbs
Plate
Three Casters Snuffers & box 40 ounces 4: p. wtt.
ffoure Candlesticks 58 ounces 10 p. wtt.
One Ladle Snuffers & box 3 Spoones wtt: 20
ounces
15 penny wtt:
Six Candlesticks Britannia 86 ounces:04 p.wtt.
Eight Candlesticks old Sterling 82 ounces 18
p.wtt

For the first time we encounter wall-mounted sconces as well as lanterns and silver candlesticks, some of the old sterling standard and some of the new Britannia, introduced following the Act of Parliament in 1697. The Mohaire Chamber was probably the principal bedchamber in the west wing of the house (known today as the Blue Damask Room), the Dyneing Roome was the Jacobean Great Chamber, over what are now the Great Hall and Chinese Drawing Room: four sconces would have provided very little illumination in such a large room on their own, so presumably they were fortified by the addition of silver candlesticks on the table, brought from the kitchen on important occasions.

Edward, fourth Viscount Irwin, succeeded to the title in 1702 but made few discernible alterations to the lighting, except perhaps in the chapel which seems to have gained 'Six chappel candlesticks...' He was succeeded in 1714 by his brother Rich who married Lady Anne Howard, daughter of the 3rd Earl of Carlisle, four years later, ordering in anticipation '10 pr of Square Candlesticks Snuffers & Stands wt 270:17 at 7/7/ per oz' at a cost of £98 3s 7d from Daniel and Joseph Norcott of London in 1717.

Rich employed an agent, an Italian named Matteo Bianchi, who purchased light fittings for him in London, as an interesting little episode illustrates. Bianchi wrote on 22 May 1718:

> ...Since in Town, I have Bought the Copper Cesterns, which shall be sent with Ten Dozen of ye best ffrench whit wine that I could fin'd in Town. and the twelve pair of Glass Sconces, if they can be got ym. ready.

A second letter, dated 24 May, gives a detailed description of the sconces:

> ...I have bespoke ye 3 pair of Silver Candlesticks. Next week I shall be sure to send ye Wax candles Tea, & Coffe, the Candles shall go by Sea with ye Coach, ffrench whitwine & ye Cestern, and ye Tea & Coffe I will send by ye Carrier, to prevent Damage wch. they will be liable to by Sea, also ye Glas Sconces I hope they are what Yr Ld.sp means, they are one peece of round Glass, which hung to ye Wall with a white lacker'd Sockett which they turn in, and have a Nosell of ye

Fig.7. Temple Newsam, the Picture Gallery prepared for a banquet in October 1894, with temporary electric lights hanging in the windows and some picture lights

Same, and are all ye ffassion now, and I have agreed for ten Shillings a pair; paying for all those things hath taken up all my Money...

They have long since disappeared but were probably quite simple, with circular looking glass plates in a metal frame from which the candle arm protruded. On 29 May Bianchi wrote again to Lord Irwin:

...Yesterday I see on Board ye Marget & Eliz: Robert Ranns Master for Hull, three Hampers of ffrench whitwine containing 10 Doz: one hampr. with ye Cestern one Box with ten Doz of Waxcandles. 5 Doz are 6 in ye pound & 5 Doz. are 4 in ye pound, ye Candles is put in ye Body of ye Coach, every thing is carefully pac't up...

Bianchi clearly took considerable trouble to safeguard the expensive wax candles but his precautions failed to secure the sconces from damage, as a note appended to the bill submitted on 31 May to 'Mr Byanky' by the supplier Ann Lewin indicates (TN/EA 12/7):

The bottom of ye nostle fixt to ye back and the bottoms of ye arms that goes into it are crackt both alike that they may makt so fitt...

Bianchi's sconces seem to be identifiable in the inventory taken on the fifth Viscount's death in 1721, which shows

them divided between the 'Great Hall...7 glass Sconces' and 'Mr Wattertons room...a parcell of glasses and glass Sconces'. Also listed were some candles in a passage known as Smithfield and in the Kitchen two sconces. The picture is completed by items in a second inventory that year, of '...the Goods and Chattells now remaining att Temple Newsame and which were of the personall Estate of the late Lord Edward Machell Viscountt Irwin..':

Dressing roome...2 Candle Sticks to the Chimney
Mohaire roome...2 Candle Stickes and Chinay over Chimley
Inner Closet...11 pair of brass candle Stickes
Great Dineing roome four Sconces...
Mr Wattertons roome...4 candle Stickes...

The candlesticks were kept in a servant's room ready for use after dark.

The first mention of a room specifically designated for the storage of lighting comes during the 1730s: it was high up amongst the servants' rooms on the second floor of the north wing over the Jacobean Gallery, inconveniently distant from the candlesticks, silver presumably in a plate closet in the Butler's pantry, base metal in the Kitchen. Here is the list:

In the Kitchen...
New Copper from London
  2 Flat Candlesticks...

9 Flat Candlesticks for Above Stairs...
3 High Candlesticks...
Pewter
    2 Lanterns
1 Brass ch [?chamber] Candlestick
Mr Watterton's Room over the Kitchen...Several Glass
    Sconces with Tops
The Pantry...2 Pair of Steel Snuffers
In the Hall..9 Glass Candlesticks, ye Sconces fix'd
The Study...A Tinn Sconce at the Door in the Passage.
The Great Parlour...4 Sconces
The Mo-hair Room... 2 Sconces
The Damask Room...2 Sconces
The Candle Chambr. Room...1 Large Box, with 14 Dozen of
    Mowld: Candles, 1 Do. 10 pound of Ditto...2 Dozen of
    Wax Candles
An Acct. of Plate...
6 Large Silver Candlesticks
2 Pair of Suffers [?snuffers] in Cases
2 Silver Sconces
16 Silver Candlesticks

Fig.8. Temple Newsam, gas light fittings in the kitchen 1922

Sometime between his succeeding to the title in 1736 and the prising of yet another inventory in 1740, Henry, seventh Viscount Irwin, must have commissioned for the 'Greate Dineing Room' over the Hall in the south wing the set of '10 stands for branches' (candelabra). The branches may have been 'In the Houskeeper's Room...1 Mohogmy Box with Guilt Branches in it...1 Box to put Candles in'. They are no longer at Temple Newsam but four torcheres from another set made ten years later were bought back in 1976. These were supplied in pairs between August 1745 and August 1746 by the immigrant French cabinet and frame maker, James Pascall, for the newly finished Picture Gallery. The cost, 'for a Rich pair of Carved Stands ['Gilt in burnished gold']', was £26, or £28 13 6d including leather covers and a case.

They are a remarkable set, described in 1902 as 'carved gilt Stands, 4ft-high, on tripod supports with carved busts of Females in the centre & triangular shaped tops' (TN 1902). The combination of female busts and naturalistic foliage suggests that Pascall had Ovid's *Metamorphoses* in mind, in particular the story of Phaethon. This mythical character is associated with light for he asked his father Helios for permission to drive the chariot of the sun for a day: losing control, he was killed by a thunderbolt from Zeus and when he fell dead from his chariot into the river Eridanus, his sisters mourned until transformed into trees. This interpretation is lent support by the even more remarkable *girandoles* or 'massive carved gilded Wall lights, elaborately carved with representation of a Stag Hunt & each having 6 Candlebranches' which also survive in the room. These were itemised by Pascall as '...two Rich Gerandolls with two branches and Six Lights Gilt in burnished gold' for which he charged £50 in August 1745. Here another Ovidian association may evoke the idea of light: Actaeon, a famous legendary huntsman, inadvertently caught a sight of Diana bathing naked, was turned by her into a stag and was torn to pieces by his own hounds.

Of approximately the same date or a little later are two handed pairs of eagle sconces in the rococo manner. In 1808 they were in the '5th. Room — 1st Floor...2 carved and gilt Eagle Gerandoles...' with the other pair in Lady Irwin's dressing room — both rooms are on the first floor of the west wing.

In 1758, Henry, seventh Viscount, retired to Bath in favour of his younger brother George, leaving belongings in the house, listed in *An Inventory of the Plate Left at Templenewsam Jan:ry 1758*:

Eleven pair of Candlesticks
Six Pair of French Plate Candlesticks Gilt
Four Single Branches of Do.................Do...
Eight Double Branches of Do.............Do...

George, eighth Viscount, was an elderly canon of Windsor and never moved north so Temple Newsam was occupied and in 1763 inherited by their nephew Charles who had restored the family fortunes with a singularly advantageous marriage. It was probably he who first installed lamps in the house, and his widow who (after his death in 1778) introduced neo-Classical style fittings. The evidence is the 1808 '...schedule of the Ornamental China Household Goods Furniture Linen and other Articles at the Mansion House at Temple Newsam...' which was drafted by Thomas Chippendale the younger after the death of the last Viscount's widow the previous year. The full list illustrates the variety of lighting, traditional candlesticks evidently being used alongside new models:

Passage A Square brass lanthorn with brass balance weights and shade...

10th. Room, Dark room [a lady's maid's room]...8 japanned night lamps

11th. Room, Sir John Ramsden's Bed Chamber...2 old brass Argaund lamps in the passage a japanned do. fixed in do..

16th. Room or Nursery...a large side lanthorn and [on?] the stairs and white lamp...

22nd. Room Lumber...5 side lanthorns a vase lamp 6 glass shades...6 glass burners a queen's ware lamp...2-1 light brass Girandoles...2 high brass lamps...

3d. Room First Floor...a tin night shade...

5th. Room — 1st Floor...2 carved and gilt Eagle Gerandoles...

9th. Room Lady Irwin's Dressing Room...4 brass brackets for 2 lights each, 2 black and gold papier mache brackets 2 carved and Gilt Eagle Brackets...2 marble candlesticks...2 Cut glass candlesticks two china figures 2 light candlesticks 2 ditto setting [sitting] figures 2 one light Gerandoles...

10th. Room Picture Gallery...8 large carved and gilt candle-stands with heads and 8 covers to ditto lined with serge 2 very large Gerandoles with carved hunting ornaments with 6 branches each...4-2 light lustres...

Middle Passage...a green and white painted term with a vase lamp in ditto mounted with brass and brass feet and brass burner...

3d. Room Best dining room Ground Floor...2 white Holland rolling blinds and racks...3 Brass argaund lamps with 2 burners each finished in Bronze and Or Molu mouldings on round pedestals... 4th. Room Great Hall Ground Floor...a vase lamp with brass balance weight and chain and brass Argaund lamp

5th. Room New terrace room Ground floor...2 glass candle-sticks...

6th. Room or Breakfast Parlour...2 japanned argand lamps with brass arms...

Great Stair case — 2 rich carved forms painted green and white with Vaselamps and brass ornaments and glass burners...a brass argand lamp one light

Long passage...three japanned argand lamps a large tin side lanthorn...

Back Stairs — a Hexagon brass lanthern and strong iron chain...

17th. North Hall...a small square brass Lanthorn at the door...a blue painted tin Lanthorn...

Kitchen...13 flat brass candlesticks 9 high Ditto...3 high iron candlesticks 8 flat iron ditto 5 japanned Ditto...a Lanthorn [tin]...

Scullery...16 lamps and oil can...

Passage — A side Lanthorn

Dairy...an iron flat candlestick...

Fig.9. Temple Newsam, brass spider and sconces in the Dining Room, October 1894

Fig.10. Temple Newsam, the Darnley Room c.1910

Fig.11. Temple Newsam, gas bracket in the staircase and hanging colza lamp in the south corridor c.1910

Coachmans Stable...2 stable Lanthorns...
Bed-Chamber [in the Stables]...a candlestick
Candles and Soap — 46lbs of Mouldcandles 429lbs of Common candles...

The 'Great Stair case' was a recently-constructed classical interior with a coved ceiling and glazed lantern through which daylight came; during the evening, light was provided by benches incorporating light fittings which must have been remarkable objects even in their time, so it is particularly frustrating that these have not survived.

Sculptural light fittings had become fashionable for staircases and other formal rooms by the beginning of the 19th century and parts of those provided for the Great Hall in the Regency period survive. A chaste 1790s room, this was transformed into an impressive Jacobean-revival interior by the last Viscountess Irwin's eldest daughter, Isabella, Lady Hertford, in the late 1820s. Lamps — latterly of both colza oil and paraffin type — provided the illumination and were placed on term-figure stands positioned on marble-topped tables (Cat.5). Discarded in 1939, they have recently been restored by Dick Reid in York and two retain their original oak graining. Against the north wall a pair of two-burner colzas stood on plaster lamp stands

based on Antique models: these were broken up after the family had left the house in 1922 but parts of both survive. Hanging by an open chain from the central cartouche in the ceiling was an eight-branch sinumbra chandelier whose characteristic circular reservoirs and supply tubes can clearly be seen in early photographs (Fig.5).

Photographs also show that the Chinese Drawing Room, which opens off the Great Hall to the east, was lit by a pair of wall-mounted two-light colzas, one either side of the overmantel glass (Fig.6), while the Red Drawing Room beyond was lit by a pair of two-light colza table-lamps.

The Picture Gallery itself was always the most problematical room both by day and night: Dr Waagen, who had visited the house in 1854, described the room as

'...one of the largest and grandest drawing rooms that I have yet seen in England. As it is, however, lighted on both the long sides, many of the pictures are seen to great disadvantage...'

In the eighteenth century it must have been lit after dark by the great girandoles and by 'branches' placed on the eight stands ranged in pairs either side of console and pier tables along the long north and south walls: lustres were added by 1808 on the mantel-shelves. But light levels must still have been low so, when Mrs Meynell Ingram held a banquet in the Picture Gallery for the Duke and Duchess of York and forty-one other guests in October 1894, the room was lit by the candelabra on the table and by clusters of naked electric light bulbs suspended over the centre of each window; picture lights are visible over the portraits flanking the Venetian window, over the chimney-pictures and beside the portraits on the extreme left and right (Fig.7). Power must have been supplied by batteries and this temporary installation had been removed before the Gallery was photographed for Fletcher Moss's *Pilgrimages to Old Homes* in 1910. The candles in the girandoles were sometimes provided with shades, visible in at least one 19th century photograph.

Mrs Meynell Ingram recorded some of the light fittings in a manuscript inventory she compiled from 1880 onwards. There were many ornamental vases whose secondary purpose was for lighting (some of them illustrated in R.L.Hobson's article 'Meissen Figures at Temple Newsam' in the *Art Journal* in 1912), but it must be doubtful if these were actually used to provide light.

During the 1890s gas was introduced into the house (supplied by the Crossgates, Halton and Seacroft Gas Co., founded in 1884) and the enormously detailed inventory of October 1902 gives a full picture of the hierarchy of lighting in a country house at the end of the Victorian era. It also demonstrates that Temple Newsam under Mrs Meynell Ingram had hardly kept pace with improving technology. By no means every room was lit by gas — its use was mostly confined to rooms occupied or used by servants, like the kitchen (Fig.8), and no fittings are visible in photographs of the main bedrooms in 1894, probably because gas was thought unsuitable.

The only major interiors in which it was tolerated were the Great Hall (where the sinumbra lamp was converted, along with the other lamps whose stands were

Fig.13. Candle Box used at Temple Newsam, japanned tin, 19th century

bored through with red-hot pokers to take the pipes), the Oak Staircase and Oak Passage where the fittings can be seen in photographs taken in 1894. There was also a 'Pair of female figure gas pedestals, resting on a square base, standing 7ft-high with 2 gas jets' in the top-floor corridor of the west wing, and — probably on the top landing of the late 18th century north-west stairs — a '4ft-6in-painted wood Pedestal with gas jet & globe in ormolu frame...', conceivably adapted from an earlier fitting. Unhappily neither of these intriguing objects has survived.

Most of the rooms were still illuminated by portable candlesticks or oil lamps. However, G.F.Bodley's 1877 Chapel, and C.E.Kempe's Dining Room (1889-91, Fig.9), were both lit by a 'spider' (chandelier) and brass wall sconces. The 1896 Darnley Room had 'Six embossed silver wall Candelabra' two of which are visible in a photograph taken for Moss's *Pilgrimages to Old Homes* (Fig.10), while the Victorian staircase and passage to the Picture Gallery, dating from 1894-97 and 1889 respectively, were lit by spiders and wall-mounted wrought-iron gas brackets. There was a 'massive brass chandelier' in the Billiard Room (which might have been the 'brass hanging candlestick wth twelve branches...' listed in the Great Hall two hundred and fifty years earlier), but there were never glass chandeliers in the house. In the south wing corridor there were 'Three French ormolu suspending Chandeliers with cut Glass bowls...': one of these hanging colza lamps can be seen in Fig.11.

The lamps were tended not in a dedicated lamp-room in the spacious cellars but in a small lamp-closet off the Great Hall (where abundant traces of lamp-black remain on the walls); its contents included a 'Stained Tray with zinc liner for lamps. Mahogany Tray...Hand Extinguisher...' The lamps seem to have been stored in a closet or cupboard in the ground-floor domestic corridor, which contained

Fig.12. Temple Newsam, the Library in 1922, with gas lamps on wall-brackets

8 Copper Lamps. Two opal glass oil Lamps. One Wedgwood double oil Lamp. One bronze suspending oil Lamp. Two blue & white china oil Lamps. One brass oil Lamp. Two fine old brassoil Lamps. on triangular bases. Thirty various glass chimneys. Ten globes. Two double brass oil Lamps. Stable Lamp. Ten japanned Reflectors...

There was another cache, including '...Two Lamps...13 Various old Lamps & sundry Lamp fittings', in the Brush Room in the cellar of the south wing.

After Mrs Meynell Ingram's death in 1904 her nephew the Hon. Edward Wood (later Lord Halifax) seems to have extended gas lighting to rooms, like the Dining Room, which had previously been lit by candles or lamps. When Lenygon's converted the Red Drawing Room into a Library in 1912 they lit it with three-branch gas lamps on wall-brackets (Fig.12). During the First World War the house was used as a VAD hospital: the more valuable fittings were removed altogether and brass spiders replaced by hanging paraffin lamps. The continual fear of fire in a house still lit by naked flames is evidenced by an ill-spelt note attached to the swell-box of the chapel organ, which reads:

> *Notice to Organ builder*
> The men not to use naked
> light when tuneing or repairing
> the Organ Lamps is kept
> for them in Butlers Pantry
> _____
> By Order of *the Honble E.F.L. Wood*

The Hon. Edward Wood sold Temple Newsam to the city of Leeds in 1922 having first dispersed the contents (including all the portable lighting) in a seven day sale. The house may have continued to be lit by gas — although it closed to the public at dusk — until electricity was first introduced in 1938. Like gas before it, electric light was restricted to the domestic rooms and only extended to the parts of the house visited by the public in 1946. Most of the old gas fittings, including the chandelier in the Great Hall and the wall-lights in the Oak Passage were sold for scrap during the War. However, a few components have been recovered from the cellars (together with a japanned tin candle box from a domestic part of the house, Fig.13) and show that, instead of the more efficient incandescent mantle type with overhead supply, most of the gas burners were fed from below; nevertheless, their controls were sophisticated and they were equipped with a bar-operated on-off valve and automatic ignition by means of a pilot light.

1 Torchere (from a set of four, originally eight)
1745 or 46
Made by James Pascall, London
Gilt pine, walnut
H 49½in (126)
Shaped triangular platforms supported on carved columns with consoles fronted by sculptured female busts; stems decorated with full repertoire of rococo motifs, standing on asymmetrical tripod bases with volute feet.
LIT. David Hill, 'James Pascall and the Long Gallery Suite at Temple Newsam', *Furniture History*, XVII (1981), pp.70–74.
PROV. Temple Newsam

Supplied by Pascall in pairs, as recorded in his Bill:

1745		
Agust 16	for a Rich pair of Carved Stands Gilt ditto	
	[in burnished gold]	26.00.00.
	for Leather Covers	01.16.00.
1746		
June 27	for a Paire of Stands as Beffore	26.00.00.
	for Leather Covers	01.16. 6.
	for Case	00.17. 6.
Jully 18	for a Pair of Stands, and ditto as beffore	28.13. 6.
Agust 8	for a Pair of Stands and ditto as beffore	28.13. 6.

The stands were removed by Lord Halifax to Hickleton Hall in 1922 and sold from there in 1947; four were bought by Leeds in 1976, the remainder belong to a private collector in Germany. The carving may refer to the sisters of Phaethon, son of Helios, see above. Examination of nineteenth century photographs makes it certain that the torcheres were originally intended to flank each of the four tables in the Picture Gallery — side-tables against the south wall, console tables against the north wall — enabling

candle light to be distributed fairly evenly around the room after darkness fell. This contrasts with the more general practice (at least in smaller interiors) of placing torcheres in the corners of rooms.

Leeds City Art Galleries (Temple Newsam)

2 Girandoles, a pair
1745
Made by James Pascall, London
Gilt pine
H 83in (211)

Asymmetrical composition of rococo scrolls and curved brackets incorporating a hound chasing a stag amidst bulrushes and foliage garlanded with fruit and flowers; the framework supports six spiralling candle-branches enriched with leaves and terminating in circular pans; brass liners and sockets of later date
LIT. David Hill, 'James Pascall and the Long Gallery Suite at Temple Newsam', *Furniture History*, XVII (1981), pp.70–74.
PROV. Temple Newsam

Supplied by Pascall on 16 August 1745 as recorded in his Bill:

> for two Rich Gerandolls with two branches and
> Six Lights Gilt in burnished gold   50.00.00.

They are recorded in inventories in 1808 ('2 very large Gerandoles with carved hunting ornaments with 6 branches each...') and 1902 ('Two very large gilt six light Girandoles on centre of south wall with stags & bulrushes...'). As in a Matthias Lock design for a girandole, the hunting imagery here may have been chosen as a reference to the story of Actaeon and the misuse of Sight, see above.

Leeds City Art Galleries (Temple Newsam)

3 Eagle sconces (two from a set of four)
*c.*1760
Carved and gilt pine, the stem of stiff wire bound with felt and covered with gesso; brass nozzles modern
H 21in (53)
In the form of an eagle displayed, rising from scrolls, flame borders and rococo sprays; gripping in its beak a twisted branch embellished with leaf scales and florets, terminating in a brass socket.
LIT. Gilbert, II, No.312.
PROV. Temple Newsam

Recorded in the inventories of 1808 ('5th. Room — 1st Floor...2 carved and gilt Eagle Gerandoles' and '9th. Room Lady Irwin's Dressing Room...2 carved and Gilt Eagle Brackets') and 1902 ('Miss Ingram's Room...A Pair of carved wood Eagle wall Candle-holders'. 'The Gallery Corridor... In Cabinet...Pair of Carved Wood Eagle Wall Sconces').

The eagle was the traditional attribute of Jupiter, the king of the heavens, and was thought to be the only creature that could look at the sun; here, however, it probably evokes the idea of light or lighting by being the attribute of Sight, one of the Five Senses, and Eagle-sconces were not uncommon in eighteenth and early nineteenth century England: Thomas Chippendale the younger supplied Lady Heathcote in March 1800 with two eagle girandoles with large wreaths of flowers and four lights each, with gilt nozzles and rich cut glass pans, for the sum of £23 (Monson Papers, Lincolnshire Archives Office).

Leeds City Art Galleries (Temple Newsam)

3

4 Vase lamp
H 19¾in (50)
Glass shade, gilt wood, brass and marble
English, late 18th century or early 19th century
Square plinth of veined grey marble supporting reeded column in gilt wood applied with four vertical bands of ribbon and wreath ornament in gilt composition; brass collar with an applied band of egg and dart in composition supports vase-shaped storm-shade of glass with folded rim. Inside, a circle of embossed gilt paper may conceal the scars of the candle holder (now missing).
PROV. Temple Newsam.

Perhaps associated with the 1792-96 alterations to the south wing (the 1808 inventory records a vase lamp in the '22nd. Room Lumber' on the second floor of the north wing) or with Lady Hertford's redecoration of the house in the 1820s.

Comparison with printed designs for vase lamps by George Hepplewhite (*The Cabinet-Maker and Upholsterer's Guide*, 1788, Plate 112) and Thomas Sheraton suggests that there may once have been some openwork decoration perhaps of pierced brass around the storm-shade. Vase-shaped lamps were sometimes used on staircase handrails, as at Wardour Castle, but this example may once have been associated with the lamp stands, Cat.5.

Leeds City Art Galleries (Temple Newsam)

against the south wall, they were bored through with a red-hot iron to take gas pipes, and stood on box-plinths when the lamps were converted in the 1890s. Perhaps they were intended as a compliment to the terms supporting vase lamps which form part of the balustrade of the staircase gallery at Carlton House, with which Lady Hertford, as an intimate of the Prince of Wales, would certainly have been familiar (Watkin, p.107). The latter supported vase-shaped candle-lamps similar in form to Cat.4 but equipped with a cover.

Leeds City Art Galleries (Temple Newsam)

5 Six lamp stands

19th century, second quarter
Oak, pine and composition
H of largest 48½in (123)
Demi-figure supporting an Ionic capital; tapering pedestal decorated with fruit, flowers and foliage, on square splayed base; oak-grained finish
LIT. *Leeds Arts Calendar*, 106 (1990), Pl.6
PROV. Temple Newsam

These lamp stands were made for the Great Hall after the alterations for Lady Hertford in the late-1820s; they are visible in the earliest view of the room, a watercolour of the 1850s. The composition ornament on the pedestals was cast from that of the genuinely early-seventeenth century (probably continental) central term on the hall overmantel. Originally intended to support lamps (fuelled by paraffin when photographed before the 1890s) and placed on marble-topped tables at either end of the Great Hall and

'As Full of Lamps as Hancock's Shop': Lighting in the Royal Pavilion at Brighton 1815–1900

The Pavilion forms a fascinating subject for the study of lighting in historic houses, spanning a period of royal occupation (1787–1845), followed by municipal ownership from 1850 onwards. Through the innovative attitude of George IV it became a pioneer in the field of gas lighting in the early 1820s, and under municipal control became one of the earliest historic houses to be lit by electricity in the 1880s.

For some contemporary observers the over-heated interior of the Royal Pavilion was excessively opulent and theatrical, and the design concept and rich decorations too grand for its size and location, outside London. Lighting played a key role in the overall effect: 'the lights are dazzling' noted Princess Lieven in 1822, whilst also commenting on the luxurious and 'effeminate' atmosphere of the

Pavilion. Lighting by day (and by night) was crucial in creating the dramatic atmosphere of the elaborate interiors designed by Frederick Crace and Robert Jones between 1815 and 1822.

The form of lighting was determined by the size, location and function of different rooms, providing in each area a particular and individual atmosphere. Nash introduced dramatic light sources from above to illuminate both the chamber and ground floors. By day the Long Gallery, for example, resembling a bamboo grove of pink and blue, was lit by three tall windows of painted glass at each end, and a large central skylight (flanked by two vertical painted windows) which pierced the first floor to allow muted natural light to illuminate the central area of the Gallery, where visitors entered (Fig.14). All the galleries and stairwells on

Fig.14. The Long Gallery from Nash's Views of the Royal Pavilion, 1826, showing the central painted laylight and the chandelier

the Chamber Floor were also lit by large painted skylights (Fig.19). The main rooms on the east front (Saloon, Music and Banqueting Rooms) had full-length arched french windows; the latter two rooms were also illuminated by clerestory level painted glass elliptical windows. The overall effect created was of a colourful, light interior, reminiscent of a garden pavilion, and full of sunlight softened by the hues of the painted glass.

Chandeliers and Lamps

The designs of the chandeliers in the major rooms are integral to each scheme, and form dramatic decorative features. Perhaps the most flamboyant is the chandelier in the Banqueting Room designed by Robert Jones, thirty feet high and weighing nearly a ton (Fig.15). Hovering in the apex of the domed ceiling is a carved and silvered dragon, flanked by six dragons, their heads arched to exhale light 'each bearing a large painted ground glass lotus for a lamp with burners' (Royal Pavilion Inventory 1828). The size and weight of this chandelier is said to have frightened Queen Adelaide who feared it might fall on the assembled company. It was removed to store by William IV in 1833, not to be reinstated until 1842 by Queen Victoria.

Fig.15. The Banqueting Room from Nash's Views

Fig.16. Detail of the Banqueting Room from Nash's Views, illustrating the Spode torcheres, designed by Robert Jones, with ormolu dragon mounts and painted lotus glass shades. The torcheres, four on each wall, stood nine feet, nine inches high

Lighting the chandeliers must have been a considerable task for the lamplighters, who were supplied with robustly built pairs of very high steps with platforms for use in the Banqueting Room. It seems that lighting the spectacular chandeliers was an event in itself for visitors: Charles Greville recalls in 1821 that after dinner Lady Conyngham requested that the Saloon be lit up as Lady Bath was due to visit the King later that evening; the Saloon was 'lit by hundreds of candles' (*The Greville Memoirs*, ed. Henry Reeve, 1874, vol.1, p.46). Each room was furnished with appropriately designed chandeliers, lanterns, oil table lamps, torcheres or candelabra to such a degree that Croker was moved to describe the Pavilion as being 'as full of lamps as Hancock's shop' (*The Croker Papers*, 1884, p.127) (Figs 16 and 17).

The Great or King's Kitchen, top-lit by day by twelve high-level sash windows, was artificially lit by four large bronze and brass hexagonal lanterns, on a rise and fall

Fig.17. Detail of the King's Bedroom from Nash's Views, showing table lamps made of 'Japan Jars' with metal stems painted green and tinted ground glass lotus shades. Similar types of lamps were used to illuminate the Long Gallery

Fig.18. Detail of the Great Kitchen from Nash's Views, showing the hexagonal bronze and brass lanterns, fitted with Argand lamps

mechanism. The twin-branched Argand fitting in each is clearly visible in contemporary illustrations of the interior (Fig.18).

Supplementary lighting for the staff was supplied by tin wall candle sconces. The inventory made during George IV's reign contains no list of portable lamps used in the Pavilion. The Denew's inventory (in the Royal Collections), compiled following Queen Victoria's decision to sell the palace, includes three and four-branch brass Argand lamps and telescope bracket lamps.

The Lamp Room, located at the south end near the kitchen and household offices, was fitted with floor to ceiling closets and presses, a dresser, shelves and a lead sink. Lamp stools, with carpeted tops, and mahogany lamp steps were stored here for use by the lamp-lighters. The inventory of 1828 records the contents of the Oil Cellar: '9 large oil vats with their brass cocks, 2 tin oil pumps and 5 large oil cans, 26 gallon tin measures, 2 one gallon ditto and 2 funnels'. Another lamp room was located in the north end basement, as a store and for trimming lamps.

The smoke from the numerous chandeliers, lanterns and lamps that brilliantly lit the interior inevitably caused damage to the paint-work and ceilings, necessitating regular cleaning. The Crace accounts, for example, include bills for the Saloon for 'cleaning and repairing the whole of the

ornamental painting, being very much injured by smoke of lamps' (Crace Accounts, 1819, p.105) and for cleaning paintwork and skylights in the Long Gallery, 'much damaged by the smoke of lanthorns' (ibid, p.85).

Gas Lighting in the Regency Period

Gas was little used in England to light interiors in the first decades of the nineteenth century. Abbotsford is an early example (c.1823), but the Pavilion preceded it by two years. The manner in which gas lighting was used in the Pavilion is interesting. It was not installed in a conventional manner, for example to replace the oil in lamps or chandeliers, but rather to illuminate at night from the exterior the decorative architectural features of painted glass windows, which during the day suffused the interior with soft, coloured tones. This may have been a deliberate choice on the part of the pavilion's architect and decorators, or simply result from the impracticality of gas lighting such complex chandeliers as those designed by Crace and Jones for the Music Room, Saloon and Banqueting Room.

Possibly innovations proposed by Humphrey Repton for Uppark, the home of Sir Harry Fetherstonhaugh, a friend of the Prince of Wales, might have been a source of inspiration. In 1813 a painted glass window was installed in the north wall of the Serving Room. Clearly Repton was most concerned with the decorative impact of the coloured glass both by day and night. He decided to illuminate the panel from behind; he wrote 'the effect will be magic as all the light may proceed from this window from Argand Lamps properly adjusted from behind' (M.Meade-Fetherstonhaugh and O.Warner, *Uppark and its People*, 1964. p.80).

For over a century publications have so frequently recorded that the Music Room and Banqueting Room were lit by gas by George IV that the term 'gasolier' has crept into recent literature on the Pavilion, used to describe the chandeliers in the Music Room. It would seem from contemporary information that in fact these rooms were only lit by gas from the exterior, at high levels, and that the chandeliers themselves were lit with oil lamps or candles.

The possibility of using gas-lighting in Brighton was first mentioned in May 1816, when Sir Benjamin Bloomfield (Private Secretary to the Prince Regent) informed the Town Commissioners that, if they decided to light the town with gas, the Prince Regent would contribute to the lighting of the exterior of the Royal Pavilion and its outbuildings. Two years later the Brighton Gas Light and Coke Company was established and undertook to light the Pavilion gardens with gas. Further research needs to be undertaken on the subject of lighting the gardens during George IV and William IV's reigns. Original gas standard lamps, surmounted with crowns and cast with William IV's monogram, have survived. These are still in the use in the Pavilion grounds, but fitted for electricity.

A letter dated September 1818 from their agent Jonathan Taylor, refers to the laying of necessary pipes to supply the Pavilion. It would seem that at this time lighting was restricted to the gardens of the Royal Pavilion as the building itself was undergoing extensive remodelling by John Nash (letter from J.Taylor to J.Watier at Carlton House dated 29 September 1818; collections of British Gas South Eastern).

In December 1820, the Governor of the Brighton Gas Light and Coke Company anxiously wrote to Sir Benjamin Bloomfield on the subject of lighting the Royal Pavilion (Minutes of the Committee of Management of the Brighton Gas Light and Coke Company, 20 December 1820, East Sussex Record Office GBR1/2). He was concerned that, although George IV had signified his interest in having the Pavilion lit by gas, no further action had been taken; a gas works had been erected for the Pavilion, at some cost to the Company. The letter stated that the Company was only formed by the members of the Management Committee as they has considered that they could, with confidence, calculate on the patronage of the King. 'Aware of the impossibility from the unfinished state of the building of lighting upon any large scale', the Committee merely requested permission 'to introduce the

gas into lamps at present at the entrance in lieu of the oil which is used in them, their object being to shew that His Majesty has not withdrawn that patronage which the company were induced to imagine they might calculate upon'. It would appear that indeed the lamp of the *porte-cochere* was lit by gas; this proposal may have included the four lanterns surmounted with small onion domes flanking the central dome of the *porte-cochere* as well as the hanging lamp. Recorded in the Royal Pavilion 1828 inventory is reference to a lantern 'belonging to the Portico formed of lackered metal with gas fittings'; this gas lamp was suspended by eight metal ropes and furnished with eight flying dragons, each supporting a glass globe on a lotus branch. In June 1821, Thomas Edge, an approved supplier and fitter of gas lamps, supplied a 'handsome scroll lamp iron' and a 'Large Lanthorn to match, with Crown for the Castle Square entrance to the Pavilion' (Account for 25 June 1821 from Thomas Edge, Royal Archives RA 25386).

In December 1821 local newspapers enthusiastically reported the lighting of the Pavilion with gas; that same month members of the Committee of the Brighton Gas Light and Coke Company visited the Pavilion to inspect the installation of piping. The Governor reported that he went on to the roof of the Pavilion 'for the purpose of inspecting the state of the lights in the Music Room', and that 'notwithstanding a high wind and very heavy rain they gave a brilliant and steady light' (Minutes of the Committee of Management of the Brighton Gas Light and Coke Company, 14 December 1821. East Sussex Record Office GBR1/2). It would seem that the only gas lighting for the Music Room was from the exterior, that is behind the high-level painted glass elliptical windows. A somewhat irritated report in the *Brighton Gazette* the following month stated 'it is still said, in many quarters, that the interior of the Pavilion is lighted with gas, but it is erroneous — in no single instance has gas been used within the walls of the palace; exteriorly it is so illuminated, and most brilliantly, when needed, and the stained glass of the Music and Banqueting Rooms, together with that of the hall etc are made to display their rich variety of tints inwards by the blaze of gas without — but no further is it used at the palace, nor is it intended that it ever should' (*Brighton Gazette*, 17 January 1822).

Brayley, in 1838, also refers to the clerestory windows in the Music Room 'which are so contrived as to be illuminated from the exterior' (E.W.Brayley, *Illustrations of Her Majesty's Palace at Brighton*, 1838, p.8). By illuminating the eight high-level glass windows, painted with Chinese devices, some light would have been cast on the richly gilt and reflective surface of the domed ceiling as well as other high-level gilt ornaments.

From other references, it appears that the sets of three painted glass windows above the North and South Staircase, which illuminated the stairs, the Chamber Floor Galleries and the Long Gallery, were also lit from behind at night, (Fig.19) and possibly also (as the newspaper report above suggests) the painted clerestory windows in the

Fig.19. The Gallery on the Chamber Floor from Nash's Views, showing the painted ground glass skylight and, in the background, one of the back-lit windows which illuminated the gallery and the stair well

Entrance hall. An account from the joiner, B.Tuppen, early in 1820, records 'assisting Lamplighter in lighting up the transparencies to the Dining and Music Room' (Account for the quarter ending 5 April 1820. Public Record Office LC11/24); this was prior to the introduction of gas and presumably lit with oil lamps. Another account from Tuppen a year later, refers also to lighting up the painted windows in the Long Gallery and 'finishing inclosures to windows each end of Long Gallery to light the same up' (Account for the quarter ending 3 April 1821. Public Records Office LC11/31). It is unclear as to whether these painted windows were lit by gas or, as at Uppark, by Argand lamps (Fig.19).

The Development of Gas Lighting in the 1850s

Following Queen Victoria's decision to sell the Royal Pavilion it was purchased in 1850 by the Commissioners of Brighton. Before it was sold the magnificent interior was completely stripped and left in a dilapidated state. All the furniture, wall decorations, decorative fixtures, chimney-pieces and chandeliers were removed to Kensington Palace. A Pavilion Committee was established in 1850 to oversee the redecoration and refurbishment of the interior and to manage the building.

In September 1850 a report by the Surveyor, resulting from a survey of gas fittings present at that time throughout the Pavilion, was submitted to the Pavilion Committee (Proceedings of the Pavilion Committee, 1850, Vol.1. Royal Pavilion Archives); it provides additional information regarding how the Music and Banqueting Rooms were gas lit. The report concludes 'that with the exception of illuminating the coloured windows of the principal domes, gas does not appear to have been much used in the interior of the Pavilion'. By 'coloured windows of the principal domes' reference is made to the elliptical painted windows of the Music Room and Banqueting Room.

According to this report the extant four inch gas piping ran from the south-east corner of the Great Kitchen, up over the roof of the pavilion on the west side, along to the north-west corner of the Music Room, where it descended into the underground passage leading from the Pavilion to the stables. The report proposed to supply gas lighting to the Banqueting Room Gallery, the Music Room Gallery and the Long Gallery from a new main, laid in the eastern lawns which would also allow the Commissioners to 'light the lawn and public walks on the East in the same manner as has been done on the opposite side'. The lights in the main rooms, being at considerable elevation and pendant, could be supplied from the original high level mains. Subsequently gas was also introduced into some of the first floor exhibition areas, as well as the King's Apartments.

This extensive installation of gas in the Pavilion was occasioned by the first major restoration of the interior, undertaken by the artist-decorator Christopher Wren Vick in 1850. Of the £4,500 spent on redecorating and refurbishing the interior, £1,251 was spent on fifty gas lights, fitted in total with 481 burners, and supplied by Messrs Apsley Pellatt. The Music Room was supplied with nine gasoliers, the central gasolier illuminated by forty-five burners (Fig.20). According to a contemporary newspaper the Pellatt gasoliers were said to comprise some 35,000 cut-glass drops.

The use of gas in the Pavilion in the 1850s caused considerable anxiety. During an exhibition of the paintings of the 'Immortal Heroes, Wellington and Nelson', the jets of the gas fittings were deemed dangerous, ascending some four inches toward a deal board, installed to reflect the light. The Surveyor informed the Pavilion Committee 'that nearly the whole of this splendid building is constructed with timber and no doubt of the best quality which, should a fire occur, would burn faster than inferior timber' (Proceedings of the Pavilion Committee, Vol.2, letter dated 10 December 1855, from the Surveyor's Office. Royal Pavilion Archives). The major concern was that if there was a fire on the first floor that the roof would collapse and with it the roof mains which was constantly charged with gas;

THE MUSIC-ROOM, IN THE PAVILION, BRIGHTON.—(SEE PAGE 70.)

Fig.20. The Music Room, from the Illustrated London News, January 29, 1856, showing Wren Vick's restoration of the interior and the gas-lit Apsley Pellatt chandeliers

the whole system might then explode. It was agreed that the gas supply to the Pavilion would be turned off when the building was not used and at night.

The complex history of the pavilion since 1850 has resulted in curious features combined from different periods, many of which remain *in situ* today. The present chandelier in the Long Gallery is such an example. The chandelier, originally in the Saloon, was moved to its present location *c.*1820. When the Pavilion was sold to Brighton in 1850 all the contents were removed to Kensington Palace. In 1864 a large number of items, including this painted glass chandelier and all but four of the Music Room chandeliers were returned by Queen Victoria and incorporated in Antoine Dury's restoration of the interior. That same year gas was installed to light the central chandelier in the Long Gallery. It seems that, somewhat inappropriately, one of the rod supports with gilt metal leaf and glass tulip decoration from the Music Room chandeliers (either an original or one of Palmer and Green's contemporary copies) was inserted between the ground glass painted bowl of the chandelier and the dragon canopy top, presumably to conceal the piping for the new gas supply.

The introduction of Electric Lighting

The Pavilion followed closely on the pioneers of electric lighting; electricity was installed early in 1883, less than three years after Cragside. In the autumn of 1882 Magnus Volk, a local electrical engineer and creator of Volk's Electric Railway (1883), offered to light the pavilion by electricity. The system decided upon was Swan's incandescent lamps, with a forty horsepower Robey engine located adjacent to the Corn Exchange in Church Street. The cables ran under the Corn Exchange and Dome, through the subterranean passage (built by George IV to provide access from his private apartments to the stables) to the roof of the Pavilion.

On April 2 1883 the Music Room and Banqueting Room were lit with electricity. The central chandelier of the Banqueting Room was fitted with ninety-six lamps, the four small chandeliers with thirty each. The rest of the ground

Fig.21. Design by J.Pain and Sons for the proposed illuminations of the east front of the Royal Pavilion to celebrate Queen Victoria's Diamond Jubilee in 1897. Reproduced by courtesy of East Sussex Records Office (East Sussex Record Office DB/B46/6328)

floor principal rooms were illuminated with electricity during the following weeks. In May the public were admitted to view the new electrical installation, which caused great interest. That autumn further electrical installations were introduction into Pavilion, Dome, Library and Art Gallery, making a total of 900 incandescent lamps and ten arc lights used in the principal rooms, with the gas system retained in less important area such as passages and anterooms.

In summer of 1884 the Pavilion gardens were lit with 400 incandescent lamps arranged in festoons, reflecting the enthusiasm for the decorative effects that could be achieved with electricity. An unidentified newspaper cutting (dated August 6 1884) described the lighting for a summer garden fete which was attended by more than 3,000 residents: 'For the first time the electric light was employed, and the result was highly satisfactory. The lamps are incandescent, giving a softer and more welcome light than the powerful arc lamps usually used out-of-doors. Strings of lamps bordered the eastern lawn and encircled the clumps of trees, and, the globes being of different colours, the effect was a soft subdued light corresponding somewhat with that of the Japanese lanterns hitherto used...For the first time some illumination was attempted on the western lawn, glow-worm lamps being hung round the pedestal of the Statue of Sir J Cordy Burrows, and dotted about amongst the flowerbeds'.

Queen Victoria's Diamond Jubilee celebrations in 1897 provide an opportunity to create spectacular illuminations at the Pavilion using both gas and electricity. J.Pain and Sons created an enchanted palace illuminated with thousands of coloured lights and oriental lanterns: 'A palace of glowing gems', a local paper observed, praising Pain and Sons' design as 'dazzlingly beautiful' (*Brighton and Hove Herald*, 26 June 1897). 30,000 prismatic gas lamps and hundreds of Japanese lanterns were employed, with festoons of crystals hung on the domes (Fig.21). The practice of illuminating the exterior of the building with coloured lights continued until the 1960s, to be replaced shortly by plain concealed floodlighting to highlight the Pavilion's elaborate architectural features.

Jessica Rutherford, Head of Museums and Director of the Royal Pavilion, Brighton

Candle Lighting

Silver Sconces

Sconces made of silver represent only one aspect of that most luxurious manifestation of Baroque art — silver furniture. The reflecting quality of the metal made it, as ever, an obvious vehicle for this form of candle lighting and its effect in the wainscotted rooms of the late 17th and early 18th century can be imagined. Prior to the Civil War they were known as 'hanging wall candle-sticks', 'candleplates' or 'candlestick plates' and Cardinal Wolsey, Queen Elizabeth and Charles I all possessed examples in silver. It was only after the Restoration however that the vogue really emerged in country houses and town mansions either for silver or 'silvered' sconces. In general they are of two types: those whose branches spring from a back reflector plate, usually in the form of a shaped oval or shield (Cat.8); and secondly, those with branches springing from a narrower upright back plate (Cat.7). An early version of this latter type are those where the base of the plate has a fixed horizontal gallery or stand holding a socket.

Other types include the rare examples whose branches are in the form of a human arm (probably deriving from mediaeval prototypes in wood or base metal). In addition there was the fashion for silver bordered looking glasses with branches, like the eight ordered by the Earl of Bristol from David Willaume in 1699 for his Drawing Room, or the four surviving examples at Chatsworth with silver gilt gadrooned borders, made by John Boddington c.1700.

By far the most usual however are those with back reflector plates whose oval or shaped borders form a cartouche for an engraved or chased armorial device, a monogram or a figurative scene in the centre. Some of the earliest are the set in the Duke of Buccleuch's collection, 1668, in the late auricular style (a collaboration between Robert Smythier and IN above a bird). More usual however are those with embossed naturalistic ornament often incorporating leafy and foliate motifs, and, if intended for a bed chamber, pairs of cupids. Their design follows the general development of English silver, changing in the 1690s under the influence of the Huguenots, and later, Daniel Marot, towards a sophisticated classicism with symmetrical scrolls and lambrequins. At Knole there are no less than 26 silver sconces in all, in at least three different sets of the earlier type. The finest examples of the later types are inevitably the work of immigrants: Pierre Platel, David Willaume, Philip Rollos and Paul de Lamerie.

Probably the most informative source for researching silver sconces is the plate list of the royal palaces drawn up in 1721. This itemised a total of 195 and mentions a large number of different types without fully describing them. Some were clearly intended to flank the fireplaces while others were for the walls of the State Apartments or for private rooms: 'Chimney sconces' (average 16oz each) or as 'small' (30oz), 'round' (12oz) or 'round knurld' (25oz). Other smaller types were 'heart shaped' (14oz), 'small heart' (11oz), 'sun sconces' (26oz), or 'small sconces with crowns' (26oz). Of the weightier types, often in large sets, there were 'starr & garter' sconces (71oz), large sconces with the cyphers of deceased monarchs 'CR' (112oz) and 'WR' (45oz and 92oz). There were also a large number described as 'acorn' sconces which appear to be those delivered in 1686 and 1689 'with oaken leaves with branches and stands to be hanged upp in her Majs new lodgings in Whitehall' (147oz) and were en suite with a chandelier similarly decorated with 'oaken leaves'.

Among these various types there were also a large group of 'picture sconces' — 10 pairs at 587oz and four at 216oz — which almost certainly incorporated an engraved or chased subject within their cartouche-like borders. Early examples of these include a set with figures of Athene, Juno, Mars and Ceres made 1668 and 1670 and which later passed to the Lowther and Swinton Castle collections after the sale of the royal plate in 1808. At the other end of the time scale there are the spectacular set of six made in 1730 by Peter Archambo for the Great Bedchamber of George Booth, Earl of Warrington, at Dunham Massey. The significance of their careful iconographic programme has defied analysis to date, although one of them represents the plight of Tantalus — after a lost painting by Titian — and may well be a veiled allusion to the Earl's unhappy marriage. His other sconces were a set of 14 in the Great Gallery (491oz in full), 'a pair of small sconces in the velvet bedchamber' (49oz), and 'a pair of small sconces with coronets at top in the Drawing Room' (48oz).

By the date Lord Warrington drew up his famous plate list (c.1750) silver sconces had been out of fashion for some 30 years. Their disappearance was due to a number of factors. First, they were often made of very thin silver and were prone to frequent damage by heavy handed servants. In addition carved giltwood chandeliers were beginning to appear, as well as more portable and efficient cast candlesticks. As etiquette became more informal there was less need to flaunt one's wealth in the traditional ways, and the new sociable activities required brighter interiors with the light concentrated on people's activities in the centre of the room. Nevertheless some splendid examples continued to be made including a set of 18 for Frederick Prince of Wales in 1738. After this date, however, this particularly attractive use of silver for lighting disappeared almost entirely. There was however a continued use of brass and gilt brass sconces in modish styles and a minor vogue for imported French ormolu (for example, by the Earl of Coventry in 1763). A short revival among the antiquarians of the Regency period never amounted to more than a passing whim.

6

This is a particularly elaborate example of a type of silver sconce introduced by the Huguenot goldsmiths during the 1690s. It appears to be one of a group of at least ten almost identical and all with a royal provenance. Others were recently on the art market and at Colonial Williamsburg (1700–1, by Philip Rollos, formerly at Keele Hall); at Thrumpton Hall; and on loan to Birmingham City Art Gallery and Museum.

In 1808 the Treasury hoped to raise some funds to defray the cost of new plate required for the apartments of the Princess of Wales at Kensington Palace now that she and the heir to the throne had decided to live apart. Thus it was decided to dispose of certain plate from the Jewel Office which was 'neither available for service in its present form nor valuable from its antiquity of workmanship'. It was hoped that some £900–£1,000 might be obtained in this way. George III gave his consent and the pieces were removed by the royal goldsmiths Rundell, Bridge and Rundell in September. Instead of melting them down Rundell's offered the better pieces to some of their leading clients including the Duke of Buccleuch, the Earl of Lonsdale, Walter Sneyd and the 1st Earl Brownlow. Another client was William Beckford who wrote as early as September 16th 'The old pieces from the royal silver are divine'. Rundell's must indeed have appreciated the worth of this newly fashionable 'antique' plate for some days later Beckford wrote that he was not 'in a state to spend two or three thousand pounds on silver, however royal or beautiful it may be'.

Other ex-royal silver sconces acquired by Lord Brownlow included a set with interlaced W and M royal monograms by George Garthorne and Arthur Mainwaring (copied by Lutyens in 1928 for the Vice-Regal Lodge, Delhi).

In 1698, the year previous to these, the Earl of Bristol acquired a set of eight 'great silver sconces weighing 491 oz at 7s per oz & for graving etc in all £175'. As they appear to have been almost exactly the same weight — 56 oz each — it is tempting to think they may have been the same model as these.

Lent by the National Trust (Belton House)

6 Sconce (from a set)
1699–1700
David Willaume
Silver
The double scrolled branch with sconce and drip pan springs from a console shaped vertical back plate with richly cast and chased ornament, including at the top, a royal crown, and below, two sceptres, scrolls and leafy foliage.
H 15¾in (38)
LIT. John Davis, *English Silver at Williamsburg* (1976), pp.17–19
PROV. Royal Collection; probably sold to Rundell, Bridge and Rundell 1808; bought by 1st Earl Brownlow and thence by descent.

7 Sconce (from a set of six)
1730–1
Peter Archambo
Silver
The double scrolled branch with sconce and drip pan springs from a shield shaped back plate with richly cast ornament including, at the top, an earl's coronet flanked by cast winged cupids. The borders below have foliage, scrolls, and flowers surrounding a chased oval 'picture' of Tantalus with Ixion and Sisyphus in the distance.
H 16in (41)
LIT. Timothy Schroder, Sotheby's sale catalogue 3 May 1990, lot 156
PROV. George Booth, 2nd Earl of Warrington and by descent; sold Christie's 20 April 1921, lot 59; sold Sotheby's 3 May 1990, lot 156 ('Property of a member of a Royal family').

figurative scenes — must be the 'picture sconces' referred to in contemporary inventories.

These sconces were commissioned by George Booth, 2nd Earl of Warrington for his seat at Dunham Massey where they originally hung in the Great Bedchamber. They were later removed by him to Enville Hall, Staffordshire. The huge quantity of plate of all kinds amassed by the earl over a long period included over 7,000 oz during the years 1728–30 alone. His taste was very conservative and he relied almost entirely on Huguenot craftsmen. Although these sconces are very old fashioned as a type, nevertheless their decoration is entirely up to the minute and unusually elaborate. Indeed they recall the design of holy water stoups for Catholic churches. The pattern of the drip pans is identical to the sconces made 1713–16 by Paul de Lamerie for Lord Foley.

Lord Warrington's inventory of 1750 recorded 24 sconces at Dunham Massey in 1750. In addition to these, there were 14 in the Great Gallery — obviously very much smaller than these and weighing 491oz in total. Others averaging 24oz each were in the Velvet Bedchamber and in the Drawing Room. The sconces here each possess their scratch weights, varying between 100 oz 11dwt and 102 oz 16 dwt. The mythological scenes have been shown to represent the following: Diana and Actaeon; Prometheus bound; Perseus and Andromeda; Tantalus with Ixion and Sisyphus in the distance; the death of Phaethon; and Narcissus and Echo. Whether these represent a coherent iconographic programme of particular significance to Lord Warrington has yet to be proved. To date only the source of the Tantalus scene has been identified — from a lost painting by Titian — and it has been suggested that this may be an oblique reference to the earl's unhappy marriage.

Lent by the National Trust (Dunham Massey)

Sconces with oval or shield shaped back plates are by far the most usual type and date from the beginnings of this form of lighting equipment. This variation — with chased

Chandeliers

Hanging lights have been described by a variety of different names between mediaeval times and the 18th century, including 'branches', 'lustres', and 'hanging candlesticks'.

The word 'chandelier', — from the French *chandelles* (tallow candles) — however, is known from at least the 15th century but only became usual in the early Georgian period. John Gumley advertised 'Glass Schandelieres' in 1714, while William Stukeley, the antiquarian, referred to 'branches or chandeliers, as we now modishly call them', in 1736.

Silver Chandeliers

Silver chandeliers were arguably the most extravagant form of lighting ever devised, and, like silver sconces, ought to be considered within the context of the luxurious silver furniture of the Baroque period. Indeed they were often the star items of a suite including tables, candlestands and firedogs as can be seen in Pyne's view of the Ballroom at Windsor in 1819. Not surprisingly very few have

survived owing to the high melt-down value represented by their weight. Probably the earliest surviving example dates from *c*.1670 now at Drumlanrig. It has two tiers of eight cast branches of dolphins with figures emerging from their mouths. It is said to weigh 2061 oz, and so its value in bullion during most of the 18th century (at 5/6d per oz) would have been over £470, not counting its value for fashion or as an 'antique' curiosity. In fact it was bought by the Duke of Buccleuch as late as 1835 from Garrard's for £1,750, although his ancestor the Duke of Montagu had indeed possessed a 'silver sconce with 16 branches' in the

Great Closet at Montagu House in Bloomsbury in 1707 (information from Tessa Murdoch).

Inevitably it was only the grandest in the land who possessed such things. There were five in the royal palaces in 1721, two of which survive today. One is at Hampton Court, made by royal goldsmith George Garthorne, *c.*1690. It is almost en suite with its smaller mate (Fig.22) made by Daniel Garnier, weighing 721 oz, recorded in the lodgings at St James's in 1721, and shortly afterwards in the 'little drawing room' (it is now at Williamsburg). They are both entirely in the Huguenot style with baluster shaped stems, fluted scrolling branches with gadrooned knops and drip pans. Another royal example, apparently delivered in 1687, was the now-vanished 'Great Branch Candlestick with Oaken leaves' which was en suite with a set of wall sconces. The earlier examples tend to have elaborate naturalistic and heraldic ornament, like the (possibly Dutch) chandelier at Chatsworth. By 1700 the transition to French classicism was complete as can be seen by the somewhat austere example at Knole. Indeed Daniel Marot included a group in his *Nouveaux Livre d'Orfeuverie* (1703, 1713). The surviving 18th century examples include those of 1703 by John Boddington (Ortez Patino Collection); 1734, by Paul de Lamerie (now in Russia); 1734, by Peter Archambo, made for George Booth, Earl of Warrington, weighing 529 and 532 oz each (private collection). A rococo example of 1752 by William Alexander, the great brass chandelier maker, was made specifically for the Fishmongers' Company, while a pair by Behrens of Hanover, 1736, after a design by William Kent for George II's use at Herrenhausen, is now in the Fairhaven Collection at Anglesey Abbey.

Fig.23. Silver Chandelier, by Robert Garrard II, 1837–8. made for for the first Duke of Abercorn

Despite their scarcity today silver chandeliers must not have been entirely uncommon. At least two conversation pieces by Hogarth — of the Cholmondeley and Woolaston families — may have these in the backgrounds. Alternatively they may have been of silvered base metal, sometimes described as 'French silver' or 'mettle lustres silver'. The extent to which imported French ormolu chandeliers, like those in the style of Boulle on the West Stairs at Chatsworth, were found in the 18th century England remains a mystery.

Keeping silver chandeliers clean must have been a nightmare. A small example at Ham in the Withdrawing Room in 1679 was 'blakd over' (possibly tarnished?) while 'paragon' and 'white serge covers to draw close above and below to cover the Chrystall and two Silver Branches' were supplied to Hampton Court in 1700 and 1701.

After an eclipse in fashion of nearly a century this extravagant form of lighting had one final blaze of glory in 1837 with the 18 light chandelier made by Garrard's for the Marquess of Abercorn (Fig.23). It is in the most luscious Rococo revival style with scrolls and heraldic ornament weighing 2,332 oz (and is one of the largest ever made). Not surprisingly its original owner became overwhelmed by such *folie de grandeur* and having sold his main English country house in 1852 died in 1885 leaving debts of £340,000.

Fig.22. Silver Chandelier, by Daniel Garnier, 1691–7. Originally in the Royal Collection, later at Keele Hall, Staffs

Crystal Chandeliers

Even rarer and more princely than silver chandeliers in late 17th century and early 18th century interiors were rock crystal 'branches', 'lustres' or chandeliers. Imported examples certainly existed at Somerset House before the Civil War and they were later to be found at Chatsworth, Penshurst and Hampton Court where three survive today. These latter were probably put together in England using imported rock crystals from Bohemia, Germany and Italy. Their metal frameworks were often silvered and

elaborately festooned with great coronas forming the apex of the compositions. However the considerable number of chandeliers incorporating both glass and rock crystal which are found in a number of country houses are usually thought to be 19th century in date. Nevertheless, the 'crystal' chandelier in the Drawing Room at Kedleston, which is recorded as being hung in 1770, cannot be the only surviving example from this date. William Farington witnessed the inaugural rout at Norfolk House in 1756, mentioning the two 'cristall' branches — 'I don't know what they cost — but from what I have seen, imagine about three or four Hundred Pound a Piece...'

Brass Chandeliers

Brass chandeliers first began to be used in private houses in the late Middle Ages and were probably being made in Britain by the late 15th century. Their early appearance must have evolved from examples from the Low Countries, like the one depicted in van Eyck's *Arnolfini Marriage*, through to the more familiar cast and multi branched models seen in Dutch genre paintings. Possibly the earliest to survive in situ are those now in the Gallery at Hardwick, thought to be possibly German c.1600, and originally in the Hall where they were described in 1601 as 'too great copper candlesticks with several places to set lightes in hanging'.

From the late 17th century to c.1740 the design of brass chandeliers is characterised by moulded stems on to which are slotted tiers of branches, with a finial at the top, a globe at the bottom and often a ring pendant. The branches are made of cast elements, allowing the patterns to be re-used and accounting for a great deal of conservatism. From at least 1738 the tiers of branches came to be bolted onto the stems by separate collars, and the stems themselves came to be baluster shaped, often with a vase shape at the bottom. On the whole these types of London-made brass chandeliers were only rarely intended for private houses. The leading chandelier maker in early to mid 18th century London, William Alexander, described his stock of 'fine wrought, or plain Brass Branches or Chandeliers, & plain, or cut-glass Lusters' as suitable for 'Churches, Halls, Assembly Rooms, etc'. Nevertheless two were hanging in the Front parlour of the Governor's Palace at Williamsburg in 1770, and examples which had outgrown their usefulness in churches sometimes found their way to private houses like Cat.8 or a magnificent one formerly at Hamilton Palace. Smaller 'Brass hanging candlesticks' were also available — perhaps the 'fine wrought' variety mentioned by William Alexander — and one such is mentioned in a relatively unimportant bedchamber in the inventory of Michael Warton of Beverley in 1688.

Four out of the five hanging chandeliers mentioned in Lord Burlington's New House at Chiswick in 1770 were

described as being made of brass — two in the Gallery and singles in the Crimson Dressing Room and the Lady's Dressing Room. These may well have been to bespoke design by the architect Earl himself or by William Kent, and are likely to have been gilded. It may well have been for one of these that Lady Burlington wrote to her husband 'I hope you will remember about my branch, to have it hung up, and the poize to be covered in green silk, of the same colour as the room and like-wise cord, and the weight to be in the form of a tassell'. 'Silvered' chandeliers (and sconces) also appeared in the early 18th century houses such as at the Cannons sale in 1747 and at Hampton Court. Brass was also used in the making of the frames of hall 'lanthorns', although Chippendale was quick to point out that 'if neatly done in wood, and gilt in burnished Gold, would look better, and come much cheaper'. Further down the social scale, in 1744 a Mr Henry Watson of Clarges Street, Mayfair, steward to the Earl of Bath, had two 'French' chandeliers in metal 'curiously repaired', implying that they were silver plated.

In the 19th century the revived use of brass for chandeliers, as well as for hanging oil lamps and gasoliers, made an important contribution to antiquarian and Gothic revival interiors. In the Porden house at Eaton the Saloon had a spectacular 12-light hanging lamp with stained glass supplied by Collins of the Strand, who invoiced the Duke for two chandeliers in 1818 for £913. At the Stowe sale in 1848 Collins' equally magnificent gilt octagonal lantern in the North Hall (which had originally cost the Duke of Buckingham £400), and whose glass depicted the regal descent of its owner, was knocked down to a hotelier from Tunbridge Wells for a mere £33-12-0d. On a more industrial note Hardman's of Birmingham were supplying brass or iron Gothic revival chandeliers and gasoliers to the designs of A.W.N.Pugin well into the 1890s. Their archives and catalogues show whole ranges available to their clients for candles or gas. At Chirk this firm provided metal light fittings in the 1850s and a hanging brass gasolier (indistinguishable in design to a chandelier) has recently been returned to the Cromwell Hall.

8 Chandelier

1738

By John Giles, London

Brass

Inscribed round the base 'EDM: SMITH SURGEON GAVE THIS TO YE CHURCH OF CHELTENHAM ANO:DOM:1738'

The quadruple baluster stem of vase design supports 24 S scrolled branches arranged in two tiers terminating in nozzles and circular drip pans. It is wired for electricity.

H 50in (127)

LIT. Gilbert, pp.113–15

PROV. Given to St Mary's Parish Church, Cheltenham by Edmund Smith in 1738 where it hung in the nave until 1838 and was sold by the church wardens following the vestry meeting on 26 April 1855; acquired by John E.W.Rolls for his large country house, The Hendre, near Monmouth and shown amongst period furnishings in the Great Hall in a photograph of 1865; by descent through the Lords Llangattock to Col J.C.E.Harding Rolls; Christie's, 28 Nov 1963, lot 15; Pratt & Burgess; bought with the aid of a government grant.

This chandelier is attributed to one of the leading makers in early 18th century London, John Giles, by stylistic analogy with other documented examples at St Dionis, Backchurch, London and at Framlington Church, Suffolk. This example is of particular importance in that it is the earliest dated chandelier in which the branches are bolted onto collars surrounding the globes instead of being hooked onto the stem above a single orb.

A number of alterations were made when the chandelier was converted to gas at some date after 1866. In order to create a continuous system of tubing the suspension ring and nozzles, being solid, were removed, the two plain lengths of curve on each branch was cut away and the

8

elaborately styles parts drilled before being re-soldered on to new sections of piping, thus apart from the addition of taps, the appearance of the branches was scarcely affected; internally the central iron rod was removed and radial tubing installed. The original gilt-metal hanging rods, the suspension and terminal rings (of scrolled design matching those at Backchurch and Framlingham) have not survived.

Leeds City Art Galleries (Temple Newsam)

Wood Chandeliers

Carved chandeliers (generally gilt) began to make an appearance in England in the last decade of the 17th century. Although they were never very widely used in English houses their most successful period was probably in the years of the high Rococo after which they gave way to the increasing popularity of glass. Like carved giltwood sconces, the early designs are taken from metalwork sources although they are generally more elaborate since their medium allows for greater virtuosity. They tend to have tall baluster shaped stems, often incorporating vases, leaf clad knops and globes, with undercut bases and pendants. A delightful early pair at Speke originally had carved fringed tassels suspended from their branches, possibly echoing the cover to the counterweights used for manipulating them. Examples of these 'balance weight, lines, and pulleys' can be seen in views of interiors and a

number of originals survive, notably on the pair *c*.1740 in the Saloon at Sudbury, and also at Belvoir (belonging to Argand lamps). The Duke of Chandos had a particularly grand pair of giltwood chandeliers with two tiers of double scrolled branches with wyvern heads one of which was acquired at the 1747 Cannons sale by Cholmley Turner for Kirkleatham Hospital where it hangs in the chapel to this day (Fig.24).

The single printed design for a chandelier by William Kent — executed in silver in a modified form — may have been influential on a small group of 'Palladian' carved chandeliers. Sir Thomas Robinson, arch-exponent of the new style, was in charge of the Board of Works and placed huge orders for furniture for the royal palaces with Benjamin Goodison, including a 'gilt branch to hold 12 candles in' for King William's Eating Room at Hampton Court in 1728. At Holkham Goodison hired out three gilt chandeliers in 1739 and when the house was nearing completion in 1757 he charged £12-16-0d for 'four carvd

Fig.24. Carved giltwood Chandelier, early 18th century. made for the Duke of Chandos at Cannons, moved to Kirkleatham Hospital, Yorkshire, after 1747

rich acanthus leaves, Vitruvian scrolls and egg and dart mouldings.

However it was the Rococo style which lent itself most successfully to chandelier design. It was as though the scrolling plasterwork of the ceilings now extended itself downwards and into a new dimension. The flickering quality of the candlelight lent itself to the asymmetrical lines of the new style, the deep undercutting of the carving and the exaggerated and unpredictable shape of the branches. This can be seen on a particularly fine group, two of which were formerly at Hornby Castle and at St Giles' House. This latter, with its eagle finial, was en suite with a pair of wall brackets and candelabra. Perhaps the most elaborate of all is the example in the Stone Hall at Houghton, replete with playful putti holding leafy festoons which seem to echo the same figures in the coving of the ceiling. It was bought second hand from Lord Cholmondley in 1748 and replaced Sir Robert Walpole's celebrated lantern which had been the subject of contemporary pasquinades and which was sold to Lord Chesterfield soon after Walpole's death.

As the Rococo period advanced so the forms appear to become lighter often with the bottoms of the stems becoming pierced, like the three superb examples at Lyme. Both Lock and Copland and Ince and Mayhew produced similar designs, the former with a slightly chinoiserie profile and the latter with a stem in the form of a sprouting tree (which we are assured, 'has been worked and looks very grand').

and gilt branches for candles' presumably in an approved Kentian manner. One of these may survive in the State Sitting Room. The style was sufficiently adaptable for less purist tastes and a variant can be seen at Tabley with

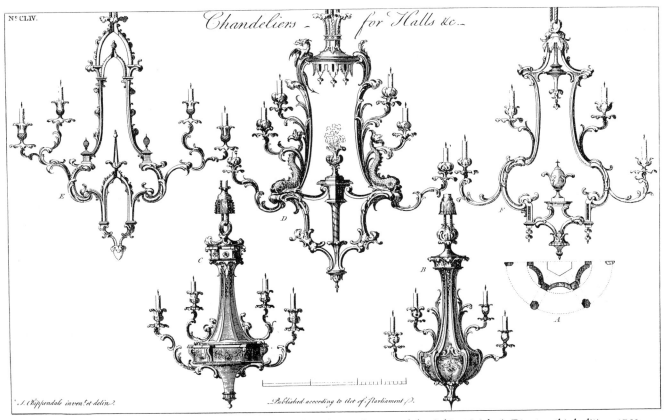

Fig.25. Designs for Chandeliers, from Thomas Chippendale's The Gentleman and the Cabinet Maker's Director, third edition, 1762

Despite their obvious magnificence giltwood chandeliers never seem to have been enormously popular. Only one example has yet come to light based on one of the two designs for solid chandeliers in Chippendale's *Director* (Fig.25). Obviously they were very fragile and a great number must have become irreparably damaged and discarded when they were no longer fashionable. But in addition they were never very effective. Isaac Ware, writing in 1740, declared that a room 'which if wainscotted will take six candles to light it, will in stucco require eight or if hung ten'. Thus for a grand room like the Ballroom at Bedford House in 1757, intended for occasions when a blaze of light was *de riguer*, it was necessary to have as many as 'three large carved and gilt chandeliers with twelve branch lights each, hung with green silk lines and balance tassels'. It is hardly surprising that when such rooms did eventually become brilliantly lit people complained loudly of the resulting heat. The same Duke of Bedford also provided Woburn with its first giltwood chandelier for the Saloon in 1760. It was probably one of the last great examples to be made in England and is still in situ. It has 18 lights and was specifically mentioned by Arthur Young who even noted its dimensions ('35 x 22 and of good height').

9 Chandelier
c.1755
Gilt pine

9

The elaborately flared and pierced lower member is carved with swirling Rococo ornament; the stem supports eight double scrolled branches with turned candleholders which are incised with Roman numerals. An iron rod passes through the hollow body ending in a buckle shaped pendant.
H 30$\frac{1}{2}$in (77)
PROV. Alfred Jowett; bought 1950

Leeds City Art Galleries (Temple Newsam)

Glass Chandeliers

The first makers of glass chandeliers in England were the specialist cabinet makers who dealt in mirror sconces with glass arms, like the well known John Gumley who first advertised 'Looking glasses, coach glasses and schandeliers' in the *London Gazette* in 1714. In many ways it was only an extension of the work of their specialist journeymen to assemble such branches in the same form as hanging brass chandeliers and to ornament the stems with cutting in the manner of bevelled mirror glasses. Thus by 1720 Gumley and his partner John Moore were supplying 'brackets' as well as sconces to Lord Burlington, this former term quite possibly referring to chandeliers. Certainly by 1725 the Duke of Chandos had 'four glass chandeleres' with three branches each, with pullies, weights and lines, in his library at Cannons, as well as two pairs of glass sconces with glass frames.

Probably the earliest glass chandeliers to remain in their original location are those in the galleries flanking the Vanburgh Hall at Grimsthorpe Castle, finished in 1726 (Fig.26). These have eight plain scrolled arms each, attached to gilt gesso receivers with stems comprising large cut glass globes surmounted by gilt gesso finials with pendants below. They obviously recall the appearance of contemporary brass chandeliers with the exception of the globe being on the stem instead of on the finial. The gesso elements are en suite with the five chandeliers in the Hall below which suggests that they are by the same maker.

Soon after this date Lord Burlington presented the Assembly Rooms at York with a chandelier whose stem was 'crinkled' or diamond moulded (less risky than cutting) and with arms with twisted rope mouldings. It was not long before cutting was extended to the arms which also began to be double curved, while drip pans became scalloped and new elements such as pagoda-like canopies began to appear. The globe and other elements of shaped glass in the stem could of course be re-arranged quite easily and fashionable new additions inserted. In 1750 for instance Mrs Delany was said to have 'pulled her old lustre to pieces, and is going to make one just like the Duchess of Portland's'. At Boughton there is an example with a somewhat old fashioned stem, but with cut glass arms holding the new style of pendants, as well as a tazza-like form at the bottom.

During the Rococo period the design of chandeliers became ever more adventurous and attuned to the spirit of the times. The inventory of the specialist glass cutter Thomas Betts in 1765 not only recorded chandeliers of various sizes (18 lights at £30, smaller ones between £15 and £20, at trade prices), but thousands of 'shades', 'panns', 'arms', 'scrolls', plus ornaments including 'drops' (often described as 'paste'), 'pillars', 'balls', 'fleur de lis', 'moons',

Fig.26. Glass and gilt gesso Chandelier, c.1726, Grimsthorpe Castle, Lincolnshire

Fig.27. Cut glass Chandelier, made by Maydwell and Windle, c.1760, Holkham Hall, Norfolk

'prisms' (spires), and 'stars'. These were not only for chandeliers but also for table lights and girandoles of all sorts. One of the best documented and least altered pairs of chandeliers of this date with just such features are the ones in the Gallery vestibules at Holkham of *c.*1760 and supplied by the prestigious firm of Maydwell and Windle (Fig.27). Another firm was Christopher Heady who advertised in 1775 'festoons of entire paste' which, as Martin Mortimer has suggested, may correspond to examples at Uppark (Fig.28), Badminton, Goodwood and Alnwick.

The 1770s however saw the rise of William Parker as the pre-eminent London maker and the development of a supremely elegant style of chandelier associated with his name. This came about by his receiving the commission for three 40 light chandeliers for the tea rooms at the Assembly Rooms in Bath, followed by another five for the ballroom. Their style was new in having tall but simple stems with vase elements, double scroll arms, and being comparatively simply dressed. As these chandeliers were so conspicuous, and in the very centre of the most fashionable place in the British Empire, Parker was indeed destined to prosper. For his aristocratic patrons he was able to supply a complete range of objects for lighting in a sophisticated neo-Classical style. At Chatsworth in 1782–3 he supplied the Duke of Devonshire with two 12 light 'lustres' 'richly cut and ornamented' for £210, in addition to six candelabra at £252 and various 'side gerandoles', some 'with front scroles'. His most important client at this time however was the Prince of Wales for whom he supplied over £4,000 worth of items for Carlton House 1783–9. Although these had been dispersed from their original

Fig.28. Cut glass Chandelier, possibly made by Christopher Haedy 'with festoons of entire paste', c.1775. Formerly at Uppark, Sussex

locations by the time Pyne's *Royal Residences* was published in 1819, other contemporary examples can be seen in the views of Buckingham House and the newly revamped King's Apartments at Hampton Court.

An important development of the late 1780s was the use of vertical chains originally linking the uppermost canopies with perhaps a tier of spires or prisms which themselves might alternate with a tier of lower candle bearing arms like the pair at Arbury delivered in 1788. Here the canopies, pans and nozzles all have vandyck borders, while the festoons are composed of graduated pear shaped drops. It was clearly a very successful design and Sir Roger Newdigate placed an order for another very similar but slightly larger model in 1804, although this time with plain fluted arms now 'more generally approved' (Fig.29). These are of course some of the grandest examples, but it was also possible to have small and indeed simple designs such as those supplied to the Marquis de Marigny in France by an unknown English supplier in 1779.

Until the early 19th century it seems that a single glass chandelier was sufficient in most country houses, in the same way that it is rare to find more than one Axminster or Moorfields carpet in any but the most extravagant houses. However, if the owners were particularly grand or their houses were important centres of hospitality there could be considerably more than one. Thus at Northumberland House there were four with 25 lights each in the Great Gallery, and at the Governor's palace at Williamsburg in 1770 there were three in the Ballroom ('with six branches each & gauze covers') and another one with twelve branches in the Supper Room.

It was the development of the vertical chains into tent-like compositions which led the way forward to the grandiose designs of Regency chandeliers. A drawing from Burton Constable of a most interesting transitional type, signed by Panton, and on paper watermarked 1794, shows the chains suspended from a domed canopy and framing the central vase-shaped stem but now descending to a circular ring made of gilt metal (Cat.13). This holds the candle arms and underneath are suspended additional festoons which are centred on another pendant canopy. The next step was to pack the chains more closely and to dispense with a visible central stem entirely. The upper canopies and candle arms had icicle pendants while a 'waterfall' of graduated pendants fell in concentric circles from under the principal ring. A series of these can be seen in the views of Frogmore which was remodelled for Queen Charlotte by James Wyatt 1792–5. A particularly unusual one consisting of a great circular 'waterfall' and which can be moved up and down like a skirt has recently been reinstated there.

By the time the Prince Regent received his new 56-light chandelier for the Crimson Drawing Room at Carlton House in 1808 the new style was entirely developed. Its huge cost, 1,000 guineas, was entirely characteristic of this extravagant and optimistic age. A tent with 30 chains with 30 drops on each (900 in all), in 6 or 7 sizes, cut with 16 facets on each side was obviously labour intensive and

Fig.29. Cut glass Chandelier, made by William Parker, 1804, nearly identical to one supplied in 1788. Arbury Hall, Warwickshire

costly, but this was not apparently a significant factor among the fashionable in Regency England.

Parker and Perry (as the firm had become in 1802-3) did not by any means have the monopoly of these grand objects. John Blades of Ludgate Hill supplied lustres for Eaton between 1808 and 1810 to the value of £2,600 although the Grosvenors acquired their magnificent metal chandelier for the Music Room from Collins. Blades' emporium was illustrated in *Ackermann's Repository* in 1809 which shows the full range of fashionable glass wares for this date (Back Cover). The firm made considerable use of the architect-designer J.B.Papworth at this date and was also responsible for designing their premises and for gilt bronze Argand lamps in a rich classical style (Cat.66). Among other architects who are said to have made designs for their client's glass chandeliers was Sir Jeffry Wyatville whose name appears in the Badminton accounts and who may have been responsible for the pair in the Great Drawing Room.

10 Pair of table candelabra

(or 'patent girandoles')
c.1784
Made by William Parker
Cut glass and ormolu
The shaped square bases are painted blue and gilded and stand on gilt ball feet and platforms. The central stem has

0

metals, enamels, paintings, varnishings or engravings, and a screw goes through the whole capital to fasten it together'.

Parker's bill to the Duke of Devonshire in 1782–3 includes similar items still at Chatsworth:

2	Large 12 light lustres richly cut and ornamented	£210
6	Candelabrums	£252
4	Pair of side Gerandoles with 3 lights each	£58-16-0
3	Pair of ditto with 2 lights each	£22-1-0
4	Pair of ditto with 2 lights and front scroles	£42
13	Very large vase lamps	£11-14-0
1	Pair of elegant Patent Gerandoles	£28-7-0

The last item on this invoice may have been similar to the example here. The style of the glass painting is reminiscent of James Giles (d.1780) and is generally on a blue ground, but examples with red and green ground colours have been noted (information from Martin Mortimer).

Lent by Oldham Art Gallery

11

a tall spine rising to a canopy with pendant drops and a cone finial. Two scrolled candle bearing branches and two further branches supporting smaller spires spring from a receiver on the stem. The latter have festoons linking them to the upmost canopy and each of the branches have graduated pear shaped pendant drops.
PROV. Given to Oldham Art Gallery from the Cook bequest via the NACF, 1955

These table candelabra may well be the type patented by the great glass chandelier maker William Parker on 28 March 1781 (no1287). This was for a new way of assembling 'the pedestals or supporters for candlesticks, girandoles, chandeliers, candelabrums, lamps, candle shades, eparns, clocks...'. They had 'A base, a die, a cornice or capital, with an ornament on the top thereof of various forms; some of the pedestals stand on feet of various forms, and some without feet, and the whole are composed of metals, wood, crystal, or coloured glass, ornamented with

11 Chandelier
Late 18th century
Cut Glass
The bowl is fitted with a silvered liner and brass receiver plate into which the 24 notched S-pattern arms, arranged

in two tiers, are socketed; the arms terminate in modern star shaped drip-pans and sconces. The stem centres on a fluted classical vase set between baluster components with an elaborate base element ending in a richly faceted cone. The corona is festooned with prismatic bead chains connected to the arms which are themselves linked by and suspend further cut glass drops ending in faceted pear shaped pendants. It is wired for electricity.
H 48in (122)
LIT. Gilbert vol.1, p.115
PROV. The Earls of Halifax, Hickleton Hall, South Yorkshire; Hickleton Hall Sale (Hollis and Webb, Leeds) 18–22 March 1947, lot 22; Thornton (Antiques) York; bequeathed by Sir George Martin 1976

The chandelier may be a contemporary with some of the alterations undertaken at Hickleton in an elegant neo-classical style probably in the 1770s.

Leeds City Art Galleries (Temple Newsam)

bead-chains and cut pendants; the silvered metal suspension rod is mounted with a socketed wheel into which the branches, masked by the dished base, are set.
H 48 (122)
LIT. Gilbert, vol.1, p.115
PROV. The Earls of Halifax; bought at the Hickleton Hall sale (Hollis and Webb, Leeds) 18–22 March 1947, lot 119

The elongated design of the stem and the more complicated cutting of the drops suggests a later date than the previous example. The receiver bowl covering the arm plate is almost certainly a replacement and appears to be a Regency flat dish light. Many chandeliers of this type have been re-assembled incorrectly often after electrification.

Leeds City Art Galleries (Temple Newsam)

13 Design for a Chandelier
*c.*1800
Paper watermarked 'J Whatman 1794'
Inscribed on the verso 'Drawings of Lantern & Chandelier from Panton & Co, New St Square, London'
Pen and wash
23 x 14½in (53 x 37)
PROV. Burton Constable

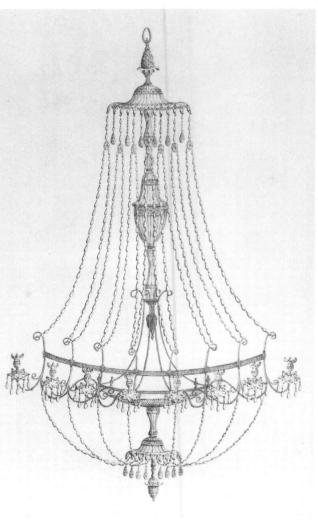

12

12 Chandelier
*c.*1800
Cut glass
The central notched stem ornamented with a wrythen knop is crowned by a slice-cut corona fringed with cut bead-drops and carries a smaller medial corona; the 14 cable twisted branches of S scroll design supporting rosette drip-pans and lights, radiate from a broad small star-cut dish ringed with a diamond pattern band; the stem terminates in a small chain-hung finial and a large faceted drop; the arms are profusely festooned with wired

13

The drawing shows an extremely interesting transitional type of chandelier mid way between the elegant neo-Classical designs of William Parker and the richly dressed confections of his successors in the Regency period. The arrangement of vertical chains which are now suspended from the domed canopy have assumed a tent-like profile framing the vase shaped central glass stem. They descend to the circular gilt metal ring which has attached scrolls some of which sweep inwards to support the stem while others hold the candle bearing arms. An inner gilt metal ring supports a glass tazza shaped stem the pendant of which receives the festoons which descend from the candle arms.

Within a very short period the design of chandeliers had developed so that the tent-like chains entirely enveloped the central stems, while the lower festoons gave way to descending and concentric 'waterfalls' of icicle drops.

This drawing was found in the archives at Burton Constable but the circumstances of its commission are not known. Very little appears to have happened at this house between the death of William Constable in 1791, and the tenure of Sir Thomas Aston Clifford-Constable (succeeded 1823, died 1870)

Lent by Leeds City Art Galleries and the Burton Constable Foundation

Portable Candlesticks and Candelabra

Although the basic purpose of the candlestick is simply to provide a receptacle for a candle it has always had more subtle functions when used in a country house. The most popular material favoured by the affluent for candlesticks for their own rooms has always been silver, which, being a precious metal, combines the qualities of a conspicuous status symbol with monetary investment. The reflective nature of the metal made it ideal for lighting, particularly when combined with ornamental surfaces. Throughout history therefore the goldsmiths have developed an ever-changing repertory of fashionable styles which makes a study of this category so rewarding. Many of these styles are represented in the exhibition so this introduction will merely serve as a broad overview.

Silver candlesticks must have been used in considerable quantities in country houses before the Civil War but very few early pieces have survived. It would seem that the general form of the early 17th century had trumpet or bell shaped feet and wide circular drip pans. This was imitated in pewter and delftware, and possibly also in Chinese porcelain (Cat.21). The bases sometimes unscrewed and could be up-ended to form fruitstands (or drinking bowls) and some must have survived into the later 17th century. In his inventory of 1688, the rich Beverley merchant Michael Warton had 15 silver candlesticks '1 of them with scrues to make fruit dishes', and which was obviously of this type. His total holdings of silver was valued at £2,000 and it also included '4 snuffers and plates for them, 4 extinguishers, 1 tinder box and..., 1 wax candle box, 1 salver for the same, 1 hand candlestick'. Most of the rest of his lighting equipment was in brass but there was also a small proportion in tin.

The style of candlesticks in both silver and brass which appeared most popular in the first twenty years after the Restoration are those with cluster column stems, recalling the short lived Gothic revival in church plate of these years. Indeed the majestic examples lent from Harthill church (Cat.14) may always have been altar candlesticks — perhaps from the Duke of Leeds' great house at Kiveton

nearby — or alternatively they were secular objects which were given to the church when they became unfashionable. The brass pair from Farnley (Cat.15) are an altogether simpler variation on this theme and typical of what Michael Warton may have possessed.

From here the next step was its development into the 'monument' candlestick of the 1680s and 90s, imitating classical columns with capitals, bases, flutings and steps. They are described as 'monument' sticks or of 'monumental fashion' in the royal accounts and remained popular until they were superseded by cast candlesticks. They were just the kind of charming but (by Continental standards) somewhat unsophisticated objects which the native English goldsmiths could turn out competently but which were to appear so provincial by comparison with the work of the Huguenot refugees. As early as 1683 Pierre Harache gained the freedom of the Goldsmith's Company and in the same year produced the set of baluster shaped and cast candlesticks at Althorp. They must have appeared revolutionary not only in the eyes of his clients but also his English fellow craftsmen. They were in fact a type which had been developed in France for nearly fifty years. These were presumably the 'ffrench fashion candlesticks' mentioned in the royal accounts from at least 1686.

In this exhibition there is an extraordinarily interesting pair in gilt brass with the arms of the third Earl of Carlisle, the builder of Castle Howard and just the kind the kind of enlightened nobleman who was to encourage the skills of these Huguenot craftsmen (Cat.17). Indeed Lord Carlisle patronised Pierre Harache for a number of pieces of silver in an advanced style which suggests that these baluster shaped sticks, albeit in brass, may be by the same man. Plated objects such as this, either silvered or gilded, were highly acceptable in country houses long before the advent of Old Sheffield Plate. In 18th century inventories they are somewhat confusingly described as 'french plated'. As late as 1758 Henry, seventh Viscount Irwin of Temple Newsam, who was particularly fond of his plate cupboard, had six pairs of 'French plate Candlesticks Gilt, Four Single Branches of Do'. As he spent most of his life being hard pressed for money he could never have afforded these in real silver gilt and was obviously content with the next best thing.

It seems that at Court the new baluster shaped candle-sticks were being delivered concurrently with the old fashioned 'monument' variety well into the 1690s. Variations of the baluster type had appeared by then — for example with lion masks on the knops (Cat.18) — and also the characteristic faceted profiles in hexagons or octagons which became known as 'square' candlesticks. In 1695 the King was provided with three varieties for his own use: '18 white candlesticks, 8 of them monument fashion, 4 of them square and 6 small FFrench fashioned...540oz 3dwt'. A number of the '8 pairs of candlesticks and nozells (square and polished)' supplied to the Duchess of Marlborough by Thomas Farrer in 1719 have survived, showing them to have been octagonal baluster shaped and 6¼in high.

Another two types are also described in the documents of this time: 'bassett' and 'pottin' candlesticks. The former were probably associated with a popular game and both were fairly substantial to judge by those delivered to the Queen's Withdrawing Room in 1689 '2 large bassett candlesticks weighing 106oz...3 pair of white pottin candlesticks weighing 139oz'.

It was also at about this date that 'standing branches' or candelabra began to be delivered both to the Court and to the aristocracy. Lord Bristol received a pair in 1688 weighing 78oz 2dwt at 7/6d per ounce (the same charge per ounce as a monteith), and the following year the Groom of the Privy Chamber took delivery of a pair weighing a massive 182oz and a smaller pair at 84oz. Originally they would probably have been only two-branched but by the end of the century triple-branches were also being made like the pair of 1697 at Welbeck. They were not to become particularly common until after 1770 (probably then because of the ever-later hour for dinner) but certain houses were exceptional. At Ickworth there is a set of 12 by Simon Le Sage of 1758, and Lord Warrington (who had no fewer than 45 domestic silver candlesticks at Dunham in 1750) listed four 'standing branches or Girandoles' for three candles each at 193oz, and another pair for four candles each, specifically described as for the Drawing Room.

The English goldsmiths of the early 18th century had to adopt the styles and techniques of the Huguenots or 'necessitous strangers' or else sink without trace. It is interesting to see how some of them developed over this transitional period: Thomas Ash (Cat.19) began his career making hand raised 'monument' candlesticks but by 1700 had adopted the new styles and by the time he died (by 1715) he was almost certainly supplying the trade as a specialist. Indeed the early 18th century saw the emergence of specialist candlestick makers: James Gould, Thomas Merry, William Cafe, John Quantock, Ebenezer Coker, John Carter. By the 1760s however the goldsmiths of Birmingham and Sheffield were sending candlesticks to London both in silver and in fused metal. Even after the establishment of assay officers in these cities in 1773 the London retailers were over-stamping the provincial maker's marks in the belief, often misplaced (see Cat.40), that their clients would prefer to see a London maker's mark. A consistent offender was John Carter (Cat.31).

The great majority of portable candlesticks were not of course intended for any particular function or location in the house. Certain types however did have a specific purpose. Foremost among these were chamber candlesticks, intended for taking to and using in the bedroom after dark. Thus they always had short stems with wide pans and originally long saucepan-like handles. It became the practice to combine them with an extinguisher and a pair of snuffer scissors, usually by inserting the latter in a slot under the sconce. They appear to have been known as 'flat' candlesticks early in the century, and somewhat later as 'hand' or 'night' candlesticks. By the early 19th century they were being made in large sets.

Accompanying all candlesticks were snuffers and stands, essential for the development of self-consuming wicks in the 19th century. There does not seem to have been a recognised ratio of sticks to snuffers, although in the higher reaches of the Civil Service it appears that for every pair of candlesticks supplied by the Jewel Office there was an accompanying snuffer and tray or stand. For toilet services (which usually included a pair of candlesticks) snuffers were optional. Those supplied with Queen Charlotte's in 1762 (perhaps the service seen in Zoffany's famous picture) were returned three days later. Lord Warrington's (needless to say) were particularly fine (Cat.25) and were made by John Quantock, a specialist who also supplied the candlesticks, while the rest of the service came from Magdalen Feline.

Yet another form of sticks for 'lighting' were tapersticks intended for the desk and principally for melting sealing wax. Their minuscule size meant that they could hardly have provided significant amounts of light. They may have been the 'wax candlesticks' referred to in inventories. Another use for them may have been for holding tapers for lighting pipes for tobacco: at Powis in 1745 there was 'a small pair smoking candlesticks'. Until the middle of the 18th century they imitate table candlesticks almost identically, sometimes to a scale of 1:2. From the 1760s the spindle type (Cat.30), and the 'bougie box' supersedes the older form.

The arrival of the Rococo style from France in the 1730s provided the more virtuoso goldsmiths with fine opportunities to display their skills, not least in candlestick making. As in the previous generation it was those with first hand links with the Continent who made the greatest impact: Paul de Lamerie, Paul Crespin (Cat.22) and Frederick Kandler (Cat.24), often by reviving the use of figurative motifs for stems (Fig.30). The source of much of the advanced work of this time can be found in European goldsmiths' work or design. Uniquely English is the strange if memorable experiment by William Kent to produce a Palladian alternative to the all-pervading Rococo style (Cat.22).

The specialist English candlestick makers, while not attempting the virtuoso style of the leaders of their craft, nevertheless adapted the baluster form very successfully for more moderate English tastes. An extremely popular type had semi-auricular spreading lobes on the bases, knops with faintly pagoda-like profiles, and nozzles

Fig.30. Candelabra, by Frederick Kandler, 1738–9, with figures of Hercules and Iole

suggestive of budding flowers (Cat.29). A slightly later variation consisted of spiral gadroons and flutings giving the appearance of bat's wings, and thus giving its name to this type (Cat.33). More conservative, and produced in great numbers, were the 'nurl'd' or 'gadroon'd' patterns (Cat.26). Other types were encrusted with shells on the base and nozzles ('scalloped' pattern), while an elegant rococo style was the 'waiv'd pattern' delivered to Speaker Cust in 1762.

The architect Robert Adam is often credited with causing the 'revolution in taste', which brought about a new interpretation of classicism in the 1760s. Despite his great importance in popularising the new style and in designing completely harmonious interiors (particularly dining rooms) it was often the patron who dictated the style of his silver. Thus the strangely austere design by the youthful Carr of York, in the form of an Ionic column, must surely have been dictated by his patron, the avant-garde William Constable who was in the forefront of taste and fashion (Cat.28). It represents the return, after nearly seventy years' absence, of the 'monument' candlestick.

Adam's own attempts at candlestick design represented here (Cat.31) seems not to have been enormously successful. It appears that his clients preferred a more pragmatic approach to their lighting equipment. The French version of neo-Classicism became known and popular: the Duke of Bedford's candlesticks by R.J.Auguste (supplied in 1766) were copied with variations by several different makers (Fig.31). Equally, Matthew Boulton at Birmingham commissioned James Wyatt, and possibly Robert Adam and William Chambers, to provide designs for candlesticks for large-scale production in silver as well as fused plate. Boulton also had an important trade in ormolu, combining it with fluorspar and painted glass (Cat.36) and white marble (Cat.37) to create some of the most luxurious objects of the age.

As the country prospered so the habits of the aristocracy filtered down to the ever increasing numbers of merchant and industrial families who abandoned city life for their own new country houses and estates. For the middle classes the new fused plate gave them 'silver looking' objects at a fraction of the price of the real thing. Yet Old

Fig.31. Candelabrum (one of a set). The candlestick was supplied by Parker and Wakelin 1770–1, and is derived from an original by R.J.Auguste; the branches 1780–1. Triple branches were added in 1826

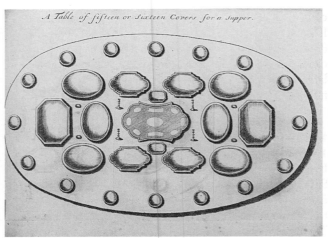

Fig.32. 'A Table of fifteen or sixteen Covers for a supper'. From Vincent La Chapelle, The Modern Cook, 1736

Sheffield Plate was strangely democratic: at Nostell in 1784 there were seven pairs of plated candlesticks, two 'with fluted columns', five 'more upright'. One example from Castle Howard is shown here (Cat.38). Likewise, provincial-made candlesticks — albeit in the most refined possible taste — were entirely acceptable in even the grandest households (Cat.40).

During the last years of the century the hour for dinner became ever later, so that by the final decade the main meal of the day was often eaten after dark (certainly in winter). In 1736 Vincent La Chapelle had suggested only four baluster shaped candlesticks for a table plan for a supper for sixteen (Fig.32). Now the response from the goldsmiths was to provide increasing numbers of branched candlesticks or candelabra intended for the table. In the past these had sometimes been provided as part of a centrepiece (Cat.20) and were to be so again in the Regency period. Lord Carlisle's French style candlesticks, adapted from Auguste in 1770, acquired a pair of *double* branches in 1780 and a set of *triple* branches in 1826 when dining habits changed yet again. Time and again at this period branches were added to existing sets of candlesticks. Often these were in fused plate.

By the turn of the century the variety of candlesticks to be found in a country house plate cupboard could be very extensive. Arthur Grimwade has made a fascinating study

of the types at Althorp and the different routes by which they arrived there. At Harewood the silver had been amassed by the family only since the 1730s at the earliest, but by 1803 there were a bewildering number of different types (some are identifiable from the 1965 sale catalogue):

6 chas'd lion mask candlesticks [4 by Thomas Heming 1774]
6 do branches to do with nozzles
4 plain scallop candlesticks [by William Cafe, 1762]
4 therm triangular chasd do
4 plain pillar square gadron do [by William Cafe, 1762 or 1758]
4 do do flowered do
8 scallop table candlesticks
2 black boy candlesticks, gilt with branches
6 hand candlesticks, with nozles and extinguishers
4 flowered foot fluted pillar table candlesticks [possibly by de Lamerie 1736]
4 plain do
2 short fluted pillar do
2 snuffer stands
2 pair steel snuffers
1 pair do with silver bows
6 night candlesticks and extinguishers

The 'lion mask' candlesticks are particularly interesting, possibly deriving from French prototypes in the 'gout grec', and were first developed by Matthew Boulton in the 1760s. It has been estimated that he could make his versions at the cost of £17-2-0d by using the economical new machinery (flatting mills, fly-punching, advanced die-stamping) while a London maker, using manual skills, would charge £44-11-0d. Despite this Boulton was obliged to abandon goldsmith's work as unprofitable and the silver-buying public continued to go to the traditional makers.

'Lion mask' candlesticks continued to be made well into the first decade of the 19th century by a number of different makers, often copying and augmenting earlier sets. Indeed this is a feature of much early 19th century silver, reflecting a more expansive lifestyle and greater hospitality among country house owners in these optimistic years (Cat.47). It also accounts for many of the revival styles which flourished at this time. But the great pioneering years of candle lighting were over. The huge success and popularity of Argand lamps was to make the category more interesting to observe from this date onwards.

14 Pair of candlesticks

1675–6
By Jacob Bodendick
Silver gilt
Each is inscribed 'Ye gift of Peregrine 2nd Duke of Leeds to Harthill Church'.
The raised octagonal bases are chased with acanthus foliage at the angles and at the bottom of the stem which rises to similar octagonal platforms (or vestigial drip pans). The vase shaped knops have further cast acanthus foliage and rise to fluted octofoil stems with further chased leaf ornament.
H 13$\frac{7}{8}$in (35.2)
LIT. T.M.Fallow and H.B.McCall, *Yorkshire Church Plate*, vol.2 (1915), pp.114–15; Charles Oman, *English Church Plate* (1957), and *Caroline Silver*, p.54, pl.61B
PROV. Given to Harthill Church by Peregrine, second Duke of Leeds (succeeded 1712, died 1729)

These are some of the most outstanding silver candlesticks of the Restoration period. They were made by Jacob Bodendick, originally from Limburg and one of the most distinguished goldsmiths working in London. His workshops included highly skilled foreign craftsmen and his style is often characterised by Germanic details.

It is difficult to know whether these examples were originally intended for secular or ecclesiastical use. They may well have been acquired by the first Duke of Leeds (1632–1712) and used as 'altar candlesticks' in the chapel at his lavish country house, Kiveton Park, South Yorkshire (built 1694–1705, destroyed 1812). If so they are further examples of the Duke's taste for magnificent works of art. Alternatively, they may have been in use within the house, placed on grand torcheres, and were later presented to the church at Harthill (adjacent to the Park) once they became old fashioned. The gift originally included a communion cup, paten and flagon (date unknown) which were subsequently sold. It should be noted that most 'altar candlesticks' of this date are not only distinguished by their abnormal height, but also by the use of prickets (Staunton Harold Church), or tall curving bases (Untermyer collection).

Lent by the Parochial Church Council of Harthill

15 Pair of candlesticks

c.1680
Brass
The square bases rise to similar square platforms (or vestigial drip pans) and square fluted cluster column stems.
H 10in (25)
PROV. By descent in the Horton-Fawkes family of Farnley Hall, Yorkshire
The design is taken entirely from silver prototypes but is unusual in having the stem placed at 45 degree angle to the platform or base. A nearly identical pair in silver (H 8in) with a maker's mark BP with an escallop below dates from 1670 and is engraved with the arms of Chichester.

Lent by Nicholas Horton-Fawkes Esq.

15

16 Snuffer stand, snuffer scissors, extinguisher and candle socket

1685–6

Maker's mark IL with coronet above (John Laughton)
(Extinguisher probably by John Sutton)

Silver

The octagonal base rises to a baluster stem with spiral fluting supporting a receptacle for the snuffer which has pierced decoration in the form of a shield surrounded by a garland of fruits and flowers. The scrolled handle is on an axis with a further scrolled candle extension. The extinguisher has an unidentified coat of arms.

Max L 6¾in (17.1)

LIT. *Silver from the Assheton Bennett Collection* (1965), p.34; Michael Clayton, *The Collector's Dictionary of the Silver and Gold of Great Britain and North America* (1985), p.359

PROV. Untraced; Mr and Mrs Edgar Assheton Bennett; given to Manchester City Art Gallery 1957

Snuffers were an essential part of lighting equipment until the development of self consuming wicks in the 19th century. Since at least the Restoration they have appeared en suite with a tray or pan — in 1661 Samuel Pepys received a gift from the sail-makers of 'two large silver candlesticks and snuffers and a slice to keep them upon'.

Combinations of vertical stands and snuffers are only found between *c*.1680 and 1725. This is a particularly rare example also combining a small candle socket and an extinguisher (also known as 'podkins').

Lent by Manchester City Art Gallery

16

17 Pair of candlesticks

c.1690–1700

Brass, with traces of gilding

The octagonal bases have sunken centres, baluster stems and vase shaped sockets all with simple moulded decoration. The bases are engraved with the armorials of Charles, third Earl of Carlisle.

H 6⅛in (15.5)

PROV. Charles, third Earl of Carlisle; private collection

The form of these candlesticks is once again in a simplified Continental Baroque style, and in stark contrast to the columnar 'monument' sticks being produced by native-born craftsmen. Indeed, these appear to be precisely the same pattern and size as a set of four in silver made by Pierre Harache, 1683–4, at Althorp, and described by Arthur Grimwade as the earliest recorded baluster candlesticks in England. He suggests that this form was first made by French goldsmiths in 1636 and notes a Parisian pair also at Althorp, 1678, with near identical stems and sconces.

This is particularly interesting in view of Lord Carlisle's known patronage of Pierre Harache, the Huguenot craftsman who was one of the first to obtain his Freedom from the Goldsmiths' Company in 1682. A pair of highly sophisticated ewers or 'decanters' by him 1697, are at Temple Newsam, and a two handled cup and cover, 1701, is in the civic collection at Carlisle. The evidence tends to suggest that these candlesticks may also have been made by Harache, or a close follower or associate.

Although there appears to be no record of Lord Carlisle's holdings of brass objects, his inventory of Henderskelfe Castle (the modest forerunner of Castle Howard, and a secondary property at this date), dated 1693, describes eleven pairs of silver candlesticks, including two 'gilt' which may possibly refer to gilt brass such as these.

More revealing of the possessions of a great Whig nobleman of the early 18th century is the plate list of Castle Howard drawn up in 1730. This itemises over 20 pairs of silver candlesticks variously described: 'large candlesticks' (average weight 19oz each), 'lesser' (17oz) 'plain' (14oz), 'small' (10 1/2oz), 'null'd' (15oz), '4 flatt candlesticks wrought at the bottoms' (16oz — annotated 'these have no sterl.mark') '4 flatt candlesticks plain bottoms and round sockets' (11oz). In addition he had 'two branch candlesticks' (23oz), a 'wax candlestick' (6oz — possibly a taperstick), and two gilt candlesticks (6oz 18dwt and 7oz) listed among the 'Guilded plate for the side board'.

Among other nearly identical examples to these in silver are a pair by Philip Rollos, 1697, and a pair (with an additional ring below the knop) by Ralph Leake, 1690. During the first and second decades of the new century the baluster form became slightly more elongated and the heavy mouldings gave way to faceted shapes or decoration with classical Regence motifs. Another similar pair by Harache, 1703, is illustrated by Wills (p.57)

Lent anonymously

8

18 Candlestick (from a set of four)
1692–3
David Willaume I
Silver gilt
The circular base has a sunken centre, a baluster stem and vase shaped socket, cast and chased gadroons and flutes,

chased foliate ornament, and the stems have applied lions' masks.
H 5½in (14)
LIT. Arthur Grimwade, 'Family Silver of Three Centuries', *Apollo*, December 1965, p.501; Philippa Glanville, 'The Silver of John, fourth Duke of Bedford', *Apollo*, June 1988, p.413
PROV. By descent from Wriothesley, second Duke of Bedford

The candlestick is from a set of four supplied to the second Duke of Bedford apparently by David Willaume. Two date from 1692–3 and another two from 1701–2. Another set of ten at Woburn, with baluster stems and scale ornament, date from 1708 and 1728 and also have Willaume's maker's marks although in this latter case it may represent that of Willaume *fils*. These goldsmiths certainly appear to have been the Russells' favourite suppliers from at least 1703 to the late 1720s: a bill of 1709 to the Duchess refers to 'boittes a poudre' presumably for a toilet service. The small scale of these candlesticks and the fact they are gilded (although renewed) suggests that they may also have been from a toilet service.

These highly elegant cast candlesticks are entirely in an anglicised Baroque style and in contrast to the columnar style 'monument' candlesticks being produced by native-born English goldsmiths at this date. This type, with its baluster stem (with or without lion masks), may well have been described in the contemporary Jewel Office records as 'FFrench candlesticks', like the six supplied to the King's bedchamber in 1686 (weighing 21oz each), or like one of the two pairs delivered to the Duke of Berwick in 1687 'one pair of them monumental, ye other FFrench fashion'.

This model appears to have been used by a small group of leading goldsmiths at the turn of the century including J.Bird (1694 and 1699), formerly at Hornby Castle, John Laughton (c.1695), John East (1702) and Benjamin Pyne (1692). Willaume produced the same design at least once again in 1706 as well as simpler candlesticks with straight tapering stems.

Lent by the Marquess of Tavistock and the Trustees of the Bedford Estate

19 Pair of candlesticks
1710–11
Thomas Ash
Silver
The wide octagonal and moulded bases rise to cast baluster octagonal faceted stems and octagonal faceted vase shaped sconces. The bases are engraved with an unidentified coat of arms and the initials W under the bases.   F*S
H 6⅓in (16.1)
LIT. Lomax, pp.155–56
PROV. Unknown; Viscount Camrose; bought 1976

These candlesticks represent the further advance of candlestick design from the squatter baluster form introduced by

19

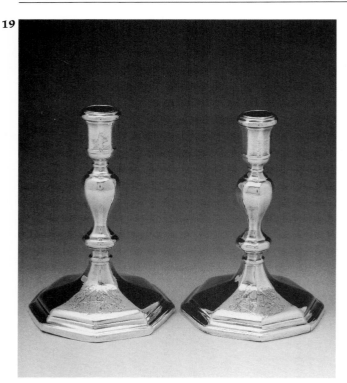

the Huguenots in the 1680s. This plain faceted design was to have a short life before being overwhelmed by richer ornament on the knops and stems.

The shortness of these examples suggests a possible origin as part of a toilet service, as do the armorials which are contained within a lozenge — a device associated with spinsters or widows.

Thomas Ash is an example of a goldsmith who successfully came to terms with the new style and techniques of the Huguenots. Early examples of his candlesticks are of the 'monument' type, but by *c*.1700 he was making more fashionable baluster shaped patterns. Recent research has shown that, on his death in 1715, he was owed sums of money by fellow goldsmiths including Paul de Lamerie, Benjamin Pyne and Anthony Nelme. Clearly therefore he was working as a specialist sub-contractor to these big workshops.

Leeds City Art Galleries (Temple Newsam)

20 The Kirkleatham Centrepiece
1731–2
David Willaume II and Anne Tanqueray
Silver

21

The structure consists of four cast feet supporting a central frame with a covered tureen, two pierced caster stands, two branches for cruet frames, and four branches for candle sockets. The ornament comprises rich cast, chased and engraved motifs in the Regence style. Engraved variously with the armorials and crest of Cholmley Turner of Kirkleatham
H (tureen) 11¼in (28.5)
LIT. Lomax, pp.87–91
PROV. Probably William, fourth Earl of Coventry; Cholmley Turner; by descent through his wife's family the Marwoods of Busby Hall; bought 1988.

This celebrated centrepiece, the earliest and most complete example to have survived, could have been used in one of two principal ways; at dinner (in the early afternoon), as a fruit stand, with the caster stands and cruet frames removed, and with the candle sockets replaced by small dishes and the central tureen covered by a large oval dish. This would have remained on the table for the duration of the first courses and until the guests could begin to use it for the dessert. Its alternative use was at the more informal meal of supper in the late evening when candles would be required. Here it served as a dumb waiter complete with a central tureen, casters and cruets. No doubt the richly chased ornament was seen to great advantage in the flickering quality of the candlelight.

Eating after sunset has obviously always required candlesticks for the table. Being portable however, most candlesticks were usable anywhere in the house, unless, as here, they were integral with a piece of table silver. Vincent la Chapelle (1736) shows a table for supper with four baluster shaped sticks (Fig.32). By the 1780s however, when dining was getting later (and in winter would have taken place after dark), 'branched' candelabra became more common, and owners frequently augmented their simple earlier sticks with new double branches. By the Regency period, with its taste for greater opulence, triple branches were often added to create an even more dazzling effect. At Castle Howard for example the fifth Lord Carlisle's 'rams head' candlesticks, bought from Parker and Wakelin in 1770, were augmented by double branches in 1780, and with triple branches in 1826 (Fig.31).

Leeds City Art Galleries (Temple Newsam)

21 Pair of candlesticks
Ching dynasty, reign of Chien Lung (1736–95)
Chinese porcelain with underglaze blue decoration
The circular foot supports a baluster stem with a wide central platform or drip pan and an upper stem with a pricket.
H 5¼in (13.3)
PROV. The Gascoigne family of Parlington Hall, Yorkshire

The style recalls earlier European examples in metalwork.

Leeds City Art Galleries (Lotherton Hall)

22 Candlestick (from a set of four)
1741–2
Paul Crespin (designed by William Kent)
Silver
The shaped octagonal base has cast and chased gadroons and scrolling leaf ornament rising to a baluster shaped stem with four oval masks on a lower knop, further leaf ornament and fluting, surmounted by an implied Corinthian capital and a shaped octagonal sconce which is engraved with the Howard family crest.
H 10¼in (26)
LIT. John Hayward, 'Silver made from the Designs of William Kent', *Connoisseur*, 174 (June 1970), pp.106–10; James Lomax, 'Silver at Castle Howard: Three Hundred Years of Investment and Fashion', *The Art Quarterly of the NACF*, 9 (Spring 1992), pp.32–5
PROV. Possibly Henry, first Duke of Newcastle; bought 1790 by Frederick, fifth Earl of Carlisle from Wakelin and Taylor; by descent.

22

these which must have been traded in at the goldsmiths by a recent client. At 7/- per ounce they were considerably cheaper than new ones for which he might have expected to pay some 8/6d per ounce including 'fashion'.

Lent from the Castle Howard Collection

23 Pair of candlesticks
Mid 18th century
After a design by one of the Slodtz brothers
Mahogany with brass nozzles
The shaped circular bases support swirling baluster shaped stems rising to sconces and leafy nozzles. The richly carved decoration comprises raffle leaves and fronds on the base, asymmetrical cartouches on the stem with further leafy scrolls on the sconces.
H 9¾in (25)
LIT. *Rococo: Art and Design in Hogarth's England* (1984), p.112

The design source for this pattern of candlestick, which is not uncommon in French ormolu, has often been attributed in the past to Juste-Aurele Meissonnier (1695–1750) who

2

The candlestick was designed by William Kent, and engraved and published in John Vardy's *Some Designs of Mr Inigo Jones and Mr William Kent* in 1744, three years after its manufacture. A further three by Paul Crespin, and of the same date, are at Castle Howard. An additional eight have also been traced — four more by Paul Crespin, 1745; two by Edward Wakelin, 1757; and a further two by Wakelin and Taylor, 1775. All these latter examples are associated with the Dukes of Newcastle and first surfaced at the Clumber sale in 1922. The ones dating from 1757 and 1775 were clearly copies of the originals by Crespin. It seems likely therefore that the four at Castle Howard were part of a large bespoke set.

The surviving ledgers of the goldsmiths Wakelin and Taylor reveal that the fifth Earl of Carlisle spent considerable sums between 1787 and 1793 building up a new dinner service mainly consisting of octagonal shaped dishes and covers. It also included matching tureens, sauce boats and salts in an elegant style recalling the simpler designs of R.J.Auguste. On 1st May 1790 he was charged 'To 4 Fine Chas'd second hand candlesticks 155oz @ 7/- per ounce, £54-5-0d'. This weight corresponds almost exactly to the total weight of this set of four at Castle Howard (156oz 5dwt). The discrepancy can perhaps be accounted for by the obvious alterations to the sconces which were probably altered and re-engraved at this time.

Clearly Lord Carlisle required a set of octagonal candlesticks to be approximately en suite with his new octagonal dishes. He must have taken the opportunity to purchase

indeed executed many designs for candlesticks. However, a pair of very similar ormolu candlesticks in the Wallace Collection is considered by Sir Francis Watson as bearing a general resemblance to a pen and ink drawing by one of the brothers Slodtz (Furniture Catalogue, F.76). This is in a volume in the Bibliotheque Nationale (Champeaux, *Portefeuille des Arts Decoratifs*, nd, pl.134) which also contains drawings in many different hands, and as Michael Snodin states (*Rococo*, p.112) even those recently connected with the Slodtz seem to be by several hands (F.Souchal, *Les Slodtz* (1967).

The taste for French silver in England was voracious throughout the 18th century, whether for imported pieces, copies of originals, or pieces deriving from engraved sources. This model was made by a number of goldsmiths including Paul de Lamerie in 1742, William Gilpin in 1744 (now at Althorp), and Paul Crespin in 1750–1 (for the fourth Earl of Dysart).

It has been suggested that this remarkable example of virtuoso carving may have been a goldsmith's pattern.

Sebastien Antoine Slodtz (1695–1754) was a son of the sculptor Sebastien Slodtz, and a grandson of the royal cabinet maker Domenico Cucci. He became Dessinateur de Cabinet du Roi in 1750 and was followed in that post by his brother Paul-Ambroise.

Lent anonymously

24 Candlestick (from a set of four)

1744–5
Charles Frederick Kandler
Silver
The shaped circular base and baluster stems are cast and chased with flowers, scrolls, shells and insects, the vase shaped sockets have detachable nozzles with similar borders, and it is engraved with the armorials of Sir William Heathcote, first Bt, of Hursley, Hants (1693–1751)
H 12in (30.5)
PROV. By descent at Hursley Park, Hampshire to Sir Michael Heathcote, Bt; sold Christie's 22 May 1991, lot 245; private collection.

The candlesticks are in Kandler's spectacular Rococo style albeit on a smaller scale to his celebrated Jerningham wine cooler of 1734 (Hermitage, St Petersburg) or his Hercules and Iole candelabra (see Timothy Schroder, 'The Kandler Candelabra', *Partridge's Recent Acquisitions 1991*, pp.11–13) (Fig.30). The extreme naturalism on the base here recalls similar features on the latter candelabra. This feature may be associated with the modeller Michael Rysbrack who worked to George Vertue's designs on the Jerningham cooler 'for the figures and base relievos, besides several chasers imployed to finish it'. The extraordinary high quality of Kandler's modelling and chasing suggests a foreign training and a continuous and up-to-date knowledge of the Continental trends.

24

It is interesting to compare these candlesticks (weighing *c*.36oz each) with the four pairs ordered by Viscount Fairfax of Gilling Castle from Kandler in January 1754. The first two were described as 'new fashion'd' and were charged at 7/10d per ounce, their weight being 29oz each. The second pair were somewhat heavier at 35oz each, and were also described as 'new fashd'. These must have been considerably more elaborate and were charged at 10/- per ounce. Lord Fairfax's bill was partly paid by turning in old plate including 'a pair of old candlesticks' weighing 22oz 12dwt for which he was credited at 5/7d per ounce (Peter Brown, *Pyramids of Pleasure*, (1990), p.36).

From the number of surviving pieces it seems that the Heathcote family were keen supporters of the Rococo style.

Lent anonymously

25

2

25 Pair of candlesticks, snuffers and snuffer stand
1754–5
John Quantock
Silver

The candlesticks have shaped square bases, baluster stems of faintly discernible octagonal profile, vase shaped sconces and detachable drip pans. The snuffers are of scissor form standing on three ball feet, and the stand is of shaped rectangular form standing on hoof feet with a scrolled handle and thumbpiece. Each item is profusely engraved with borders of scrolls, shells, diaper patterns, and with the arms of the Countess of Stamford and monograms on the drip pans.
H (candlesticks) 8in (21)
L (snuffer stand) 7¾in (19.5)
L (snuffers) 6¼in (15.75)
LIT. John Hayward, 'The Earl of Warrington's Plate', *Apollo*, July 1978, pp.38–39
PROV. By descent from Mary, Countess of Stamford at Dunham Massey, Cheshire

These candlesticks, snuffers and stand are part of a 28 piece silver toilet service traditionally said to have been presented to Mary, Countess of Stamford by her father, the second Earl of Warrington for her 50th birthday. All the other pieces bear the maker's mark of Magdalen Feline (except two waiters by Richard Rugg). These pieces of lighting equipment have the mark of John Quantock, a specialist candlestick maker whose mark has not apparently been found on any other category of plate. The whole toilet service however has been uniformly engraved, probably by yet another specialist craftsman. It is in a late Régence style, some 30 years at least behind the times, but entirely in the taste of Lord Warrington's youth. For further discussion of his silver see Cat.7

Lent by the National Trust (Dunham Massey)

26 Pair of candlesticks (from a set)
1760–1
Edward Wakelin
Silver

The candlesticks have raised square bases with cast gadrooned borders and circular depressions which rise to cast baluster shaped octagonal tapering stems with lobed knops and cast vase shaped sconces with nozzles.
Inscribed 'No 6' and 'No 7' and with scratch weights 25oz and 25oz 14dwt.
H 9½in (24.2)
LIT. Lomax, p.157
PROV. Bequeathed by Agnes and Norman Lupton 1952

This is one of the most popular designs for silver candlesticks found in the middle years of the 18th century. Identical and very similar examples were made by a number of different makers over the years c.1750–80, notably by Ebenezer Coker, Eliza Godfrey, William and John Cafe, as well as by John Perry, Makepiece and Carter, Hannam and Crouch, John Carter and Simon Le Sage. Some of the later examples may be copies made to augment existing sets.

It seems possible therefore that these candlesticks may have been produced by a sub-contractor and that Edward Wakelin's mark only represents his activity as a retailer. Ebenezer Coker, in particular, is known to have supplied large quantities of plate for Edward Wakelin and John Parker. This pattern may well have been described as 'nurl'd' or 'gadroon'd' in contemporary documents. The inscription 'No 6' and 'No 7' indicate that they were once part of a larger set.

Leeds City Art Galleries (Temple Newsam)

27 Pair of candlesticks
c.1760–5
Bow factory

The porcelain figures of a boy and a girl stand in front of bocages and are painted in enamel colours and gold and

27

rest on four scrolled feet. Each is fitted with a metal candle branch with a porcelain sconce and is pierced for attachment of a second branch.
H 9½in (24.1)
PROV. Bequeathed by Mrs Frank Gott 1923

At Temple Newsam in 1808 Lady Irwin's dressing room contained 'two china figures 2 light candle sticks 2 ditto setting [sitting] figures'.

Leeds City Art Galleries (Temple Newsam)

28 Design for a candlestick

*c.*1762
John Carr (1723–1807)
Ink and wash
Inscribed in ink 'No1' and on the verso 'Drawings By Mr Carr'.
The simple design comprises an Ionic column on a stepped foot surmounted by a vase sconce.
21 x 14½in (53 x 37.5)
LIT. Ivan Hall, *William Constable as Patron* (1970), p.34
PROV. William Constable (of Burton Constable) and by descent

The design (which is en suite with a drawing for a branched candelabrum) shows an early return to the 'monument' form which had been popular in the last years of the 17th century. Here, however, the inspiration is the new approach to neo-Classicism with which William Constable, Carr's client, was entirely conversant. The candlesticks may have been executed in silver by An. Carmey for £22-1-0d in 1762.

Lent by Leeds City Art Galleries and the Burton Constable Foundation

29 Two candlesticks

1759–60 and 1760–1
William Cafe
Silver
The raised hexafoil bases have chased spreading lobes, partly imitating shells, and rise to cast circular hexafoil stems with knops, cast vase shaped sconces with rope mouldings and detachable drip pans with wide cast borders and shell decoration.
H 5¾in (14.4)
LIT. Lomax, p.157
PROV. Bequeathed by D.D.Schofield 1962

28

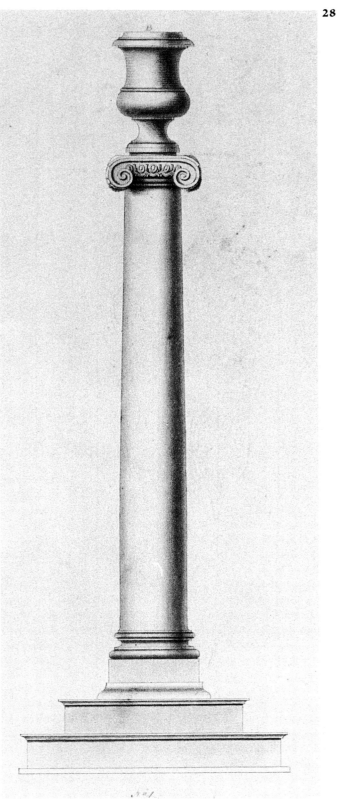

The design was a very popular one for both candlesticks and tapersticks over the period *c.*1745–70 and is found on examples with the makers' marks of James Warren and Michael Fowler (Irish), Ebenezer Coker, Hyatt and Seymore, John Carter, and probably several others. Later

29

3(

examples were probably made to augment existing sets made earlier. A variation with shaped square (as distinct from hexafoil) bases was also very popular. There are a pair of tapersticks also by William Cafe, 1759, at Temple Newsam, of an identical pattern but on a scale of 2:1).

The prolific brothers John and William Cafe who must also have worked as sub contractors for large firms, made candlesticks to a number of designs. More sophisticated examples of their work are figure candlesticks, examples in the French taste, and numerous more Rococo pieces (with shell and scale decoration, or with naturalistic or rocaille forms). Both were apprenticed to distinguished gold-smiths and candlestick makers — the elder brother John to the specialist James Gould, and the younger to the more versatile Simon Jouet. Likewise both passed on their skills to the next generation of candlestick makers via their own apprentices, notably Thomas Hannam and John Perry.

Leeds City Art Galleries (Temple Newsam)

30 Wax Jack
1766–7
Maker's mark indistinguishable (probably William Cafe)
Silver
The pierced circular base has a gadrooned border, scroll grip and the three paw feet. The central spindle supports the taper holder of scissor form.
H 6$\frac{3}{8}$in (16.2)
LIT. *Silver from the Assheton Bennett Collection* (1965), p.40
PROV. Unknown; Mr and Mrs Edgar Assheton Bennett; given to Manchester City Art Gallery 1957

Wax jacks of this form, or the alternative 'bougie box', appear to supersede tapersticks of the miniature candlestick type from about 1770. The wax taper would be treated in turpentine and should not crack when bent. Later examples, also made in Old Sheffield Plate, consist of a vertical circular or oval frame with a horizontal spindle to hold the wax taper, resting on a chamber candlestick base.

Lent by Manchester City Art Gallery

31 Pair of candlesticks (from a set)
1767–8
John Carter (designed by Robert Adam)
Silver
The square bases have acanthus leaf borders and rise to circular feet with guilloche bands, beading, acanthus leaf decoration and vertical flutings. The baluster stems have a calyx of acanthus leaves, spiral fluting, a beaded and foliate horizontal band and are surmounted by tall vertical stiff leaves. The vase shaped sconces have similar ornament and gadrooned nozzles. Two corners of each base are engraved with different crests: one (contemporary) for the Philipps family of Picton Castle, Pembrokeshire; and the other remains identified. Under the bases are scratched numbers '7' and '8'.
H 13$\frac{3}{4}$in (35.4)
LIT. Robert Rowe, *Adam Silver* (1965), p.37; Lomax, pp.158–160

PROV. Picton Castle, Pembrokeshire; Harrods Silver Department 1915; Dr HF Marshall; bought Leeds City Council 1963.

The design of the candlesticks corresponds to three drawings by Robert or James Adam in Sir John Soane's Museum. Unfortunately these are not dated, nor do they have any indication of the client for whom they were intended. The contemporary armorials on these however indicates that their first owner was Sir Richard Philipps, later Lord Milford, who is not otherwise known as a client of Robert Adam's.

The candlesticks, which are marked '7' and '8' were clearly part of a large set; numbers '5' and '6' were also made by John Carter in 1767; numbers '1' to '4' by Sebastian and James Crespell in 1769 (two with branches added, 1791); another two were made by Daniel Pontifex in 1796 (sold in 1965 with the Temple Newsam pair and clearly made at a later date to augment the set). In addition to these there are another two made two years earlier than any of these — in 1767, by David Whyte and William Holmes, now at Manchester City Art Gallery. These have no visible armorials but cast paterae applied on the bases where the crests may have been engraved.

Certain elements and variations of Adam's design for these candlesticks can be seen on a large number of examples by a variety of different makers in the 1770s and 80s. However, the design as a whole was not widely plagiarised. It has been suggested that there is too much ornament for a reflecting material like silver, and that this is a classic example of an architect's design for a medium of which he has no practical experience. Possibly the simpler

designs of Adam's rival James Wyatt, intended for mass production in both silver and Old Sheffield Plate by Matthew Boulton, were more successful.

John Carter was a specialist maker of candlesticks and salvers. He produced a wide variety of pieces over the period 1767–77 including Rococo, cluster column and 'monument' types. He was also a sub-contractor of Parker and Wakelin's, and his mark is also found over-striking pieces made by Sheffield or Birmingham makers.

Leeds City Art Galleries (Temple Newsam)

32 Pair of candlesticks
*c.*1770
Silesian glass
The domes and shaped circular bases rise to cylindrical stems, sconces and detachable nozzles.
H 8$\frac{3}{8}$in (21.3)
PROV. Bought 1987

At Temple Newsam in 1808 Lady Irwin's dressing room contained '2 cut glass candlesticks'.

Leeds City Art Galleries (Temple Newsam)

33 Two tapersticks
1771–2
Ebenezer Coker
Silver
The stepped square bases have alternating cast gadroons and flutes and rise to cast tapering stems with knops and

33

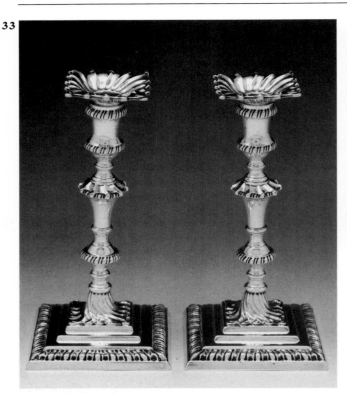

34

spool shaped sconces. The lower part of the stems, upper knops, and detachable sconces have spiral bats' wing motifs, while the lower knops and sconces have alternating gadroons and flutes.
H 6¼in (16)
LIT. Lomax, p.161
PROV. Bequeathed by Agnes and Norman Lupton 1953

Another very popular candlestick design, interchangeable for tapersticks but on a greatly reduced scale, and made by a number of different makers over the period *c*.1760–80. Other makers who produced identical examples include William Cafe, John Hyatt and Charles Seymore, Jonathan Alleine, John Carter, William Turton, William Holmes and Nicholas Dumee. They were also made in Old Sheffield Plate by Matthew Boulton. This pattern could conceivably be the one described as 'step pillar and bats whing' which was being supplied to Parker and Wakelin by John Winter of Sheffield in 1760s (information from Helen Clifford).

Ebenezer Coker was a prolific specialist maker of candlesticks and salvers (like John Carter, see Cat.31). He is also recorded as a sub contractor to the large firm of Parker and Wakelin.

Leeds City Art Galleries (Temple Newsam)

34 Chamber candlestick
Mid/late 18th century (?)
Brass
The rectangular pan has a roll-over rim and a closed ring handle and plain thumbpiece. The stem has moulded decoration and a slide ejector and mechanism. The handle has an aperture for an extinguisher hook (now lost).

H of stick 5in (12.7)
W of pan 7¾ (19.7)
PROV. Chatsworth, Derbyshire

This was probably once part of a large assemblage of chamber candlesticks of different dates and intended for the domestic staff at either Chatsworth or Devonshire House. This may account for some anomalies of design. John Douglas has recently shown that closed ring handles of this profile appear in the 1750s ('English Brass Chamber Candlesticks Pre 1800', *Base Thoughts: The Journal of the Antique Metalware Society*, 4, pp.38–46.) On the other hand the depth of the pan (1½in) suggests an earlier date while the shape of the stem is similar to late 18th century examples.

Lent by the Trustees of the Chatsworth Settlement

35

35 Chamber candlestick
Late 18th century
Brass
The oval pan has a roll-over rim and an open scroll handle and thumbpiece engraved DD34. The stem has moulded decoration and a slide ejector and mechanism. The handle is riveted with copper studs and has an aperture for an extinguisher hook.

H of stick 5½in (14)
W of pan (max) 7¾in (19.7)
PROV. Chatsworth, Derbyshire

The number on the thumbpiece indicates that this must have once been part of a large assemblage of similar chamber candlesticks. The oval shape of the pan and the open handle suggest a late 18th century date.

Lent by the Trustees of the Chatsworth Settlement

36 Pair of candle vases
c.1771–2
Made by Matthew Boulton
Fluorspar, ormolu and glass
The fluorspar vases have painted glass pedestals, ormolu mounts and reversible candle holders in the form of leafy domes surmounted by finials.
LIT. Goodison pp.144, 150–1, figs 108, 109
PROV. Unknown; Mrs Ivy Judah; bought Manchester City Art Gallery 1985

This particular model may well have been known as the Cleopatra vase. Invoices from Boulton to his clients

indicate that these had painted glass pedestals, and versions also contained medallions with female masks. Other examples are known incorporating 'Burgoyne' candle branches (see Cat.37), including a pair at Pavlosk.

These examples were recently acquired for Heaton Hall, near Manchester, the early masterpiece of James Wyatt who also provided Boulton with designs for silver and ormolu, including candlesticks. In 1775 Lady Egerton, mother of the owner of Heaton ordered a pair of 'Ormolu Vases' from Boulton, possibly similar to this example.

Lent by Manchester City Art Gallery

37

37 Pair of candle vases
c.1772
Made by Matthew Boulton
White marble and ormolu
The circular stepped marble bases, ringed with gilt copper guilloche-pattern bands, support cylindrical pedestals ornamented with rosette paterae between female terms suspending swags of drapery. The marble vases mounted in leaf cups are raised on enriched ormolu feet and decorated with garlands, while the open scrolled foliate friezes feature rams' heads which support fronded branches ending in drip pans and fluted candles holders, the fruit finials reverse to form a fourth candle socket; the vases are lined with gilt copper.
H 15½in (39)
LIT. Goodison, pp.146, 150 and pl.105; Gilbert, vol.II p.385
PROV. Comte Stroganoff de St Petersburg, Berlin; bought 1975

Boulton's vases were sometimes named after the patron who had first commissioned them and this model appears to have been known as 'Burgoyne's', presumably after the celebrated general. Two almost identical versions but with bluejohn bodies are known. The branches relate to the arms on a pair of candelabra designed by J.C.de la Fosse at the Detroit Institute of Art. This further supports the view that, despite his xenophobic utterances, Boulton was capable of plagiarism from French sources.

Leeds City Art Galleries (Temple Newsam)

38 Candlestick (from a set)
*c.*1780
Possibly by Matthew Boulton
Old Sheffield Plate
H 12¾in (32.3)
LIT. Michael Snodin, 'Matthew Boulton's Sheffield Plate Catalogues', *Apollo*, July 1987, pp.25–32
PROV. The Earls of Carlisle and by descent

38

Old Sheffield Plate was a particularly suitable material for candlesticks and a great number of different patterns were developed which were also manufactured in silver. The main difference between the two of course lay in the price. Horace Walpole paid two guineas for a pair of plated candlesticks on his visit to Sheffield in 1760 which might have cost him six times that figure had they been made of silver. As Timothy Schroder has pointed out, the average cost of similar candlesticks in brass would have been between 6s and 12s, or the average earnings of a well paid factory worker which would not have exceeded 10s per week. Nevertheless the effect was to bring 'silver-looking' objects well within the expectations of the middle classes. Parson Woodforde of Weston Longueville, in rural Norfolk (with £400 pa) bought a pair in 1777 to use at 'Rotation' dinners. However, this example from Castle Howard demonstrates candlesticks in Old Sheffield Plate were by no means a preserve of the middle class.

The design for this example, of a revived 'monument' form, was a very popular one. It is very close to one illustrated in Matthew Boulton's printed catalogue of 1779. A near identical example by Tudor and Leader of Sheffield is in the Victoria and Albert Museum. Compare with the creamware example Cat.39D.

Lent by the Castle Howard Trustees

39

39 Five creamware candlesticks
(from left to right)
A. Impressed LEEDS POTTERY, 1780s, H 11¼in (28.5)
The eight sided openwork plinth supports two addressed seated griffins and scrolls from which rise four lobed shafts to a vase shaped sconce. These correspond to no 113 in the Leeds Pattern Book (*c.*1814 edition), 'Griffin composite candlestick, 10 inches high. The price in the Leeds Agent's Book was 4/6d. The Castleford Pottery Pattern Book (1796) illustrates a very similar design called 'Chandelier, Facon de griffon.'
B. Probably Yorkshire, Leeds Pottery, 1780s, H 10¼in (26)
The female figure holds a lamb under one arm and a wavy stem in the other which supports a pan and sconce.
C. Probably Yorkshire, 1780s, H 10⅝in (27)
A 'veilleuse' or 'beverage warmer' comprising a hollow pedestal stand, a food bowl and cover with a candle sconce.

The design corresponds precisely to one in the *Leeds Original Drawing Book No 1*. Veilleuses were made in delftware, Chelsea and Lowestoft porcelain, as well as in silver.
D. Staffordshire or Yorkshire, 1780s, H 8$\frac{1}{8}$in (20.5)
The fluted column has an entwined garland of leaves and stands on a square base with incurred sides moulded with festoons of leaves.
E. Staffordshire or Yorkshire, 1780s, H 13in (33)
The circular crustaceous base supports a dolphin on whose tail rests a sconce in the form of a bud.
The Leeds Pattern Book (*c*.1814 edition) shows a 'Dolphin candlestick 10 inches high', no 108 with a square base moulded with flowers and shells (Price in Agent's Book 1/6d reduced from 1/9d).
LIT. Walton, pp.124–27

Leeds City Art Galleries (Temple Newsam)

40 Candlestick (from a set)
1787–8
John Parsons (Sheffield)
Silver
The square upwardly curving base supports the tall four sided tapering stem, with on each side two flutings and an upper panel of fly punched festoons. The vase shaped sconce and nozzle have bands of simple beading, also repeated on the stem and foot.
Engraved with the armorials of Baron Borthwick
H 12in (30.4)
LIT. James Lomax, 'Silver at Castle Howard: 300 years of Investment and Fashion', *The Art Quarterly of the NACF*, 9 (1992), p.34
PROV. Baron Borthwick; Susanna, Duchess of Grafton; Lady Cecilia Howard

The elegant neo-Classical forms and decoration introduced into the repertory of English goldsmith's work in the 1760s became simpler and more attenuated as the century advanced. In part this was due to the development and popularity of Old Sheffield Plate and the new technology which favoured simple die stamped ornament and thin gauged 'flatted' metal.

John Parsons, like many of his colleagues in Sheffield and Birmingham, made candlesticks to the same design in both silver and Old Sheffield Plate. Certain London makers and retailers, notable John Carter, had a habit of over-striking provincial maker's marks if the latter's wares had been bought in for re-sale. Presumably this was because they imagined their clients would not value Sheffield or Birmingham pieces as highly as those made in London. However, if this candlestick is an example, Lord Borthwick obviously did not disdain a set of Sheffield-made silver candlesticks. Likewise the Dowager Lady Irwin of Temple Newsam possessed a pair of elegant branched candelabra, 1791, also by John Parsons of Sheffield.

This set of candlesticks later acquired a set of branches, a feature consistent with the later hour for dining and the

taste for more elaborate table arrangements in the Regency period.

Lent by the Castle Howard Trustees

41 Two candelabra
1794–5
John Scofield
Silver
The raised circular upwardly curving bases have a horizontal reed moulding and vertical part flutings, raised to seamed tapering stems with the lower knops part fluted and with reeded shoulders. The bell shaped cast sconces have similar part flutings and a detachable nozzle which is the pivot for the branch. These are cast in several sections and centre on a part fluted sconce with a reversible nozzle or cover. The scrolling branches are fluted and have leaf ornament while the pans and nozzles are reeded. The feet are engraved with the arms of Sir Wilfrid Lawson, Bt. of Isell

41

H 16¾in (42.9)
LIT. Lomax, pp.163–64
PROV. Bequeathed by D.D.Schofield 1962

Table candelabra are rare in English silver before about 1760 and generally speaking comprise only double branches. On the whole it appears that only the most assiduous collectors of plate acquired these: Lord Warrington at Dunham Massey had '4 Standing Branches or Girandoles for 3 candles each' but as their total weight was only 193oz they could not have been very substantial. In addition he had '1 pair of Standing Branches or Girandoles for 4 candles each in the Drawing Room' weighing 79oz. By 1760 branches appear to become more common and within a short time begin to be supplied in Old Sheffield Plate.

The design of these candelabra appears to have been very popular. Lady Irwin of Temple Newsam had a similar pair but by John Parsons of Sheffield, 1791, and a set of twelve 'threaded fluted candlesticks and sockets' at 8/6d per oz were supplied to Stoneleigh Abbey in 1787 by John Scofield.

Leeds City Art Galleries (Temple Newsam)

42 Torchere (from a set of four)
*c.*1795–1800
Possibly designed by Henry Holland and made by Alexis Decaix
Bronze

The three paw feet support a circular platform and the tall fluted shaft. The upper section is baluster shaped and supports the circular top.
H 48in (121.9)
LIT. Dorothy Stroud, *Henry Holland* (1966), pl.61, p.110; Edward T.Joy, *English Furniture 1800–1851* (1977), p.39; Frances Collard, *Regency Furniture* (1985), p.39; Martin Chapman, 'Thomas Hope's Vase and Alexis Decaix', *The V & A Album* (1985), no.4, pp.216–28
PROV. Woburn Abbey, Bedfordshire

This set of four torcheres has traditionally been associated with the work of Henry Holland for the fifth Duke of Bedford at Woburn, beginning in 1787. The most splendid surviving interior is the Long Library for which Holland almost certainly designed many of the furnishings including a central library bookcase with desks at either end and possibly these torcheres. The earliest view of this room, Henry Moses' engraving for *Vitruvius Britannicus* (1827), shows these torcheres placed at the corners of the desks and surmounted by the silver gilt swan-shaped candlesticks (Cat.43). Holland may well have been assisted by the youthful Charles Heathcote Tatham (see Cat.47) who entered his office in 1789 and whom he dispatched to Rome as a draughtsman in 1794. The few surviving drawings for furniture by Holland are contained in the two volumes at the R.I.B.A. and include designs for bookcases for the library at Woburn and 'pier tables with glass over' for the same room as well as 'an ornamental stand to support a lamp'. Clearly there were many more, for in 1796

4

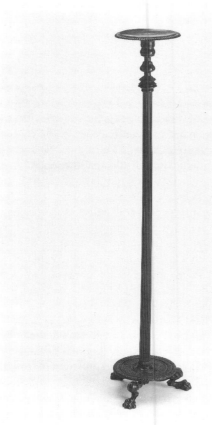

he wrote to the Duke: 'On the articles of furniture, was anyone to examine the endless number of drawings I have made, and witness the trouble I have had they would not envy me my charge on that account'.

Among the craftsmen making furniture for Woburn were Ince and Mayhew, Francis Herve and John Kean. The style was of course consistently francophile with the Parisian *marchand mercier* Dominique Daguerre acting as a supplier and intermediary, here as at Carlton House. The library chairs at Woburn, likewise associated with the bookcase and these torcheres, are identical to a set made by Jacob in Paris for the Prince of Wales, possibly to Holland's design.

Unfortunately the name of the craftsman responsible for these torcheres is not known. It is tempting, however, to ascribe them to Alexis Decaix, a Frenchman who may have fled the Revolution and is recorded working in London as a 'bronze and ormolie manufacturer' from 1794. He worked for Garrards from 1799 to 1804 and from 1800 to 1803 supplied 'bronze manufactures' to the Duke of Bedford's friend the Prince of Wales. He was taken up by Thomas Hope whose designs he executed and became highly fashionable with premises in Old Bond Street. Indeed the torcheres in the Indian Room at Hope's Duchess Street mansion were very similar to these. At Woburn 'Mons De Caix' was apparently responsible for a small amount of ormolu gilding. His association with Garrards is particularly interesting in view of the swan shaped candlesticks which surmounted the torcheres (Cat.43).

Lent by the Marquess of Tavistock and the Trustees of the Bedford Estate

43 Candlestick (from a set of four)

1800–1
John Wakelin and Robert Garrard
Silver gilt
The stick is in the form of a swan whose open plumage supports a leafy fluted sconce with a tall vertical shaft and whose head and neck are reversed to form a handle.
H 7in (17.8)
PROV. Woburn Abbey, Bedfordshire

These candlesticks, whose design must be unique in English silver, are associated with the library bookcase and side-desks at Woburn and the accompanying torcheres (Cat.42). It appears that the candlesticks have traditionally always been placed on top of these torcheres and they appear in this way in Henry Moses' engraving of the library for *Vitruvius Britannicus* (1827), and in watercolour views of *c.*1850 and 1884 (Cornforth, p.43).

While the design for the library furniture and torcheres is attributed to Henry Holland it is difficult to give him the credit for these silver candlesticks. Indeed no other silver is known to have been designed by him. It seems possible that they were designed and made by Alexis Decaix who was working for Wakelin and Garrard at this date and who may have been responsible for the accompanying torcheres. Decaix, as an emigre from France, would most certainly have been aware of the advanced style of the goldsmith Henri Auguste and the designs of Moitte which this piece recalls. The Garrards archives record his making candlesticks, candelabra, inkstands, and mounts for

43

precious objects. Also in 1800 he made 'a pair of Egyptian Slaves for a light on Bronze Pedestal with hierogliphick characters' for Garrards own shop.

An alternative designer for these candlesticks may be Jean-Jacques Boileau, another emigre designer and decorative painter working for Henry Holland at Carlton House from *c*.1787. He also worked for Garrards although, interestingly, a set of four wine coolers at Woburn, 1803–4, which closely relate to one of his drawings, has the maker's mark for Paul Storr (Michael Snodin 'J.J.Boileau: a forgotten designer of silver', *Connoisseur*, vol.1, 198 (June 1978)).

Lent by the Marquess of Tavistock and the Trustees of the Bedford Estate

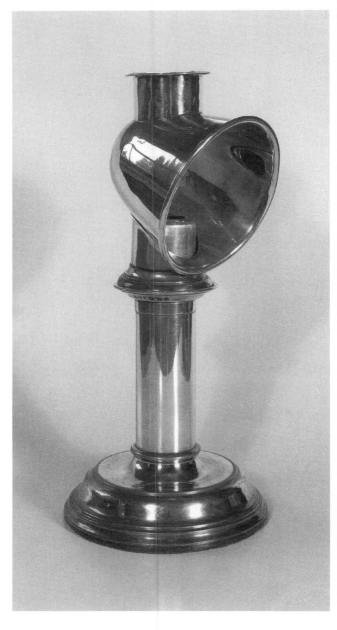

44 Chamber candlestick
Early 19th century
Ormolu
The asymmetrical stand has scrolling leafy borders, a scrolled handle, and supports a reclining cupid on a sheaf of flowers holding a stylised bud sconce
H 4$\frac{1}{2}$in (10.8)
PROV. Woburn Abbey, Bedfordshire

The design may be derived ultimately from Meissonnier and is entirely in the French taste. An example was produced in silver by Paul Crespin, 1744.

Lent by the Marquess of Tavistock and the Trustees of the Bedford Estate

45 Telescopic candle reading lamp
c.1810–20
Old Sheffield Plate
The circular moulded base supports a cylindrical shaft with a knop and a fitted circular hood.
H 15in (38)
PROV. Probably given to John Henry Inch (1877–1934), butler in service with Colonel Amelius Richard Mark Lockwood (1847–1928) of Bishop's Hall, Romford, Essex; by descent to Arthur Inch, in service as a footman to the Marquess of Londonderry, and used by him at Londonderry House, Mount Stewart, N.Ireland, and

Wynyard Park, Co Durham. Donated by Arthur Inch in 1988 (information from David Beevers)

Telescopic candlesticks, originally with a shaft containing one or more sliding pillars, were developed from the late 18th century and were made in both silver and fused plate. Richard Morton of Sheffield and Anthony George Eckhardt of London took out a patent for these in 1797. In the course of time these developed reflector hoods and spring-action self-adjusting candle mechanisms of the Palmer's patent variety (Cat.50).

The design remained popular well into the 20th century. A very similar example was advertised in the Army and Navy Stores catalogue in 1907 as a 'Candle Reading Lamp (Telescopic)...Nickel plated all over 8/3d...E.P. all over 19/-...Candles for above box of 6 1/3$\frac{1}{2}$d'.

Lent by the Royal Pavilion, Art Gallery and Museum (Preston Manor), Brighton

46 Reading light

Samuel Hennell
1813–14
Silver
The circular base supports a central spindle with an
adjustable candle arm and socket on one side and a tall
parallel cylindrical container with a sliding action for a
folded pleated shade on the other. Engraved with the
monogram of the Earl of Essex
H 10in (25.4)
PROV. The Earls of Essex; E.Swonnell (Silverware) Ltd.

The evidence for shades to accompany candle lighting in
18th century England is extremely scanty both in the documents as well as among surviving objects. However, an
adjustable arm with a candle grip attached to a vertical
tube containing a circular pleated and folding shade was
published recently (*Antique Collector*, August 1987, p.62).
During the 19th century numerous patents and designs
were registered for improved candle shades including (in
1852) a variation on this, consisting of a column with a
sliding ejector for a shade to open into a pleated fan
(no.355, by Rose Jacob of Cockspur Street).

Lent by E.Swonnell (Silverware) Ltd

47 Pair of candelabra

c.1835
Paul Storr, of Storr and Mortimer
Silver gilt bronze
The stepped square feet support tapering altar shaped
plinths with monopodia corners of chimera heads and feet
linked by husk festoons, while the fronts are engraved
with the armorials of the fourth Earl of Fife. The baluster
stems have richly cast and chased stiff leaf and acanthus
ornament with spreading palm leaves at the base and at
the top which support a further central stem and sconce,
and nine further scrolling branches with leaf ornament
and rosettes, pans, sconces and nozzles.
H 35in (89)
LIT. Bourne and Brett, p.154
PROV. James Duff, fourth Earl of Fife; John Hardy

These candelabra are somewhat unusual (for Britain) in
being made in silver gilt bronze. They were designed by
Paul Storr in the massive 'antique' style introduced by the
architect and antiquarian Charles Heathcote Tatham
(d.1842) around 1800, and were supplied in the mid 1830s
by Storr and Mortimer of Bond Street, goldsmiths to King
Willaim IV. They were commissioned by James Duff,
fourth Earl of Fife (d.1857), who served as Lord Lieutenant
of Banff and are engraved with his armorials including his
badges as a Knight of the Thistle and as a Knight of San
Fernando. This latter was granted in recognition of his
contribution during the Peninsular War to the capture of
Fort Matagorda, near Cadiz in 1810.

The ornament of the acanthus-enriched baluster stems
and 'altar' plinths primarily derives from the Vatican
Museum's celebrated Barbarini antique marble tripod
candelabra. Their basic prototype, however, are the bronze
candelabra produced by Roman goldsmiths and founders

such as Giuseppe Valadier (d.1839) in the late 18th century, and in particular from Tatham's own engraving of a 'Branch Light designed and executed in Bronze at Rome in the year 1796'. This latter was adapted from a design executed the previous year by the Roman bronze-founder Giuseppe Boschi and who based it on the Farnese antique marble candelabrum. Tatham, while seeking archaeological proto-types in Rome for Henry Holland's work at Carlton House for the Prince of Wales, had been impressed by the Italian practice of furnishing grand apartments with yellow-tinted casts or 'gesses' of such antique marble candelabra. So he not only commissioned 'perfect' copies of the seven-foot high Barberini candelabra in plaster, but also obtained reduced versions of the Farnese candelabra in gilt bronze. The Barberini candelabra later appeared in his *Etchings of Ornamental Architecture* (1800), and provided the source for the silver gilt candelabrum which he designed for John, second Earl Spencer (d.1834) in 1801. The features on this pair of candelabra which are taken from Barberini ones are the acanthus scrolled capital and the base of the palm-enriched shaft, as well as the rectangular plinth of truncated obelisk form and husk-festooned angles composed of monopodia or chimera, the ram-horned and fire breathing lion of antiquity.

Lent by John Hardy Esq (Temple Newsam only)

48

48 Two chamber candlesticks
1836–7
Robert Hennell III
Silver
The dished octofoil pans have scrolled handles with fitted conical extinguishers. The cylindrical stems have strengthening mouldings above and below the detachable hexafoil nozzles. The pans are engraved with the crest of Leatham

LIT. Lomax, p.165
PROV. By descent in the Leatham family of Ropergate House, Pontefract, to Lorna Priscilla, later Lady Gascoigne by whom given in 1970

This was a popular design for chamber candlesticks and examples are found by a variety of different makers.

Chamber candlesticks were probably made in very large sets: the Parlington plate list of *c.*1843 recorded 20 'Bedroom candlesticks' as well as 9 'Pair of dressing Candlesticks'.

Leeds City Art Galleries (Lotherton Hall)

49 Candelabrum
*c.*1855–60
Antler horn, leather, white metal
Three hoof feet support a domed leather centre encrusted with small horns and from which spring five main antler branches with six attached sconces (four surviving).
H 37½in (95.5)
PROV. Richard Watt IV of Speke

The candelabrum probably dates from the period after 1855 when Speke Hall was being refurnished by Richard Watt IV in a picturesque antiquarian style. It is mentioned in the 1867 inventory of the house (information from Roy Boardman).

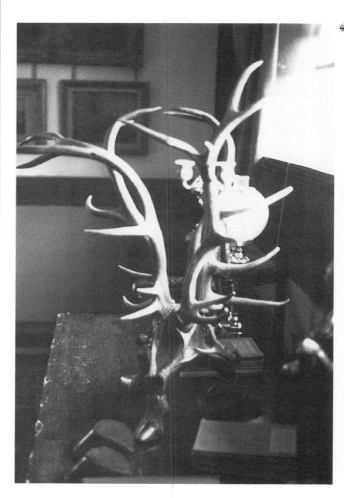

Antler furniture had a considerable vogue in the middle years of the 19th century with specialist makers encouraged by the rediscovery of the Scottish Highlands and the immense popularity of sporting artists such as Sir Edwin Landseer. Particularly memorable chandeliers exist at Blair Castle and (with heraldic overtones) at Chatsworth.

Lent by the National Trust (Speke Hall)

within the tube presses the candle upwards as it burns. Thus the light is always at an equal height, and there is no need for snuffing. They usually had some form of globe or shade, or in this case probably a hood.

These candle lamps remained popular for many years. Similar 'Reflecting Candle Lamps to burn No.6 candles' were in the 1895 Harrods catalogue, nickel plated at 5/6d or brass at 4/11d.

Leeds City Art Galleries (Temple Newsam)

50 Pair of candle lamps Late 19th century
inscribed DIBBEN/SLOANE STREET
Brass
The circular moulded bases support cylindrical shafts with a knop and a detachable nozzle with a bayonet action for removal. The interior of the shaft is hollow and contains an adjustable spring candle support.
H 11¾in (19.8)
PROV. Castle Howard; bought 1991

This type of candle lamp derives from Palmer's patent of 1842 whereby candle wicks were made to bend out of the flame to as to avoid the necessity of snuffing. Originally this was achieved by dipping only one side of the wick with a starch, but later the wicks were made in two halves which spiralled round each other and spread out laterally when burnt.

The most suitable stick for this invention was this type which is similar to the 'Soho' lamp patented in 1840, consisting originally of a more complicated hollow cylinder intended for burning fat or tallow. Here the nozzle or cap keeps the candle within the tube and a spiral spring also

51 Candle lamp
Late 19th century
Apparently electroplated
H 14in (35.5)
PROV. The Tempest family of Broughton Hall, Skipton
See notes for Cat.45

An interesting variation on the plain circular reflector hoods were the 'corrugated' or faceted types.

Lent by Henry and Roger Tempest

52 Patent candle shade frames with marble 'candles'
Late 19th/early 20th centuries
Various makers
White metal, marble
From left to right: 'DIBBEN & MARCHANTS SHADE HOLDER THE 6 CORONET'; no inscription; IMPROVED PATENT/RD NO 591336'; 'GREENS

ARCTIC CANDLE LAMP PATENTED IN THE
UNITED KINGDOM USA & OTHER FOREIGN
COUNTRIES'

The Design Registers at the Public Record Office record
innumerable developments for candle and lamp shades
throughout the late 19th century. The example second
from the left is similar to the Brass Sliding Candle Shade
Support' available in the 1895 Harrods catalogue at $1\frac{1}{2}$d
each.

Lent by Mrs Maxwell Scott

The marble 'candles' have a metal pricket at the top of each
which helps locate the detachable pyramidal cover (first
left).

Lent by Leeds City Art Galleries and the Burton Constable Foundation

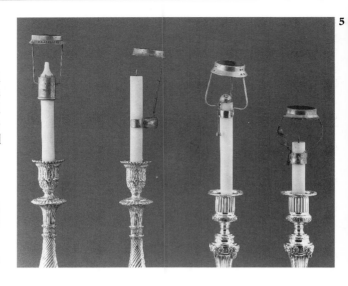

5

Lanterns

This section is not concerned with small, portable, single
candle lanterns for carrying in the hand or attaching to
carriages; it concentrates on various forms of lantern used
in entrance halls, passages and on staircases. Lanterns
protected candles from the menace of drafts and people
standing beneath them from drips of grease.

Side lanterns, usually for a single candle, were fixed to
the walls of staircases and passages; they had an open top,
glazed fronts and sides, a reflecting back and metal base
plate with a deep candle socket; access for snuffing and
cleaning was via a hinged side panel and some were fitted
with a smoke shade. The frames were fashioned either from
wood (Cat.53) or japanned metal (Cat.54). In March 1772,
Chippendale billed David Garrick for 'a Tin Side Lanthorn
with shade and burner 6s 6d'. Specially-shaped lanterns
were sometimes made to illuminate dark corners: few
however survive.

Wall lanterns were rare in 17th century country houses;
none are recorded in the Ham House inventories of 1677,
1679 and 1683, but examples are preserved at Knole on
the private staircase. There was 'a Glass Lanthorn at ye
Stairshead' at Dyrham in 1710, whilst several pairs of
'lamp sconces' were recorded in passages and staircases at
Kiveton in 1727, providing just enough illumination to
light the way. The Chapel there was provided with '2 Door
Glass Lamps/2 Irons for Do/1 Round Glass for a lamp to
hang over a Door'; these sound like exterior lights and so
strictly fall outside this survey.

The passage/staircase distribution of wall lanterns is
confirmed time and again in country house inventories
until the end of the 18th century, when candles were
increasingly superseded by oil lamps. Brass rather than
silver candlesticks seem to have been the rule even in the
grandest households; Benjamin Goodison, for example,

supplied the Royal Palaces with brass candlesticks for 15
glass side lanterns in 1737. Apart from a single design in
Hepplewhite's *Guide*, 1788 (Fig.34), side lanterns are not
represented in furniture pattern books which is curious
because they were regularly supplied by fashionable
cabinet-makers. For instance, in December 1752 John
West invoiced Holland Goddard Esq for '3 Mahog Side

Fig.34. Hepplewhite, Guide, 1788

Lanthorns, compass fronts £4 14s. 6d./3 Brass Candlesticks to the Side Lanthorns 5s'. Surviving examples are mostly 'neat' expressing their utility status; however, ambitiously styled wall lanterns were commissioned, the most famous being a richly carved, gilded and black japanned pair resting on brackets and surmounted by eagles made to place over doorways in the staircase hall at Norfolk House, London. They were carved in the workshop of Antoine Cuenot, *c.* 1755 and cost £19 17s. 6d. (Bourne and Brett, 1991, p.71).

Suspended lanterns constructed from small panes of greenish glass set in lead cames had been made at least since the 16th century — an important example of *c.* 1600 is preserved at Hardwick Hall, Derbyshire, while two apparently dating from the late 17th century hang in an upstairs passage at Ham House. Glazed lanterns only started to become common in country houses during the early 18th century. The majority were square or hexagonal with one hinged panel to form a door (Cats 55 & 56). Staircase lanterns could sometimes be serviced from the stairs, but hall lanterns were lowered by means of cords and pulleys, thus the Great Hall at Kiveton in 1727 had '1 large Glass Lanthorn with a Crimson Silk line & ballance weight'. In 1729–33, Benjamin Goodison supplied the still extant 'large glass Lanthorn with a wrought brass frame and a gold crown on the top' for the Queen's Great Staircase at Hampton Court at a cost of £138.

Mid 18th century pattern books published by Chippendale, Thomas Johnson, Ince & Mayhew and others illustrate numerous highly elaborate designs for Hall or Staircase lanterns, including several in the Chinese or Gothic taste. The majority were cast in brass but finely carved and gilt or mahogany framed examples are known. Chippendale's bill to Sir William Robinson yields a good description of a lantern and its paraphernalia:

8 Oct 1760	
A large Brass Lanthorn Glaz'd wt best crown-glass for the Hall	6 6 0
a large Crystal shade	7 6
a large Ballance Tassel cover'd wt Green worsted crepe & Hangers with a Tufted shag	1 8 0
a Do for ceiling	1 9 0
a Strong iron screw frame wt box pullies & brass collars	9 6
5 yds Cast work-line	7 6
a Jappan'd lamp wt 3 burners & crystal top	4 0
Hanging the lanthorn at your house	2 6

In a prefatory note to their *Universal System*, 1762, pl.vi which presents two designs for lanterns, Ince & Mayhew remarked they were 'calculated for being made in Brass or Wood; of the latter we have executed some that are much admired, and at much less Expence than Brass', but in his *Director* Chippendale states they 'are generally made of Brass cast from wooden Moulds'. That he not only designed but carved the moulds for brass hall lanterns is made clear from his Harewood House account which itemizes 'An Exceeding large Brass Hall Lanthorn richly ornamented in the Antique manner ... £100'; this charge included 'Carving the various

Fig.35. Burton Constable, brass hall lantern by W.Collins, 1832, adapted for gas and later electricity (H 62in)

patterns for do in wood and chasing them in Brass'. The glass for the sides and bottom, the brass oil lamp with 12 burners and the chain cost an additional £23 8s. A five foot high gilt brass lantern combining grand late Regency ornament with Gothic frets and ruby glass borders was ordered from William Collins for the Hall at Burton Constable in 1832 at a cost of £60 (Fig.35).

Not all country house owners ordered hall lanterns. In 1792 the Great Hall at Newby, Yorkshire, was illuminated by '2 Bell Lamps on Carv'd Mahy Stands'; in 1771 Sir Rowland Winn purchased from Chippendale for the Lower Hall at Nostell Priory '8 Large Globe Lamps on wrought brass Scrolls and shades to do ... £20' (Fig.36), while in the last decade of the century the Entrance Hall at The Grange, Northington contained 'An octagon lamp in a brass ornamental frame/2 globe lamps brass arms'. John Gordon's bill for equipping the Duke of Gordon's house in Upper Grosvenor Street provides a capital record of how a smart London house was lit in 1750. He invoiced for the staircase and hall: a pair of 'mahogany Sqr side Lanthorns/one mahog Compass side Lanthorn/one large Brass framed Glass Lanthorn with Iron chain painted blew' plus a spectacular set of four globe lamps for the staircase supported on carved white and gold dolphin stands (SRO. GD44/49/20/16).

Fig.36.   Nostell Priory, one of eight globe lamps supplied by Thomas Chippendale for the Lower Hall in 1771 (diam. 15in)

Hanging staircase lanterns were normally of the same style as those made for halls, but *The Universal System of Household Furniture* and *Genteel Houshold Furniture*, both published in 1762 each contain a plate with 6 patterns for 'Staircase Lights' intended to 'fix on the Hand Rail' or designed as brackets. W.H.Pyne's *Views of Royal Palaces*, 1819, includes a plate showing Wren's great staircase at Kensington Palace with six hand-rail lanterns ordered in 1729 — now unhappily lost. However, a fine set of staircase globe lamps survives on the newel posts at Houghton Hall, Norfolk, while at Heaton Hall, Manchester, a series of tall tripod vase lamps designed by Wyatt are fixed to pedestals at the banister foot (Fig.37) and on the landing. A remarkable set of sixteen hand-rail lamps, preserved at Burton Constable near Hull (Fig.38), dates from the

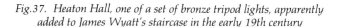

Fig.37.   Heaton Hall, one of a set of bronze tripod lights, apparently added to James Wyatt's staircase in the early 19th century

Fig.38. Burton Constable, one of 16 lights on the staircase and landing handrail, 1760s, the shades 1838

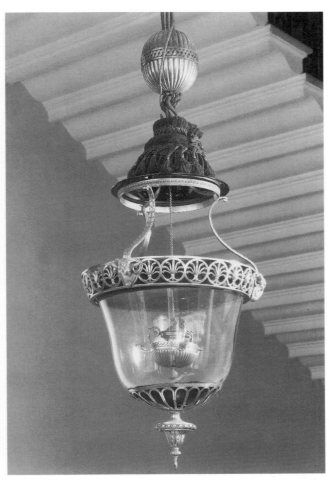

Fig.39. Osterley Park, one of three ormolu hanging lamps designed by Robert Adam for the staircase, c.1775 (H 34in)

1760s, the engraved glass shades being added in 1838 for 4s each.

The main staircase at Harewood House, fitted up by Thomas Chippendale in the highest style of elegance in 1774, was lit by '6 Antique Brass Girandoles' set on green and gold pedestals (the latter only survive) and 'A very neat wrought Brass Lanthorn ... and a large brass scroll Brackett...to fix against the half space of the Great Staircase', for which Chippendale's drawing exists. Evidently pairs of pedestals stood at the foot of the stairs, at its head and in corners on the half landing. The great staircase at Osterley Park miraculously retains the lighting appliances designed by Robert Adam (Figs 39 & 40) and recorded in an inventory 1782: 'Three elegant Lamps mounted in Or Molee with brass ballance weights, lines, Tassells and double pullies Antique burners hung with Chains compleat/A Tripod term painted green and white with an elegant glass Lamp Vase mounted with Or Molee ornaments. An Antique Lamp with two burners'. The pair to it stood in the hall passage.

Passages were frequently lit with less costly hanging lanterns. For example, in 1759 Chippendale provided a large carved and gilt hall lantern for Dumfries House costing £34 but the 'neat hexagon Lanthorn' which he supplied

for the bedroom passage cost only £13 13s. Describing her new house at 18 Lincoln's Inn Fields in January 1774, Mrs Kenyon expressed pleasure at the lighting arrangements: 'I must tell you before I proceed further there is a very handsome glass-lamp in the passage, another upon the landing, and a third by the dining room door'. (Historical MSS Commission Reports, 14th Report, 1924, Appendix IX, pt. iv). Town houses were obviously often rather gloomy. Hepplewhite's *Guide* illustrates two vase-shaped hanging lamps suspended from three chains attached to a decorative brass collar. Many modest examples of this type designed to hold a single candle, sometimes headed by a glass smoke-shade, survive (Cat.57).

Lit. G Bernard Hughes, 'Georgian Hall and Wall Lanterns', *Country Life*, 15 November 1956, pp.1132–36.

53 Compass side lantern (one of a pair)

*c.*1740

Mahogany with gilt mouldings

H 32 in (78) W 12 in (30)

The mirrored back with a lobed base and pointed crest is fronted by a hinged open-topped D-shaped glass door enclosing a shelf for a candlestick; headed by an attachment for a smoke shade.

53

5

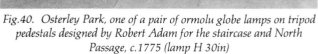

Fig.40. Osterley Park, one of a pair of ormolu globe lamps on tripod pedestals designed by Robert Adam for the staircase and North Passage, c.1775 (lamp H 30in)

PROV. Wallington Hall, Northumberland, from the Entrance Hall

Lent by the National Trust (Wallington Hall)

54 Side lantern (one of a pair)
1760–70
Gilt metal
H 44 in (112)
Of glazed rectangular design with a mirrored back and hinged door on the left hand side; decorated with a pagoda canopy and Chinese fretwork base, entwined ribbons below the shelf.
PROV. Nostell Priory, Yorkshire, staircase landing

More likely to be an example of Rococo chinoiserie than Regency exoticism. When illustrated by Percy Macquoid, *The Age of Satinwood*, 1908, p.30, the canopy and base were hung with bells.

Lent by Lord St Oswald and the National Trust (Nostell Priory)

55 Hall or staircase lantern
*c.*1760
Gilt brass and glass
H 29 in (74) Diam 18 in (46)
Of octagonal design with one hinged pane and a circular smoke shade; the frame is enriched with cast acanthus fronds, shell motifs, floral festoons and satyr masks; open canopy with perching birds headed by a flame finial concealing the suspension ring.
PROV. Carlton Towers, Yorkshire, discovered in the Lamp Room

Similar to designs published by Chippendale and Ince & Mayhew in 1760–62.

Lent by His Grace the Duke of Norfolk KG

56

55

57

56 Design for a hall lantern
*c.*1794
By Panton & Co, London
Pen, grey and yellow wash
21 x 15in (53 x 38)
Hexagonal brass lantern shown with a smoke shade and
oil lamp having a vase-shaped reservoir and four burners
with glass chimneys. Inscribed 'This Lanth'n is 2 ft 8
across from side to side & 3 ft from Corner to Corner 6 ft
High'
PROV. Burton Constable, Yorkshire

An associated drawing (Cat.13) is on paper watermarked
1794, inscribed on the verso 'from Panton & Co/New St.
Square/London'.

Lent by Leeds City Art Galleries and the Burton Constable Foundation

57 Hanging lamp
Late 18th century
H 22 in (56) Diam $10\frac{1}{2}$in (26)
The vase-shaped shade has a folded lip and a stamped
brass collar with three cast eagle-head suspension
brackets; single candle socket, smoke shade above.

The lobby and twin vestibules to the Upper Hall at Nostell
Priory are lit by a fine matching set of vase pattern hanging
lamps.

Leeds City Art Galleries (Temple Newsam)

Oil Lamps

Possibly one of the most significant events in the history of domestic comfort in Britain was the appearance of the Argand lamp in 1784. Until this date the burning of oil for lighting in country houses was not very extensive: it created smoke and a foul smell as well as being inefficient. On 15th March of that year Ami Argand, a Swiss distiller, registered a patent for a 'lamp or lantern producing neither smoke nor smell'. He had made two discoveries. First, if the wick of a traditional oil lamp were made hollow and enclosed between two tubes in such a way that oxygen could burn the oil vapour both on the inside and outside of the flame, the resulting light would be equal to ten or twelve tallow candles. Secondly, if a glass chimney were placed above the lamp so as to increase the draught further, the brightness would be even greater. Unfortunately for the inventor he was unable to manufacture his brain-child in France as he was not one of the *ferblantiers* who alone had the guild right to sell lamps, and in England the provisional patent which he took out in 1784 expired two years later mainly through the negligence of his partner Matthew Boulton, and he was left with no protection from pirates.

Within a year of its registration William Parker, the great chandelier maker, was advertising himself as the sole supplier of 'Argand's Patent Lamp Etc.'. Yet the following year Sophie von la Roche noted in her diary '...we finished tea at evening investigating Argand lamps of all descriptions' and proceeded to describe a shop in Bedford Street where they were displayed 'forming a really dazzling spectacle; every variety...crystal, lacquer and metal ones, silver and brass and every possible shade'.

It was the mechanism of Argand lamps which dictated their design. This can best be described by reference to the diagrams in *The Penny Cyclopaedia* (1839) (Fig.41). In the first, which shows the outside of the classic lamp, A is the reservoir of oil from which it descends to the cistern B and along pipe C to the burner D which contains the wick placed between two tubes and immersed in oil. The wick rises a little above the tube at E. F is the glass chimney which is wider at the base in order to increase the draught upwards. It rests on a gallery G and is held in place by four wires H. When the gallery G is turned the wick can be regulated by being raised or lowered. The wick is hollow and cylindrical and receives *two* currents of air — internally from the pierced work at I and externally from the gallery at G. K is a characteristic early Victorian lamp shade and L the handle which controls the supply of oil from the reservoir to the cistern.

The second diagram shows the internal working of the lamp. The reservoir A screws into the cistern B. When the lever at L is moved the oil passes through the hole at O into

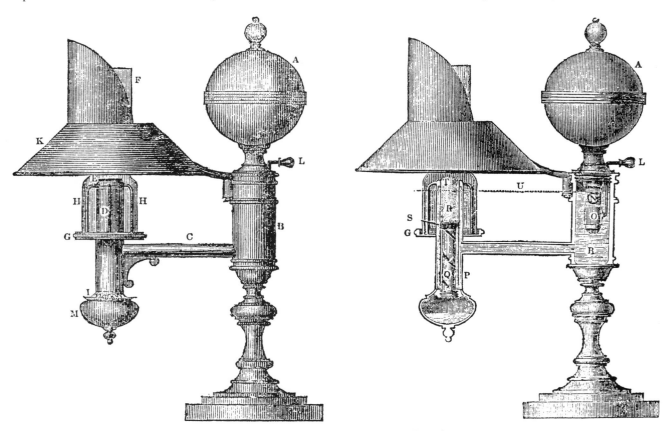

Fig.41. An Argand lamp, from The Penny Cyclopaedia, 1839

the cistern B. Inside the vertical tube P is a smaller tube Q with the oil contained in a space in between with the wick R stretched over the short tube at S and rising slightly above at T. The outer surface of the tube Q has a spiral groove in order that when the gallery G is turned the tube and wick will rise and fall and thus regulate the light.

The type of oil used was from cole seed and was known as colza oil. It was thick and viscous and had to be gravity-fed from a reservoir located above the burner.

Although Argand lamps were an immediate success and were greatly to expand the number of activities possible after the hours of darkness, they never entirely supplanted candle lighting. There seems to have been no particular rule or etiquette about lamps and their correct use in houses in the early years. Early 19th century views and inventories show a wide range of uses and combinations. Drawing rooms and parlours tended still to have candles and hanging chandeliers, dining rooms almost exclusively so unless lamps were placed on pedestals. Libraries and passages however lent themselves more readily to oil. As in so many aspects of furnishing it was probably the personal taste of the owner which dictated his or her choice of lighting equipment. At the Grange, Hampshire in 1795 there appeared to be no Argand lamps available to the new tenant, the Prince of Wales. The well-off Harden family of Brathay Hall in the fashionable Lake District are shown in a series of sketches 1803–26 to have been content with candle and firelight for their traditional after-dark activities. Likewise Henry Moses' views of elegantly clad ladies and gentlemen in ultra-'Grecian' interiors show them generally grouped around candle lighting. On the other hand in 1808 the Dowager Lady Irwin at Temple Newsam had had any number of 'argaund lamps' as well as a small number of 'night lamps' probably for the servants and of the old fashioned 'spout' variety (Cat.64).

One of the main disadvantages of Argand lamps was the inconvenient shadow cast by their reservoirs but this was no drawback for wall lamps which, often fitted with a reflector, remained popular for passages (Fig.42 and Cats 58–62). Likewise, multi-branched hanging lamps could minimise this problem by having a single central reservoir. In the second decade of the 19th century however the Astral and then the Sinumbra lamp were developed in which the oil was contained in a hollow ring which also acted as a support for the shade (Cat.67). The oil was fed to the central burner by curving tubes and the lamps were surmounted by hemispherical or flattened shades. The result was a diffused and generalised light and they were ideal for placing on centre tables, so characteristic of Regency interiors (Fig.43). They could equally well be used as branched hanging lights and early in their history Thomas Hope used them for lighting his Dutch pictures in the mansion at Duchess Street. In the Saloon at Devonshire House there was a large multi-branched Sinumbra lamp hanging from the ceiling together with the 'stork' Argand lamps on pedestals (Cat.120) and a pair of Parker's girandoles on the mantlepiece (Gere, p.214).

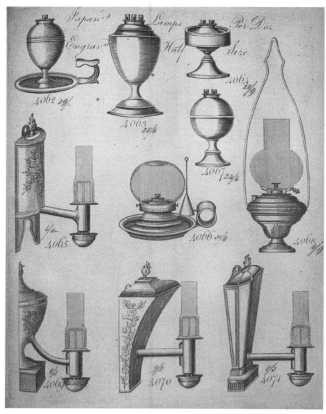

Fig.42. Page from a lamp maker's pattern book

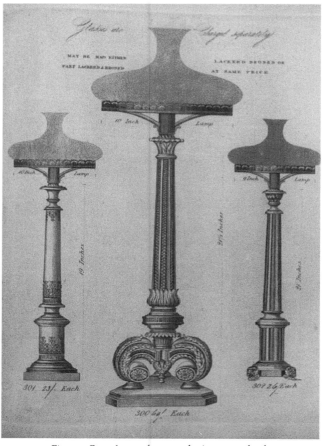

Fig.43. Page from a lamp maker's pattern book

The question of shades was obviously important. In America in 1840 *Miss Leslie's Housebook* probably echoed slightly earlier English taste: 'In buying astral lamps for the table choose shades of plain ground glass as they give the clearest and steadiest light and are best for the eyes...lamp shades painted in bright colours are now considered in very bad taste...The fashion of having shades decorated with flowers or other devises, cut on the glass and left transparent is also on the decline...though it may do well for the mantel lamps and lustres' (Bourne and Brett, p.173). Both for table or hanging Argand lamps it appears to have been acceptable to leave them with their glass 'chimneys', but more usual also to cover these with spherical or vase shaped 'globes'. Likewise tapering cylindrical shades in tin, often japanned in green, were quite common for lamps intended for reading. At Stratfield Saye these have also survived on the eight-light hanging billiard table lamp, which originally had four reservoirs for oil but was later converted to gas (Fig.44). Also at Stratfield Saye are a number of multi-branched hanging lamps with cut glass dishes beneath them, a fairly common style. Old photographs show that these sometimes had pendant flame shades above them (Fig.45).

The second quarter of the 19th century saw a number of developments on the basic Argand principle. There were several problems entrepreneurs sought to overcome in order to produce a shadow-less light: how to raise the thick and viscous oil (incapable of capillary action) from a reservoir below the burner; how to eliminate the tendency of the oil to thicken in cold weather; and how to achieve an ever-brighter combustion. From as early as 1794 the Carcel lamp had allowed the oil to be housed in the base of the lamp and to be raised by a series of clockwork pumps. It was particularly popular in France throughout the 19th century and burnt either whale or colza oil. However its mechanism was very fragile and it required frequent servicing.

Other mechanically operated lamps included the Moderator lamp, patented in 1825, where oil was raised to the burner by a spring activated piston which also controlled the movement of a wire inside the supply tube

Fig.45. *A hanging Argand lamp with flame shades, Stratfield Saye (from an old photograph)*

thus 'moderating' the supply flow. The excess oil was channelled back into the cistern. A variation of this was the Meteor lamp, where the piston or plunger worked up and down by a nut and screw mechanism from the outside (Cat.73). The Solar lamp attempted to improve combustion by having a wick which passed through a hole in the centre of a cap or cone with air directed from a horizontal direction. In addition to this the appearance of the Liverpool button, a metal cone placed in the centre of any Argand burner, deflected the central draught onto the wick. These are just a few of the many types of new lamps being developed over these years.

Birmingham, with its tradition of metal working, was naturally one of the great centres of oil lamp manufacture. Looking back in 1866, some years after the universal adoption of paraffin lamps and at a time of ever increasing use of gas, a Report for the British Association on the brass manufacturers of the city gave an interesting view of the application of design to industry:

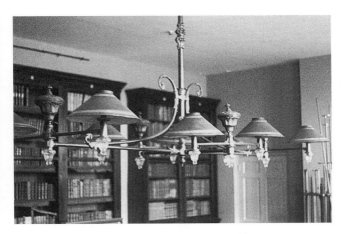

Fig.44. *Billiard table lamp, Stratfield Saye*

Gas has given the quietus to lamp making, if we except those for paraffin, and the chief manufacturers of lamps have been absorbed into the manufacture of Gas fittings. But the trade is one which claims to consideration, in so far as while the mechanical construction of the oil lamp employed and kept alive a superior class of workmen (imitative certainly,) in which proportions of the remains of classical mouldings, copied from Stuart's Athens and Piranesi, were used, and in which the pillars [sic] Corinthian, Ionic, Composite, etc., in character, supported lamps, or Caryatide figures bent under the imaginary weight of the lamp they were supposed to sustain. One designer represented 'Atlas supporting an improved brass Liverpool lamp', with arms extended, hands pressed on stomach, the lamp apparently balanced on his head, conveyed the unpleasant impression that the head of the lamp would speedily roll off. Hanging lamps were of equally strange design. Imitations of the Warwick vase formed the receptacle for the oil; the arms to which were attached the burners concealed below by heavy cast 'boats', or bodies; bearded philosophers or ivy-crowned satyr masks grinned down on the possessor of the lamp who stood below, and honeysuckles, vine leaves, fruit, etc., made up the component parts of an incongruous whole. These articles were then accepted in the days when art and taste was the exception rather than the rule, as examples of supereminent art applied to industry. Probably nothing more instructive as to progress in the direction of applied design can possibly be gathered, than by turning over the pages of the pattern books of the Messengers and Timothy Smiths of a bygone period. We learn therein the traditions on which ornament was founded, and following the traditions, we see how much originality was sacrificed on the altar of antiquity, fitness never for one moment being taken into consideration; and hence, the misapplication of forms, abstractly good in themselves, imperfectly reproduced for purposes for which they were totally inapplicable. Nor at this period were these reproduced by inferior artists or modellers. Flaxman, whose graceful, elegant, and poetic fancy illustrated so beautifully passages in Homer and Dante, whose sculpture charms from its chaste and pure, yet simple dignity, modelled for the Messengers, as did Francis Chantrey; and Wyon, a progenitor of the now distinguished mint medalist, when in connection with the Soho, lent his artistic powers to the designing of the decorations for the lamp work produced in that establishment, in addition to his avocation as a medalist. The various drawing masters in the town were also pressed into the service as 'designers'. The imperfect understanding which prevailed as to construction, or rather 'that ornament should be designed without reference to construction', does not appear to have been understood at the period, or if understood, was ignored: still, however, these gropings in the dark are entitled to respect, as the harbingers of a better time coming which has now arrived, or to which we are rapidly approximating.

The increasing cost of oil, now including whale oil, led to various attempts to distil a new fluid from mineral deposits. The breakthrough came in 1847 with James Young's process of refining paraffin (or kerosene) oil. The resulting lamps required flat wicks with good aeration, and various improvements culminated in 1865 with Hinks' Duplex Burner with two wicks. Throughout the 1870s and 80s patents for all kinds of new parts continued to be registered

— Silber's producing an average of over two each year at this time. In country houses Argand lamps were quite easily converted for paraffin and their decorative qualities must have been appreciated (Cats 66 and 69). Colza oil indeed continued to be used right up to the end of the century when the Harrods catalogue requested their customers to state whether they required fittings for their lamps suitable for Colza, Mineral or Duplex oil.

58 Wall lamp

Early 19th century
Tin, japanned black with yellow leafy and classical decoration
The hemispherical vase shaped box originally contained the reservoir and rests on a short rectangular platform; the domed detachable cover has an attached vertical part lining for the reservoir below and is surmounted by an acorn finial, while the curving feeder branch is attached to the perforated burner cylinder. The back plate has a shaped aperture for a wall hook.
H 11½in (29.2)
PROV. Chatsworth, Derbyshire

Like Cats 59 and 64 the design relates very closely to one in an anonymous printed lamp maker's catalogue in the Victoria and Albert Museum (Fig.42, M63i E1331–1899). Their wholesale price was apparently 8/6d each. The design enables it to stand upright as a torch as well as against the wall.

Lent by the Trustees of the Chatsworth Settlement

59 Wall lamp
Early 19th century
Tin, japanned yellow with black lines and ornament
The curved rectangular box contains the detachable
valved reservoir with a curved cover and cone finial. The
straight feeder branch is attached to the perforated burner
cylinder. The back has an attached plate with an aperture
for a wall hook
H 10½in (26.7)
PROV. Chatsworth, Derbyshire

Like Cats 58 and 61 the design relates very closely to one in
an anonymous lamp maker's catalogue in the Victoria
and Albert Museum (Fig.42, M63i, E1331–1899). Their
wholesale price was apparently 9/1d each.

Lent by the Trustees of the Chatsworth Settlement

61 Wall lamp
Early 19th century
Tin, japanned yellow with black lines
The rectangular hinged box forms the reservoir and had
two feeder branches and cylindrical burners complete
with their wicks between concentric tubes and twist
mechanism. It slides into the rectangular shaped back
plate with a projecting support to tray and two apertures
for wall hooks.
W 13in (33)
PROV. Chatsworth, Derbyshire

Lent by the Trustees of the Chatsworth Settlement

60 Wall lamp
Early 19th century
Tin, japanned red with yellow foliate and classical
decoration
H 12¼in (31.1)
PROV. Chatsworth, Derbyshire

See notes for Cat.59

Lent by the Trustees of the Chatsworth Settlement

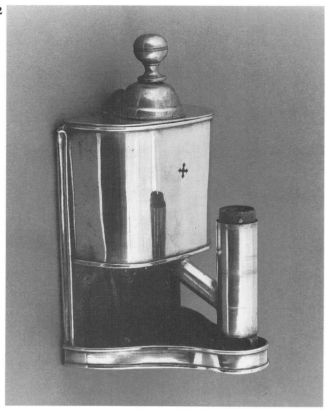

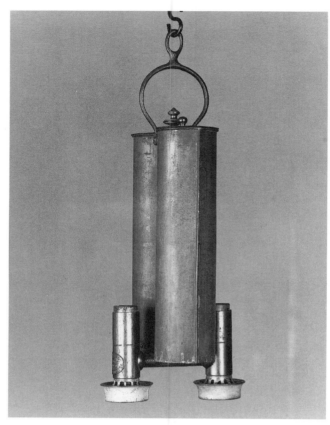

62 Wall lamp
Early 19th century
Brass
The curved rectangular box contains the detachable valved reservoir, has a bell shaped finial, a straight feeder branch which is attached to the cylindrical burner with its concentric tubes and twist mechanism. It slides onto the rectangular back plate with a projecting tray or support. The back plate has an attached plate with an aperture for a wall hook
H 9½in (24.1)
PROV. Chatsworth, Derbyshire

The design enables the box and burner to stand upright as a torch when it is removed from the sliding back plate.

Lent by the Trustees of the Chatsworth Settlement

63 Hanging lamp
Early 19th century
Brass and white metal
Inscribed on attached label HANCOCK & CO/ MANUFACTURERS/COCKSPUR ST./LONDON
The reservoir consists of a valved double cylinder contained within a similarly shaped casing with double branches and perforated cylindrical burners with concentric tubes for wicks. The top has a baluster finial and knob for adjusting the oil flow and the casing has a double looped handle
H 16in (40.6)
PROV. Chatsworth, Derbyshire

The coarse quality of the reservoir casing suggests that this was originally enclosed by a brass container. The lamp probably originally hung within a glass lantern.

Hancocks are recorded at Cockspur Street, Charing Cross throughout the nineteenth century until 1865 when they moved to Great Marlborough Street (see Cat.71).

Lent by the Trustees of the Chatsworth Settlement

64 Night lamp
Early 19th century
Brass and white metal
The circular hollow stand is heavily moulded and rises to a central detachable screw with an aperture for a wick. The circular handle has a long thumb rest and finger support and a further aperture for an extinguisher (now lost). The underside of the lamp is of white metal
W 4½in (11.4)
PROV. Chatsworth, Derbyshire

The design relates very closely to a group in an anonymous early 19th century lamp maker's catalogue in the Victoria and Albert Museum (Fig.42, M63i, E1331–1899). They would originally have had a collar around the central burner which would have supported the open glass globe shade. At Temple Newsam in 1808 one of the maid's rooms contained '8 japanned night lamps'.

Lent by the Trustees of the Chatsworth Settlement

65 Pair of lamps and stands

*c.*1806
Made by James Deville
Brass on bronzed plaster stands
Each lamp has an urn-shaped reservoir with cast acanthus decoration, a gadrooned edge and domed finial; the dish shaped body is ornamented on the top with bands of acanthus and on the sides with three human masks. The burner protrudes from one side and the whole rests on a circular socle and plinth. The integral stand consists of three flexed scroll legs with claw feet divided by lion masks, resting on a concave sided triangular base
H 21in (53)
PROV. Bought 1992

The stands are identical to a pair of bronzed and gilt plaster torcheres signed and dated 1806 by James Deville (Clifford, p.45). Deville (1776–1846) was a plaster figure maker with premises in the Strand. He was also a lamp maker, so the lamps as well as the stands can safely be attributed to him. In designing the stands he may have been influenced by plates engraved by George Smith in 1804 and 1805 subsequently published in his *Household Furniture* (1808), pls 111–12. Numerous similar examples of lamps survive at Stratfield Saye, often in bronze with gilt mounts or masks.

Leeds City Art Galleries (Temple Newsam)

66 Hanging lamp

*c.*1820
Ormolu
The cruciform design centres on a vase shaped reservoir originally intended for colza oil; the underside of the body has satyr masks in each corner with florid scrolls and leafy decoration and an acanthus rosette pendant. The four open buckle suspension brackets are supported by ornate chains to a foliate corona
H 37in (93.9) from top of corona
PROV. The Clavering family of Callaly Castle, Northumberland; bought 1986

The burners were converted for paraffin probably *c.*1880 with new reservoirs below the burners in the branches. It was again converted to electricity in 1892 when a steam generator was installed. The original chimneys survived until *c.*1950 when they were replaced by the present 'flambeaux' shades.

Several nearly identical examples survive including those at Nostell and Farnley. The former may be associated with a payment to Litchfield, 1824. Possibly the grandest of this type with masks on the undersides of the branches is the one in the entrance hall at Stratfield Saye which is traditionally thought to have been designed by Sir Jeffry Wyatville.

A drawing in the Victoria and Albert Museum by Joseph Buonaretti Papworth is also nearly identical to this (E820–1978), and the design for the chain is similar to one in an anonymous brass founder's catalogue, charged at 8/6d per yard. Papworth was closely involved in all aspects of furniture and lighting design and in 1823 designed a new showroom for the glass and chandelier dealer James Blades.

Leeds City Art Galleries (Temple Newsam)

67 Sinumbra lamp
*c.*1820s
By Bright and Co.
Bronze, partly gilt
The tall plinth supports a fluted Corinthian column with a richly cast gilt base and capital from which springs the burner with double branches connected to the circular shade support which is chased with vines and which contains the reservoir.
Inscribed by Bright and Co.
H 33½in (85)
PROV. Woburn Abbey, Bedfordshire

The 'sinumbra' principle (explained on p.80) was particularly suitable for rooms requiring a general and diffused light and such lamps were often placed on centre tables.

John Bright appears to have shared the same address as Argand and Co. at 37 Bruton Street since at least 1805 and remained there until after 1830. Argand and Co. cease to be mentioned in the directories after *c.*1825 and many lamps are found with inscriptions 'Bright, late Argand and Co..' implying that the former had taken over the entire business.

Lent by the Marquess of Tavistock and the Trustees of the Bedford Estate

68 Design for hanging lamp
19th century, second quarter
Signed W.Collins, inscribed 'No 5'
Pen and ink
The base comprises a platform with eight scrolling classical leafy branches with tall glass shades of lotus leaf design; the central plinth has a rich leafy pendant below and supports a two-handled vase shaped reservoir with Rococo revival ornament. The four tall tubular supports

67

68

appear to be rigid and rise to a corona with similar leaf ornament to the branches. The scale of three inches to a foot indicates its intended size of three feet diameter.

H 21½in (55)
PROV. Sir Thomas Aston Clifford-Constable and by
descent at Burton Constable

The design is for the hanging lamps in the Gallery at
Burton Constable. The curious juxtaposition of Rococo
revival and classical ornament on this design indicates the
carefree interchange of parts which characterises metal lamps
of this period. This however would not have been tolerated
by one of the great chandelier and lamp designers of this
period, J.B.Papworth, whose style is consistently classical.

Collins of the Strand was one of the most ambitious
chandelier and lamp makers of the Regency period. He
provided the great hall lantern at Stowe in the style of
transparencies with its heraldic glass panels and the stained
glass and two vast chandeliers for Lord Grosvenor at Eaton
in 1818 for £913.

Lent by Leeds City Art Galleries and the Burton Constable Foundation

69 Hanging lamp

19th century, second quarter
Brass, glass chimneys and shades
The central vase-form reservoir has a fluted neck, feeding
four burners having original chimneys and frosted and cut
glass shades. The body is in the form of lotus leaves,
suspended by scroll brackets and cast-link chains from a
cast and pressed brass vase-shaped counterbalance, and

by means of crimson silk cords with tassels from the
ceiling rose
H 19in (48.3) from top of reservoir
PROV. Burton Constable

The lamp hangs in the bay window in the Dining Room at
Burton Constable and was supplied perhaps in the 1830s
campaign of relighting undertaken by William Collins,
who supplied the Hall lantern in 1832 for £60 and the
hanging lamps in the Gallery.

Lent by Leeds City Art Galleries and the Burton Constable Foundation

70 Two wall lamps on brackets

Early 19th century
Ormolu
The rich double scrolling leafy branches support
detachable and angled double branches with perforated
burners and a tall vase shaped reservoir above
H 18in (45.7)
PROV. Chatsworth, Derbyshire

The lamps are part of a set now in the theatre at
Chatsworth.

Lent by the Trustees of the Chatsworth Settlement

70

71 Pair of standing lamps

19th century, third quarter
Ormolu and brass
Inscribed on the burners HANCOCK AND RIXON/
47 GT MARLBOROUGH ST/REGENT STREET/
LONDON
The square bases each support a cylindrical drum pedestal
with a leafy stem, a vase shaped reservoir and straight
cylindrical feeders with perforated burners
H 20½in (52)
PROV. Chatsworth, Derbyshire

71

7

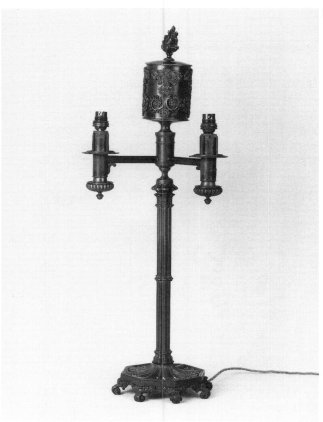

Hancocks were one of the most celebrated lighting emporia in London. From at least 1805 they had premises at 1 Cockspur Street, Charing Cross, when they described themselves as 'Hancock, Shepherd & Co., cut glass ware-housemen'. By 1810 they had become Hancock, Shepherd and Rixon and from *c.*1825 began to advertise themselves as 'lustre, lamp and glass manufacturers'. From *c.*1830 they became Hancock and Rixon and remained at Cockspur Street until 1865 when they moved to Great Marlborough Street, the address on these lamps. See also Cat.63.

Lent by the Trustees of the Chatsworth Settlement

72 Standing lamp
19th century, third quarter
Bronze, partly gilt
Inscribed on attached label HANCOCK & RIXON/
47 GT MARLBOROUGH ST/REGENT STREET/
LONDON
The octagonal base rests on eight scrolling leafy feet and is pierced with Gothic tracery. The octofoil cluster column shaft rises to a leafy capital which supports the two angled branches with perforated cylindrical burners and shade supports (converted to electricity). The cylindrical reservoir, with an attached lever for controlling the oil flow, has applied leafy and foliate mounts and is surmounted by a flame finial
H 30in (76.2)
PROV. Chatsworth, Derbyshire

Standing and table lamps in the Gothic style appear to have been particularly popular from the early 19th century. A very similar example to this has been noted at Burghley. The strange juxtaposition of the classical style reservoir above the Gothic structure may be accounted for by the easy interchange of parts within a country house lamp room. Another example of an identical reservoir still en suite with its original gilt and bronze classical shaft and pedestal inscribed 'Bright and Co.' can be seen at Woburn.

Hancocks are recorded at Cockspur Street, Charing Cross throughout the 19th century until 1865 when they moved to Great Marlborough Street.

Lent by the Trustees of the Chatsworth Settlement

73 Two 'Meteor' lamps
*c.*1870s
The stands probably Minton & Co., the burners inscribed SILBER'S PATENT No M/342
Pate-sur-pate porcelain, brass and gilt bronze
The circular mounted bases have four paw feet with classical masks and leaves between and rise to a tall vase shaped stand with pate-sur-pate decoration; on one with a maiden holding shackles being transported helplessly by a butterfly and on the back a spray of flowers and the word ABANDON; on the other a standing figure riding a butterfly holding reins and on the back a similar spray and the word DOMINATION. The two handled detachable cover contains a cylindrical reservoir which fits into the

1880 alone. It has not been possible to trace the registered specification from this patent number (which may be spurious). It would seem that he was working in collaboration with Minton's to create these integrated lamps with a pate-sur-pate body introduced to England by Marc Solon in 1870.

Lent from the Burghley House Collection

74 Back lamp
19th century, last quarter
Supplied by Messenger and Sons
Tin with traces of japanning, the fittings brass, nickel plated reflector plate
The back plate has a hook and on the front a slot for a removable circular reflector. It is integral with the curving box reservoir with a lifting burner and detachable chimney. An applied oval label is inscribed MESSENGER & SONS/ PATENTEES/ BIRMINGHAM AND LONDON
H (including chimney) $15\frac{1}{4}$in (38.7)
PROV. Watts family of Speke Hall

Messengers remained a leading firm of light fitting suppliers well into the 20th century (see also Cat.121). Their surviving literature show that they adapted to all the new forms and their catalogue of *c.*1908 is particularly

vase below and contains a tubular 'meteor' lamp mechanism contained within a cage-work sheath.
H $23\frac{1}{4}$in (59)
PROV. William, third Marquess of Exeter, Burghley House, Stamford

When dismantling these lamps for cleaning it was discovered that they had burnt a thick and viscous colza oil. Since this type of oil has generally to be fed from a reservoir placed *above* the burner and here it is below, these lamps must have originally have had a 'meteor' lamp mechanism or variation on the 'moderator' lamp principle (which partly survives in a damaged state). It was 'among the many new contrivances of the last few years' described in the 1845 *Supplement* to *The Penny Cyclopeadia* (p.204):

> in this reservoir is a kind of piston or plunger , worked up and down by a nut and screw from the outside; the rising of this piston occasions the pressure or tightening of a coiled spring, and this pressure causes the oil to be fired up a central tube towards the flame. The admission and regulation of the oil to the lamp, the adjustment of the wick, the arrangement of the air holes for admitting draught, and of the gallery which supports the glass chimney, are all of an intricate kind, and, whatever may be their efficiency while in good order, would render the repair, in case of damage, a serious matter.

A.M.Silber, whose patent number is attached to the burners, was an ambitious inventor who registered no less than 21 patents for different kinds of improvements for industrial and domestic lighting between 1870 and

ambitious specialising in 'Electric Fittings, Artistic, Original and up to date'.

The design is almost identical to one illustrated in the Harrods catalogue of 1895 and described as 'No 9744 Back Lamp, Wizard Burner 3/6d each'.

Lent by the National Trust (Speke Hall)

75 Reading lamp

Late 19th century
Impressed on applied label: SMETHURST/2/DUKE St./MANSIONS/GROSVENOR SQUARE
Silver plated on brass with opal glass shade and clear glass chimney
The circular foot supports a central stem rising to a double scroll ring finial. The short curved branch for the burner and for the cylindrical reservoir can be adjusted by means of a butterfly screw. The circular ring shade slots into the burner branch which also supports a further ring for the inner chimney. The reservoir cover is attached to an inner cylinder which removes and which has a self adjusting valve at the bottom which controls the flow of oil. The top of the burner has been partially electrified and has a hollow screw attachment.
H 21in (53)
PROV. The Earls Fitzwilliam at either Wentworth Woodhouse or 4, Grosvenor Square; removed from the Lamp Room at the former c.1940, when it had a label attached to it saying 'Lady Maud's Boudoir' (Lady Maud Fitzwilliam, b.1898, later Countess of Wharncliffe).

75

Smethursts were one of the most celebrated names in early 19th century lighting. James Smethurst of Borough, south east London, registered his earliest patents for lamps and burners in 1791, for reflectors in 1802 and for 'improvements upon lamps' in 1827. By 1810 he had progressed to Bond Street where he described himself as a 'Patent Lamp Manufacturer'. During the late 19th century and until 1891 their premises were at 175 Piccadilly; the following year they moved to 2 Duke Street Mansions, Grosvenor Square where they described themselves as 'lamp manufacturers, electrical engineers, electric light fitting makers, wax chandlers and oil merchants'.

Wentworth Woodhouse, Yorkshire, one of the largest houses in England, was electrified c.1903 when all the lamps were removed to the Lamp Room for conversion. Work clearly began on this example but for some reason was not completed.

This model was clearly a popular one with a long history of manufacture. Variations exist by a number of different makers: and early 19th century Sheffield plated pair were sold at Christie's South Kensington, 3 November 1990, lot 31, with the impressed label *Bright Late Argand, Bruton St*. Another very similar example inscribed 'Pillischers/58 New Bond St' is at Speke and traditionally thought to have been purchased from Mappin and Webb. Simplified versions are found in the Harrods catalogue of 1895 described as 'Single Queen's Reading Lamp Brass 9/4d each Nickel 12/6d each' — double versions being proportionately more expensive. The Army and Navy Stores catalogue of 1907 described them 'for mineral oil' in seven different styles, with glass shades in white, pink or green.

Lent anonymously

76 Reading lamp

20th century, first quarter
Made by Miller & Sons, 179 Piccadilly, London
Nickel-plated brass and tin
H 23½in (60)
Incised on the removable reservoir Belcher 18 Oct [?19]13.
The circular foot supports a central stem fitted with a lifting ring. The hollow branch supporting the reservoir and burner can be adjusted for height by means of a butterfly screw. Separate cylindrical reservoir of plated tin has a simple needle valve at the bottom allowing it to be filled when inverted, otherwise closing until installed in the lamp.
PROV. Port Eliot, Cornwall

This type of argand-burner lamp was apparently in use over a long period of time, although documented early examples are rarely found. The incised inscription may be the date of a repair or even of manufacture, for the *Army & Navy Stores Catalogue* for 1907 lists a virtually identical model, available in brass for mineral oil, with a white shade, for 11/3d; the nickel-plated version (as here) cost 13/6d while extra shades cost 7d in white, 1/5d in green

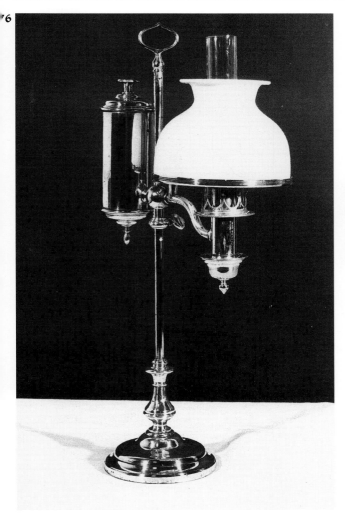

and 1/8d in pink, with chimneys of the best quality at 4/- a dozen. There was a colza-oil version at the same price. Unlike Cat.75, this lamp is entirely unmodified and burns satisfactorily using the residue of mineral oil in the wick.

Lent by the Earl of St Germans

77 Back lamp

19th century, last quarter
Supplied by Miller & Sons, 179 Piccadilly, London
Tin, japanned brown with green stringing (the back black), fittings brass
H 6in (15)
The back-plate is integral with the triangular suspension loop and rectangular reservoir, from the bottom of which emerges the tube feeding the burner tube which is of complex section and contains a flat wick which could be raised by means of a knurled knob. The chimney is missing. The slot that supported the reflector (also missing) is stamped MILLERS 179 PICCADILLY
PROV. Port Eliot, Cornwall

These back lamp were evidently hung from hooks on the walls of the basement-level domestic passage, where

one still hangs today. This model was a simple one, probably burning colza-oil; it would have given out a relatively feeble glow for the cotton is flat although air completely surrounds it. The fact that the lamp stands upright on a table-top suggests that it could be used as a torch. Compare with the domestic back lamps from Chatsworth, Cats 58–62.

Lent by the Earl of St Germans

78 Back lamp

19th century, last quarter
Supplied by Miller & Sons, 179 Piccadilly, London
Brass burner and supply tube, remainder of tin japanned brown with green stringing; silvered copper reflector
H $11\frac{1}{4}$in (28.5)
Back-plate with suspension loop and drip tray are integral, reservoir case and burner can be slid out vertically; inner reservoir of japanned tin has needle valve at the bottom. MILLER & SONS 179 PICCADILLY stamped on the burner tube.
PROV. Port Eliot, Cornwall

This type of back lamp was used in domestic parts of the house and the cleanliness of this example indicates that mineral oil rather than the heavy and viscous colza-oil was burnt. The removable reservoir and burner, whose tube is fitted with a plug to enable it to stand vertical on a table-top, suggests that the lamp could be used as a torch.

Lent by the Earl of St Germans

78

the lamp-room to be refilled and trimmed. The orifices fit the reservoirs from paraffin lamps, hence the relatively late date suggested. The lead shot in the box may once have been used to clean blackened chimneys, fragments of which also remain inside.

Lent by the Earl of St Germans

80 Oil drum, filler and bottle
Perhaps 20th century, first quarter
Japanned iron; drum has brass tap and tablet
H (of oil drum to top of cap) 22½in (57)
Cylindrical drum with two loop handles, conical spout with cap, brass tap and tablet engraved MINERAL OIL
PROV. Port Eliot, Cornwall

Harrods catalogue of 1895 indicated that they 'deliver all Oils FREE in 5 and 10 gallon drums by our own Vans (daily) except Saturday, in Town...Carriage not paid on country orders for oil'. Jars and cans were 'charged for, but returnable at the following rates; — one-gallon oil cans, 1/6d; five-gallon, 5/0d;...one gallon jars, 0/10d;...'. An oil bottle very similar to the present example was illustrated on p.394, the 8 pint size priced at 1/3d.

Lent by the Earl of St Germans

79 Lamp box (with oil reservoirs)
19th century, third quarter
Pine
W 23¼in (59)
Rectangular box of pine with removable top pierced with six circular holes.
PROV. Port Eliot, Cornwall

This appears to be a unique survival of a box used by the footmen to take reservoirs and burners from suspension, bracket and floor lamps in the main rooms of the house to

80

79

Gas Lighting

In 1846 J.Rutter, Engineer to the Old Brighton Gas Company, produced his *Treatise on the Ventilation of Gas Lights.* 'It is a remarkable circumstance' he commented, 'that while many thousands of persons had availed themselves of gas,...so small a proportion had thought it...necessary to the comfort and convenience of their families. There was a large number of persons who only required to have the subject brought judiciously to their notice in order to induce them to use gas in their drawing rooms and bedrooms as readily as they did in their counting houses and shops.' But the matter was not quite so simple and for much of gas's early audience the counting house shop and factory remained its principal sphere of use.

Following the development of gas as a light source in the 1790s its immediate take up was primarily for the illumination of factories and workplaces. In 1802 its perfecter William Murdoch used it to illuminate the exterior of Matthew Boulton's Soho works, Birmingham to celebrate the Victory of Amiens whilst firms such as Gott and Sons of Leeds were quick to follow in their wake.

The advantages of gas lighting in the factory were multitudinous. As Murdoch himself stated

the peculiar softness and clearness of the light brought it into great favour with the workpeople; and it being free from the inconvenience of sparks and the frequent necessity of snuffing...diminish the hazard from fire to which cotton mills are so much exposed. (Chandler, p.11)

Cost also provided an important incentive. At Philips and Lees Salford factory the expense of lighting the shop-floor was reduced by £1400 when the firm changed from candles to gas. This was no inconsiderable sum especially when added to the reduced insurance premiums available to gas users at the time.

Polemicists were quick to point out the relevance of gas lighting to the domestic interior as well as the workplace, *Ackermann's Repository* being an early campaigner for its adoption. In 1809 the magazine ran a series of articles *On the application of gas when compared to the light afforded by lamps and candles* and followed this up in 1813 with a detailed account of Ackermann's own gas lit library at his premises in The Strand (Fig.46). The room was described as being 'lighted solely with gas which burns with a purity and brilliance unattainable by any other mode of illumination.'

Fig.46. View of the library at Ackermann's Repository of Arts, Strand, 1813

Fig.47. Hughenden Manor, 1881, showing candles in use in the principal reception rooms

Here vestal figure lamps and table gasoliers lit the prints, drawings and artbooks on view countering one of the main early criticisms of gas use — that it was damaging to artworks and surfaces. As the Repository ambitiously stated 'gas produces no soot' and 'that the quantity of carbonic acid...is considerably less than that given out by oil tallow or wax.'

That such an important arbiter of Regency taste should take up the gas-gauntlet must have been influential. They furthered the cause again in 1815 when they published Fredrick Accum's *Practical Treatise on Gaslight* which, whilst explaining how gas was made, also illustrated a range of fashionable fittings to show that gas could be decorative as well as practical. Largely in the 'antique' taste the fittings exploited the gas-flame to decorative effect passing it through burners which transformed it into torch-like flames or classical acroteriae (Cat.79).

Despite this creative attempt to promote gas-light for domestic use many people remained indifferent or resistant to the potential of this medium. There were criticisms about the smell of gas, worries about the heat produced and concern about the damage it might cause to interiors and artworks. For some critics however, worries were increased by the notion that gas lighting was somehow socially inferior and, whilst acceptable for the 'Industrial Classes' and the town it was seen as quite out of place for the Great House

and the country. Writing of Belvoir at the beginning of this century Lady Diana Cooper commented

> There were lamp-and-candle men, at least three of them for there was no other form of lighting. Gas was despised. I forget why — vulgar I think.' (Cooper, p.35.)

A similar criticism was made earlier in the century by Benjamin Disraeli in his novel *Lothair* where the artist Mr Phoebus is made to state that he 'would not visit anyone who had gas in his house.' Certainly Disraeli seems not to have taken to the medium and illustrations of his own country house, Hughenden Manor, show only candles in the principal rooms as late as 1881 (Fig.47)

The main problem delaying the early take-up of gas light in the country house was its very newness. Until the 1840s there were few skilled technicians able to establish and run gas houses for country mansions who, unlike town houses, were unable to tap into a running public gas supply. Such a venture could be costly too and, with the increased efficiency of oil lamps and the refinement of wax candles there was little incentive to make the changeover.

There were however a few exceptions and for some science-loving country house owners gas provided an absorbing novelty. Sir Walter Scott who as early as 1810 had balked at the prospect of 'Lighting London with smoke' changed his mind in 1823 when he began its introduction at Abbotsford. Like Accum he wished to exploit

Fig.48. Abbotsford, c.1890, showing Milne's gas lustre supplied in 1823. The bowls and burners are later 19th century replacements

the decorative nature of the gas flame as created by the newly developed cockspur or batswing burners, even contemplating their completing the form of Scottish thistles or fleur de lys along the balustrades at Abbotsford. (Letter to Daniel Terry 29th March 1817.)

Although this plan was not carried out Scott, using the brass founder and patent lamp manufacturer James Milne, set about lighting his new home with gas albeit more conventionally. Many of the original fittings survive in situ including the Drawing Room gas lustre supplied by Milne in 1823 for £35 8s. Outside the house gas retorts remain, reused as gate piers at the rear of the house (Fig.49).

Scott's letters of the 1820s illustrate the costliness of installing the hi-tech gas manufacturing equipment and also its occasional unreliability. Writing to Miss Clephane on the 23rd of January 1824 he remarked 'We had a merry dance in the first week of the New Year which lasted till they burnt out all my oil gas which left them in the lurch at six next morning when they betook themselves to candles.'

In some houses confidence in the gas system could result in memorable incidents. In 1826 Mr Creevey visiting another early gas lit house, Lambton Castle, found his enjoyment of Lady Normanby's singing interrupted:

> when lo and behold out went the gas from the top of the house to the bottom. No nothing can do justice to the scene and the confusion it produced, for you must know that the house is literally lighted by gas, there is not a candle to be had for love or money.' (Gore, p.223.)

Not all houses were quite so keen to fully illuminate their houses with gas. Its role when used in country houses was often restricted to the domestic areas of the buildings on the grounds of smell and unsightliness. At Worsley Hall for example, gas was principally fitted to the kitchens and stables whilst at Louis Vulliamy's Westonbirt House, pipes were restricted to the basement only (Worsley Hall Account Books and Westonbirt Papers deposited at the

Fig.49. Gas retort, Abbotsford

RIBA). Stowe Palace,where a gas system was introduced by the 3rd Duke of Buckingham in 1864, had only the external lamps on the North Front, the bottom passage, North Hall and Marble Saloon lit by gas. In the Saloon

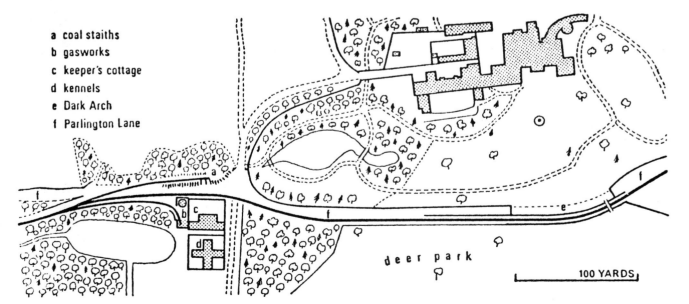

a coal staiths
b gasworks
c keeper's cottage
d kennels
e Dark Arch
f Parlington Lane

deer park

100 YARDS

Fig.50. Plan of Parlington Hall and Park showing the relationship of the gas works to the house and coal staiths

Fig.51. Gasolier by Messrs R.W. Winfield & Son of Birmingham, exhibited at the International Exhibition 1862

Fig.52. Gasolier by Mr Messenger, 1862

Fig.53. Crewe Hall, c.1900, showing 19th century armorial gas picture lights in situ in the Drawing Room

'8 upright gas burners' and 'gas jets' were 'arranged round the attic' but elsewhere lamps and candles continued to be used (*Stowe Miscellany*, May 1973).

Even when gas was fully used in the house some areas might retain candles or lamps for richness of effect. As late as 1860 the *Footman and Butler's Guide* advised that in the Dining Rooms 'even with gas, oil lamps and candlesticks are still to be placed on the table' a reserve that was to be repeated again with the advent of electricity.

By the 1840s however, J.C.Loudon's prophetic statement that 'with the progress of improvement, it will be found worth while to adopt it (gas) in all country villas' was coming to fruition. In the spate of country house building mid century gas works were increasingly seen as an all important adjunct to the house. Writing in 1871 James Kerr in *The Gentleman's House* remarked: 'it is becoming common in planning large Country Houses to include provision for gas lighting' but went on to state that 'The architects province need go no further than to accommodate the gas engineer according to his demands.'

Certainly this was the case at Hassobury, Essex and Adderley Hall, Salop where specialist contractors were

Fig.54. Burghley House, movable picture light, possibly by Silber

brought in to install an appropriate system. At Hassobury, Benjamin Verity and Sons supplied all fittings and pipes for the house itself and erected a gas holder, gas house and lime purifying room in 1870. This came to the rather alarming sum of £814 10s 7d. Such expense could however be offset by the costs saved in oil, candles and lamp-men (Gosling papers, Essex CRO D/DG1 E7/13 and Corbet papers, Salop CRO 327 Box 269).

Usually private gas works were placed at a distance from the main house largely for reasons of safety and convenience. At Burghley where a gas system was installed in the middle of the last century this was sited close to the stable block. At Parlington Hall, Yorkshire, the Gascoignes chose to place their gasworks some two hundred yards from the house by the Keeper's cottage, close to a private railway line that brought coal from the family mines to produce the gas (Fig.50) At Culzean Castle the gas works and adjoining manager's house of *c*.1880 were sited by the beach allowing coal to be brought by Clyde steamboat almost to the storehouse door.

In some instances the gas works would also be used to light an estate village as at Kelham in the 1850s but more usually it would have lit the house, stables and offices and occasionally the stable clock (Girouard, p.108)

Responsibility for the smooth running of the gas house was soon to be the province of the Gas Technician who replaced the lampmen of yore. In some early houses such as Abbotsford the system was more ad hoc. In March 1823 Scott wrote 'About twice a week the gas is made by an ordinary labourer, under occasional inspection of the gardener' (Letter to D.Terry). Day to day turning on and off of lights remained part of the Footman's duties.

Gas's increasing status is perhaps indicated by its installation at Windsor Castle in the 1850s at the instigation of Prince Albert. This work which included the setting up of vast cut glass sunlights in the Waterloo Gallery was carried out by the Birmingham firm of C.Osler and Co, one of the many companies flourishing in the wake of gas light's new found respectability (*Journal of Gas Lighting*, 17 March 1879, p.375).

Birmingham itself became a major centre for the manufacture of fittings and Samuel Timmins' book *Birmingham and the Midland Hardware District* of 1866 outlined the complicated division of labour, the cheapness of mass produced fittings and the range of lamps available to a worldwide market. The importance of Birmingham is borne out by the large number of its manufacturers exhibiting at the International Exhibition of 1862. Here such celebrated makers as R.W.Winfield and Mr Messenger showed a wide range of designs in the classical and gothic tastes (Figs 51 and 52).

Although it is true to say that some critics continued to express reservations about gas use throughout the nineteenth century its popularity in the country house context increased once important houses such as Burghley, Windsor and Chatsworth began to use it. Technical improvements also added to its acceptability. The introduction of 'governors' to maintain gas pressure, the improvement of burners and the development of new ventilation systems meant that gas was increasingly economical to run and healthy to use. The introduction of pilot lights on some fittings made lighting the gas flame easier whilst the invention of the inverted regenerative burner in the 1870s increased the strength of light which could be achieved (Cat.85)

Gas fittings were also created to accommodate an increasing range of activities and settings. At Hassobury, Verity & Sons supplied a 'polished and lacquered Billiard Gasolier with improved ring burners, large wire frames and protectors and green shades' for the centre of the billiard room's glass ceiling. A grand gothic fitting of the 1860s by an unidentified maker survives in the billiard room at Allerton Park, Yorkshire whilst early photographs of interiors at Halton House, Buckinghamshire show an elaborate example of the 1880s.

Gasoliers decorated with glass or porcelain flowers were felt particularly appropriate to the winter garden or conservatory setting whilst simple bronzed brackets were available for the domestic quarters (S.Timmins, p.343; *International Exhibition Catalogue*, 1862, p.119). Specialist fittings were also available for the lighting of paintings. At

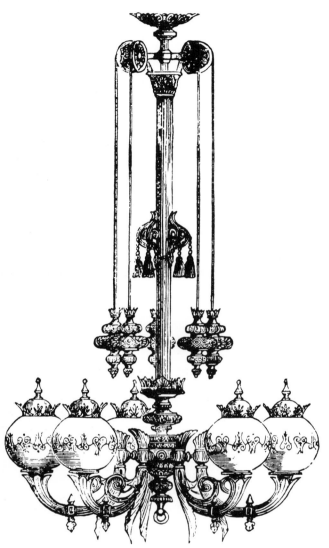

Fig.55. *Gasolier by Winfield & Co. showing ornamental balance weights. Exhibited at the International Exhibition 1862*

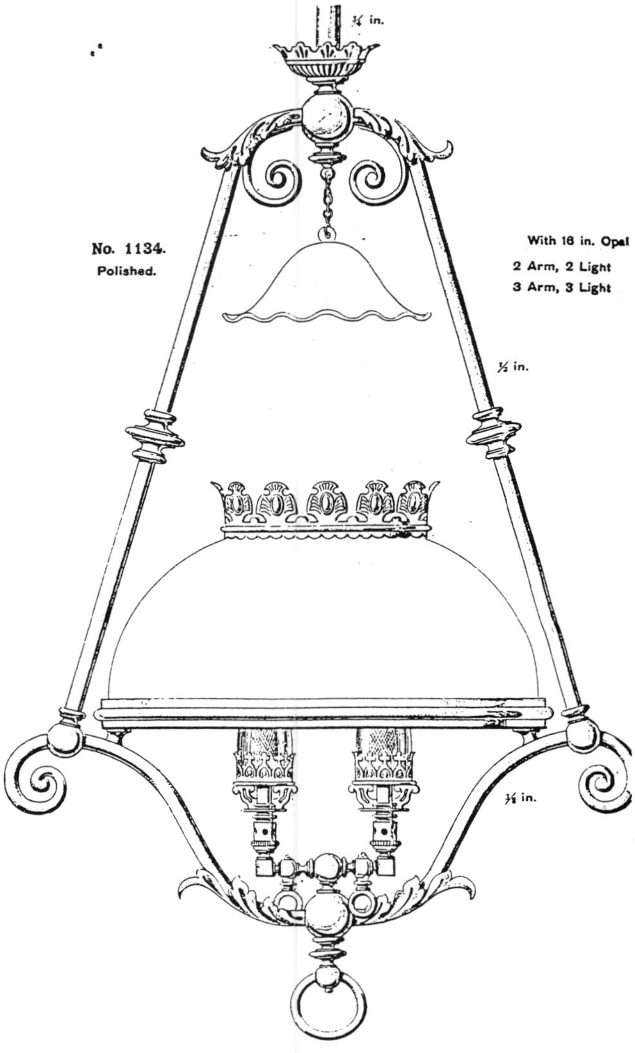

No. 1134.
Polished.

With 16 in. Opal
2 Arm, 2 Light
3 Arm, 3 Light

Fig.56. *Pendant fitting for use with Acetylene gas installed at Farnley Hall, 1901*

Crewe Hall the celebrated series of Reynolds portraits in the drawing room are shown in early photographs illuminated by double brackets, the light focussed by means of metal shades emblazoned with the Crewe arms (Fig.53). Less elaborate examples can still be seen in many of the rooms at Burghley (Fig.54). This adaptation contradicted the earlier criticism that gas was unsuitable for use with paintings.

A great technical improvement was the development of mechanisms to allow gasoliers or pendants to be raised and lowered to facilitate lighting. This involved the introduction of a simple water slide with balance weights which enabled movement without gas leakage. By the 1860s the weights were conveniently concealed amidst a welter of cast and applied ornament (Fig.55).

Flexible tubes allowed for the creation of portable table and reading lamps whilst swing brackets such as those supplied to Hassobury in 1870, could be angled as the use required. But despite this variety, Aesthetic Movement characters like Mrs Orrinsmith continued to rail against the

available systems. As she commented in *The Drawing Room* of 1878, gas 'is especially injurious to decorations be they pictures, papers ceilings or hangings, quickly making them dingy and dirty. The light they give is intense irritating and ineffective.' She did however go on to grudgingly comment that most people could not 'exclude from their drawing rooms a light which saves much daily labour, is instantly and easily available and confessedly economical', the main factors behind gas light's undoubted popularity.

Even in the challenging days that followed the practical employment of electric light, gas continued to present a viable alternative aided by the incandescent mantle and improved gas production methods. As late as 1901 Bailey and Clapham were called in to introduce a new 'Acetylene Gas Light Installation' at Farnley Hall for F.H.Fawkes (Fig.56). Acetylene, developed in the 1890s, was a hydrocarbon gas generated from calcium carbide decomposed by the action of water. It was thought ideal for 'installations in which gas has been generated more or less on the spot as in...country house installations' and around 1910 a system was set up in the newly restored Bramham Park, proving yet again that Loudon's recommendations for gas use still held true. As his correspondent Mr Robinson had remarked in 1833 'I have long looked on lighting by gas as the most elegant and comfortable of all our domestic improvements', a sentiment no doubt shared by many a country house owner (Loudon, 1833, p.1027).

81 A Practical Treatise on Gas Light
by Fredrick Accum
1815
Published by R.Ackermann
$8\frac{1}{2}$ x 6in (21 x 15)

Part of Ackermann's thrust to bring gas-lighting to a wider audience, the Treatise was written by Fredrick Accum the 'operative chemist' behind the gas system at Ackermann's own premises in the Strand.

Reviewed in the *New Monthly Magazine* for 1815 as providing 'all the information that can be desired on the subject', the Treatise contained three plates and an accompanying text reproduced here. All fittings were described as 'already in use in the metropolis' and therefore represent realised fittings of the period rather than fanciful designs. Accum went on to produce his celebrated *Description of the Process of Manufacturing Coal Gas* in 1820.

Lent by British Gas PLC, London Gas Museum

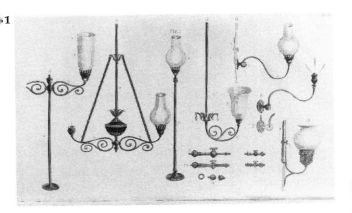

PLATE-III.FIG.1. Represents a *Rod Lamp*.
The gas passes through the rod *a*, to the Argand burner, which is surrounded by a cylindrical chimney, *c*, swelling out of the lower extremity. The construction of the Argand burner, we have mentioned already, p.94.

In all the gas-light burners, constructed on Argand's plan, care should be taken that the flame be in contact with the air on all sides, and that the current of the air be directed towards the upper extremity of the flame. This may be effected by causing a current of air to rise up perpendicular from the bottom of the chimney glass, and to pass out again through the contracted part, or upper extremity of the chimney; but no other current of air should ever be committed to come near the gas-flame, or enter the glass chimney which covers or defends the light; for if more air be permitted to mix with the flame than is sufficient for the complete combustion of the coal-gas,

it necessarily diminishes the heat, and consequently reduces the quantity of light.

FIG.2. *A Rod Gas Lamp, with branches.*
The gas passes through the hollow rod, *a*, and part of the hollow branch, *b*, the burner of the lamp. The cylindrical shaped glass, *c*, exhibited in this figure, is not so well adapted for the complete combustion of coal-gas, as the belly-shaped chimney, *c*, represented in fig.1, 3, 5, 6, because the ascending current of fresh air is not turned out of its perpendicular course, and thrown immediately in a concentrated state, into the upper part of the flame where the combustion of the gas is less perfect. The exterior current of air which enters at the bottom of the lamp, rises merely with a velocity proportional to the length of the cylinder, and to the rarefaction of the air in the same, but without being propelled to the apex of the flame, as it should do, and is made to do, in the bellied glass adapted to the lamp, fig.1.

FIG.3. *A Branch Lamp.*
a, the tube which conveys the gas to the burner; *b*, the stop-cock of the tube.

FIG.4. *A Pendent Rod Lamp;* in which the gas is supposed to come from a pipe above, through the ceiling, into the pipe, *a*, to supply the burners. The tulip-shaped chimney, *b*, of this lamp, is likewise ill adapted for gas-light burners.

FIG.5. *A Pendent double-branch Lamp.*
The gas passing through the perpendicular tube, *a*, into the brackets, *bb*; *c* shows the Argand burner.

FIG.6. *A Swing Branch Lamp.*
a, the gas pipe with its stop-cock; *b*, a brass ball, communicating with the pipe, *a*; *c*, the conducting tube, ground air-tight into the ball, *b*, and communicating with the burner of the lamp, so as to allow it to have an horizontal motion.

FIG.7. Shews the construction of the ball 6, and pipe *c*, of the lamp, fig.6.

FIG.8. *A swing Cockspur Lamp*, constructed upon the same plan as fig.6. These two lamps are very convenient for desks in counting-houses, &c.

FIG.9. A stop-cock with ball and socket, which, when adapted to a gas-light pipe, allows it to have an universal motion, so that the light may be turned in any direction.

FIG.10. Section of the stop-cock, with ball and socket.

FIG.11. Shows the ball and socket, fig.9, in perspective

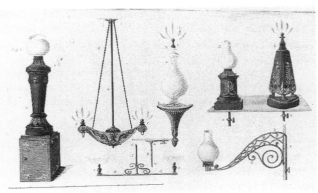

PLATE IV,* FIG.1. *A Candelabrum*; the gas pipe ascending from the floor of the apartment, through the column *a*, and terminating in the burner of the lamp.

FIG.2. *A fancy pendent Cockspur Lamp*. The gas being transmitted to the burners, *cc*, by means of the pipe, *a*.

FIG.3. *A Pedestal Argand Lamp. a,* the pipe and stop-cock, which transmits to, and shuts of the gas from the burner of the lamp.

FIG.4. *A Pedestal Cockspur Lamp. a,* the stop-cock and gas-pipe.

FIG.5. *A fancy bracket Cockspur Lamp,* intended merely to show that the coal-gas, as it passes to the burner, is perfectly devoid of colour, and invisible. *a* is a glass vessel furnished at its orifice with a brass cap, *c,* and perforated ball, out of which of the gas-flame proceeds. *b,* the pipe which conveys the gas into the glass vessel, *a.*

FIG.6. *A bracket Argand Lamp. a* and *b,* the gas-pipe communicating with the burner.

FIG.7 AND 8. *A Horizontal Branch Lamp.*
a, the gas-pipe, supposed to be concealed in the ceiling. *b,* the communicating pipe, which, together with *c,* branches out at right angles at *dd. e,* are the burners of the lamp.

PLATE V.FIG.1. *A Candelabrum,* into which the gas-pipe ascends from the floor of the apartment, the lateral branches communicating with the central tube.

FIG.2. *An Arabesque Chandelier.* The gas enters from the ceiling of the room into the rope-shaped pipe, *a,* from which it proceeds through one of the arched ribs, *bb,* into the horizontal hoop, or pipe, *c.*

FIG.3. *A Roman Chandelier.* The gas enters through the inflexible hollow chain, *a,* into the central tube, *b,* from whence the burners are supplied by the lateral branches, *cc.*

FIG.4. *A Gothic Chandelier.* The gas is transmitted to the burners through the rope, *a,* which includes a tube, and the communication with the burners is established through the lateral branches.

FIG.5. *A Pedestal Figure Lamp.* The gas is here made to pass, by means of a pipe, through the body of the figure into the lattice-work plateau, constructed of hollow and perforated brass tubes.

FIG.6. *A Pedestal Vase Lamp.* The gas-tube enters through one of the claw-feet of the altar-shaped pedestal, into the glass vase, *a,* at the bottom of which it joins the tubes communicating with the metallic corn-ears, *b,* at the upper extremities of which it forms jets de feu.

FIG.7. *A Girandole.* The gas enters through the bracket, *a,* and is conveyed to the burners by the descending tubes *bb.*

FIG.8. *A Candelabrum,* having a central pipe, through which the gas is conducted to the burner at the top.

*The gas-lamps exhibited in this plate, are employed in the library, counting-house, warehouse, and offices of Mr.Ackerman

82 Pair of converted Argand lamps

*c.*1823
Modified by James Milne, Edinburgh
The cast argand lamp is in the Gothic taste with crocketed reservoir in the form of a mediaeval lantern enriched by bronzed panels.
H 22in (55)
PROV. Sir Walter Scott, Abbotsford

Walter Scott began the installation of gas at Abbotsford in 1823 using James Milne as contractor and supplier. Milne's bills (copies of which are housed at the National Monuments Record of Scotland) list a surprising array of fittings from 'plain pendants for the servants hall' to the elaborate cut glass 'gas lustre' provided for the Drawing Room. Whilst many of the fittings were specially designed for gas use, others were adapted from existing oil lamps. Cat.82 is itemised in Milne's bill for August 1823 as 'Altering 2 1 Lt Gothic Argand Lamps for niches' and their original position may have been in the mediaeval style openings to the left and right of the sideboard recess in the Dining Room at Abbotsford. Their function was presumably to light the serving area. The conversion involved the disabling of the colza reservoir, sealing of all joints and the introduction of a pipe through the base of the lamp to the burner. A tap controlled the gas supply.

Lent by Mrs Maxwell-Scott, Abbotsford

83 Garden's Platinum Light

*c.*1830

H 24in (52)

Formed from two clear glass vessels linked by a metal collar.

Walter Scott's interest in artificial illumination probably led him to try Garden's patent lamp. Its rather complicated mechanism which used hydrogen gas is described in detail in the 1847 edition of Thomas Webster's *Encyclopaedia of Domestic Economy,* together with a diagram:

> 740.*Garden's Platinum light.* A very curious discovery was made in 1824, by Professor Dobreiner, of Jena, who found that platinum, prepared in a spongy form, possessed the singular property of causing a jet of hydrogen gas thrown upon it to inflame in consequence of its union with the oxygen of the atmosphere; and the heat thus excited is thus sufficient to render the platina red-hot, at which a match may be lighted. Upon this principle an apparatus for procuring an instantaneous light has been constructed by Mr Garden, 272. Oxford Street, London, as follows. *a* and *b, fig.*147. are two glass vessels, the neck of the upper one being fitted air-tight into the lower by grinding. A hollow cylinder, *c,* is fixed upon the neck of the vessel *a,* and reaches more than half way down into *b*: round this tube a piece of zinc is wrapped. A quantity of diluted sulphuric acid is poured into the vessel *b,* which, acting upon the zinc, produces the hydrogen, which rises to the top of the vessel, but, not being able to escape, it collects there, and forces the acid to ascend through the tube into the upper vessel, the air in which escapes through the stopper loosely fitted. As soon as the production of hydrogen has gone on so far as to occasion the acid to descend to the lower part of the zinc, all further action of course ceases, and the upper part of *a*

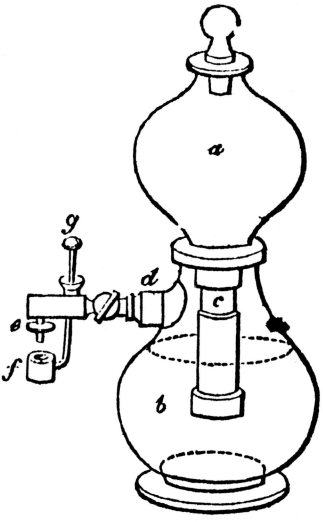

remains filled with gas. From this part of the vessel, s tube, *d,* projects, furnished with a stop-cock, and the extremity of this tube turns downwards terminating in *e,* where a jet of hydrogen issues on opening the cock. Immediately below this is a little cup, *f,* to hold the spongy platina; and this cup may be moved further off or nearer by means of a wire *g,* which slides up and down through a collar. When a light is wanted, the cock is turned, a jet of hydrogen falls upon the platina, which inflames the hydrogen, and is itself made red-hot, and capable of igniting a match.

Webster went on to state that the apparatus could be mounted in a mahogany frame to give it extra security and recommended its use for the library or bedchamber.

Lent by Mrs Maxwell Scott, Abbotsford

84 Pair of sconces

*c.*1840

Each with three S-scroll cable twist branches springing from metal sockets embraced by a fluted cup, the central arm rising to an apex; the scalloped drip — pans are hung with faceted lustres and the framework elaborately festooned with wired bead chains and prismatic drops.

84

8

H 38in (95)
PROV. Charles Thornton (Antiques) York

The hollow branches of the girandole arms suggest that they were originally piped for gas.

The Perry and Co Archive deposited in the Prints and Drawings department, V & A, illustrate a number of similar cut glass examples drawn up by the designer Mr Bartlett during the years 1867–1874. The final page of the volume explains the order in which such a complicated arrangement would be set up:

> In fixing the sidelight great care must be taken to get them upright, the best way is having screwed the metal part on the end of gas pipe in wall to put in the spire and arms, when it will easily be seen if the light is upright in front and right with the wall at the side; small wedges behind the backplate may be found necessary, if so care should be taken to cut them off even with the metal work, when it is satisfactory... put in the back plate: the arms and spire should be removed, the check screw taken out and the metal body unscrewed to put the glass piece over the back plate, replace the body, put in the check screw and screw in the arms and curls taking care that the joints are gas tight put on the glass piece screw in the spire, hang on the dropwork in the order marked finishing with the pans and drops. (V & A 95.C.85)

Leeds City Art Galleries (Temple Newsam)

85 Gas bracket
*c.*1870
Gilt and bronzed brass
The scrolling bracket enriched with classical bosses, flower heads and stylised acanthus leaves. Articulated at

the back plate. The stop-cock cast with indistinct design registration lozenge.
L $21\frac{1}{2}$in (54)
PROV. William, third Marquess of Exeter, Burghley House, Stamford

A gas supply was installed at Burghley during the middle of the last century although there is no information to suggest when and by whom it was set up. Gas brackets provided a flexible source of light, the cup and ball joint allowing the lamp to be moved to left or right as required. Often positioned at either side of the chimney piece or over the sideboard they can be seen in operation in a wide range of 19th century photographs; a more complex version is shown at Pitfour Castle of a type probably introduced in the 1850s (Gere, Fig.292) More brackets from the Burghley suite can be seen in situ in the Old Ballroom.

Lent from the Burghley House Collection

86 Table lamp
*c.*1870
Bronzed and gilded brass on an ebonised plinth
The lamp takes the form of an antique spout lamp mounted on a twisted column rising from the heavily cast base decorated with husks and renaissance ornament.
H 12in (28.5)
PROV. William, third Marquess of Exeter, Burghley House, Stamford

Following the development of flexible rubber hosing during the 1860s it was possible to connect table lamps to the supply via wall gas points. This example exploits the classical spout lamp form, directing the gas flame through the now missing burner which screwed on to the spout. The stop-cock is given bold Greek-key like decoration and beyond it a screw fitting permitted connection to the hose and wall supply. In order to maintain the antique theme it is likely that the gas flame went unshaded.

Lent from the Burghley House Collection

chimneys, used to draw away the 'products of combustion' were often given a decorative treatment, Doultons being amongst the many factories producing ceramic covers.

The present example was used at Cragside where the pre-electrification gas works seem to have had a continued use in the domestic areas of the building. The lamp is one of a pair removed from the Tower at Cragside.

Lent by the National Trust (Cragside)

87 Regenerative gas lamp
*c.*1880
Supplied by Wenham & Co.
Of inverted form with opaque glass shade and ceiling protector, the enamelled tin chimney decorated with stylised flowers and bands of gilding.
H 31in (77.5)
PROV. Lord Armstrong, Cragside

During the 1880s experiments continued to further reform the efficiency of gas lights. As Cassell's *Book of the Household* commented 'The most improved high-duty burners are all on what is called the 'regenerative' system, by which both the gas and air are highly heated before combustion by the heat of the lamp itself.' (vol.II p.188) Of these the Wenham Co's version was felt to be 'the best known and most popular'.

Leading to greater efficiency of gas consumption, the lamps were primarily used as overhead pendants. The

The Rise of Electricity

Although Sir Humphrey Davey had demonstrated the possibilities of electricity as an illuminant at the Royal Institute in 1808 it was not until the late 1870s that scientific developments transformed it into a viable means of creating a domestic light source.

Before this, arc lights (a system whereby current was made to jump between two pencils of carbon) were tried, although the intensity of light produced made it suitable for only the largest of interiors or outdoor events. At Lord Armstrong's house the vast library was lit by an arc lamp in December 1878 whilst in 1880 Jablochov candles, a simple version of the arc lamp, were tried out in the ballroom at Lord Salisbury's home Hatfield House. As Cassell's *Book of the Household* commented in 1890 the arc lamp was 'not universally becoming to colours or complections...and ladies will have to choose the colours of their evening dresses with special view to the electrical light when it becomes general. It is said that at present nothing looks so well under its influence as pink and the various shades of red.' (vol.2, p.194)

Witnesses to this early light at Hatfield commented on being 'compelled to eat their dinner under the vibrating glare' and perhaps for these reasons many people continued to use candles when dining. In the 1890s Mr Sugg the gas-light King commented on a dining room lit by electric glow lamps supplemented by candles merely for artistic effect. Reservations about the brilliance of the light produced led some innovators to set the system up outside in the garden close beside the windows. At Sir A.Ramsay's house the lamps shone through pink muslin curtains to light the principal rooms within (*The Electrician*, 1881 p.68).

With the development of the incandescent lamp a more sympathetic light was produced and presumably its take-up enhanced (Fig.57). Perfected independently by Joseph Swan and Thomas Eddison the light consisted

of a small glass globe from which the air has been exhausted, and in which is fixed a thin filament of carbon connected with two platinum conducting wires which pass through and are fused into the glass.

On passing the electric current through the carbon it becomes intensely white hot and emits a beautifully soft clear and steady light.

The lamp unlike most other lamps has no mechanism about it and when it fails...is an easily replaced by a new one as a candle is placed in a candlestick.' (*Swan Illustrated Catalogue*, 1883)

First shown by the inventors in the years 1878–79 the immediate response was suspicious, one reviewer in Cassells *Family Magazine* of 1880 cautioning readers that 'accounts are commonly written by journalists...quite incapable of forming any opinion on the subject beyond what is told them by those interested.'(p.256)

Even so by 1883 many country houses had taken up the light form, several being at the forefront of the new technology. For some the use of batteries as a power source made electric lighting an ideal means of creating temporary illumination for a grand event. This may have been the motive behind the illumination of 'Lord Butes Castle Cardiff' listed as 'Temporarily lit' in the Swan catalogue of 1883.

Permanent installations were soon to be found at houses such as Cragside, home of Joseph Swan's great friend Lord Armstrong, Hatfield House, Chatsworth House and Octavius E.Coope's home, Berechurch Hall near Colchester. At this time the fittings for electricity were either purpose built or converted from earlier fittings. At Hatfield remarkably discreet metal cups turned the plasterwork into a firmament of bulbs. At this point few attempts were made to shade or conceal the light source (Figs 58 and 59).

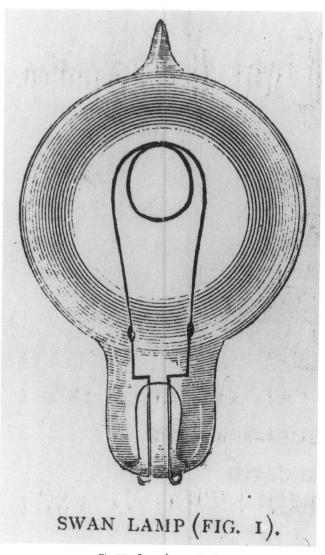

SWAN LAMP (FIG. I).

Fig.57. Swan lamp, 1883

Fig.59. Hatfield House, c.1900, showing decorative groupings of lamps and holders in the library

Fig.58. Hatfield House, c.1900, showing bulbs and lightfittings incorporated into the Dining Room cornice and ceiling

Bulbs bristled from all available cornices and brackets and, as the *Electrician Magazine* of 1887 put it, 'the Elizabethan mouldings and pendants...lending themselves very artistically to this purpose.' At Cragside paraffin lamps were turned into perhaps the earliest known electric table lamps (Cat.86).

By 1893 the installation at Chatsworth was particularly admired for its discreetness and a review in the *Pall Mall Gazette* (dated 11 December) commented:

> The original lamp fittings in ormolu or bronze have received with their old fashioned ground glass shades the brilliant Swan burners of today. The chandeliers in crystal or cut glass, the girandoles in ormolu and the many-branched silver candlesticks are still seemingly fitted with shaded wax lights. There are two new features in connection with these pretence candles. There are specially constructed of a transparent porcelain which is indistinguishable by the eye from wax and the inevitable glass bulb at the top, instead of being the conventional size, is made only just large enough to contain its flaming carbon thread. (Fig.60)

The ease with which existing fittings and indeed houses could be converted to electricity was one of its early selling points. As one contemporary reviewer noted:

electric current can far more easily be conveyed into houses than gas-pipes because they can be conveyed along walls or even between floors and ceilings, by means of small apertures; and they can also be fixed at any convenient place on the walls and conveyed...to any point where they are wanted. (Cassell's *Book of the Household*, 1890, vol.2, p.192ff)

This flexibility was another positive factor especially in the context of great houses where important or costly decorative schemes had to be preserved.

Another selling point lay in the fact that the new light which, although expensive to install, was potentially safer and cleaner than its predecessor gas. Writing to *The Times* on 16 January 1883 Octavius Coope commented:

> The cost of the first outlay for electricity is...somewhat in excess of the same for gas; but then I have no nuisance of lime or of tar or other refuse products; no leakage of gas into the house, no smell in the manufacture, or damage to my garden; and in the place of an unsightly gasometer, I have a compact little engine...which when not driving the dynamos is utilised for pumping water to the top of the house.

Added to this was its safety in conjunction with artworks and decoration. Whilst gas had long been criticised for the tarry deposits with which badly maintained systems could damage paintings and sculpture, critics were quick to recommend electricity which did not 'destroy the most elaborate gilding' and left 'ceilings and walls unsoiled.'

directed volleys of sofa-cushions rendered the summoning of a fire engine unnecessary. (Cecil, vol.III, p.7)

Even in the 1890s systems could be erratic. In 1893 Lady Emily Lutyens visited Knowsley, Lord Derby's Lancashire seat, probably electrified at the instigation of his friend Lord Salisbury. At dinner

out went the electric light. Happily there was gas in the passages, but it was a great nuisance. Everyone, though enjoyed the joke, and the light came on during dinner. These luxuries have their drawbacks.' (Lutyens, p.250)

For many country houses such luxuries were not even attempted until the servant problem of the twentieth century made it increasingly vital. Reminiscing about life at Longleat during the first war, lamp boy Gordon Grimmett outlined the Marquis of Bath's approach to the new fangled light systems, which must have struck a chord in many hearts:

The rooms had been designed for oil lamps or candle light, and if he were to change to electricity not only might it mutilate the ceilings and walls but the character of the rooms would change. He had the same feelings about central heating....' (Harrison, 1976)

Fig.60. Chatsworth, c.1900, showing 'pretence candles' in use in the Chapel gallery

But despite these recommendations, electricity could be problematic. At Hatfield its installation in the late 1870s had been rather ad hoc. As Lady Gwendolen Cecil put it:

No expert middleman had as yet undertaken the installation of the new invention. It was an opportunity for independent action under conditions which were so untried as to have all the charm of scientific experiment and Lord Salisbury did not miss it. He set his estate workmen to the task that Winter under the direction of a sympathetic clerk of works. (Cecil, vol.III, p.4)

The results are well known, especially those caused by the omission of fuses in the system. On one occasion

a party of guests, on entering the Long Gallery after dinner found the carved panelling near the ceiling bursting into flames under contact of an overheated wire. It was happily a shooting party in which young men formed a substantial element. They rose joyfully to the occasion and with well-

88 Vase table lamp
c.1880
Oriental enamel vase base with spherical ground glass
shade.
The lamp utilises an existing vase of cloisonné enamel
which supports the electrical mechanism and shade
H 24in (60)
PROV. Lord Armstrong, Cragside

Richard Norman Shaw's drawings for the New Library at
Cragside were executed in 1870 and incorporated an
illustration of the present table lamp standing on Shaw's
elaborate low bookcase unit. At this point the lamp, one of
a suite of four, is shown complete with chimney and oil
burning mechanism but in 1880 the house's conversion to
electricity ensured that the lamp was further modified.

(Fig. 3.)   The Bay Window in the Library.

Describing the Library in a letter to *The Engineer* on
17 January 1881 Armstrong wrote:

> The library...is well lighted by eight lamps. Four of these are
> clustered in one ground glass, suspended from the ceiling in
> the recess, and the remainder are placed singly and in globes in
> various parts of the room, upon vases which were previously
> used as stands for duplex kerosene lamps. These vases being
> enamel on copper are themselves conductors, and serve for
> carrying the return current from the incandescent carbon to a
> metallic base in connection with the main return wire. The
> entering current is brought by a branch wire to a small

insulated mercury cup in the centre of the base and is carried
forward to the lamp by a piece of insulated wire which passes
through a hole in the bottom of the vase and thence through
the interior to the lamp on the top. The protruding end of this
wire is naked and dips into the mercury cup when the vase is
set down. Thus the lamp may be extinguished and re-lighted
at pleasure merely by removing the vase from its seat or
setting it down again.

The lamp fitted well into the 'aesthetic' scheme for the
library (see illustrations) and, like the remainder of the suite,
remains in situ.

Lent by The National Trust, (Cragside)

89 Lea and Sons Catalogue
c.1890
8 x 11in (19 x 27)
PROV. Lord Armstrong, Cragside

Sometime after 1891 the original fittings at Cragside were
replaced by elaborate examples supplied by the firm of Lea,
Sons & Co, Shrewsbury.

Although the relevant bills do not seem to survive, Lea's
brochure remains in the Library at Cragside and many of
the existing fittings can be identified in the catalogue's
illustrations. Sheet 10 fig.6026 shows the grand electrolier
used in the Drawing Room, sheet 11 fittings from the

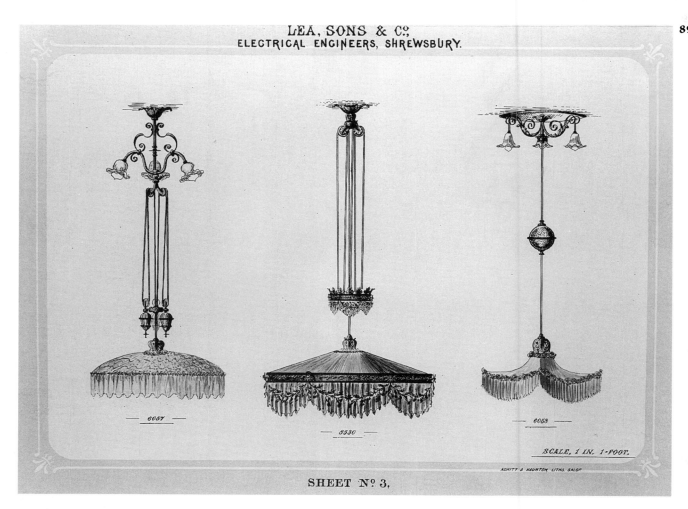

Yellow Bedroom and corridor and sheet 3 the rising light finally used in the Library.

Lea's fittings were intended to accommodate 'Ediswan' lampholders and were available in a range of finishes 'Bright Iron and Blue Steel' being 'a new and artistic combination.' They reflect the increasing elaboration of fittings towards the end of the century.

Lent by the National Trust (Cragside)

90 Standard lamp
*c.*1890
Probably supplied by Lea, Sons & Co, Shrewsbury
Lacquered brass
Lamp base in the form of a cast Corinthian column, the lampholder mounted on a telescopic tube which allows the light to be raised or lowered. The later silk shade rests on a brass corona above the multiple brass lampholder.
H 72in (180)
PROV. Lord Armstrong, Cragside

Although not illustrated in Lea, Sons & Co's, catalogue it is possible that this formed part of the suite supplied by the firm sometime after 1891. Identical examples survive in the Library at Cragside.

Lent by the National Trust (Cragside)

91 Rise and fall light
*c.*1890
Supplied by Lea, Sons & Co, Shrewsbury
Bright iron with silk shade and fringing
Of pendant form, the shade is suspended from a fringed coronet which conceals the weight mechanism. The flattened conical shade, recovered in red silk has an outer band decorated with cast ornament and further enriched by swags of naturalistic iron flowers.
H 48in (120)
PROV. Lord Armstrong, Cragside.

Not shown in Bedford Lemere's photograph of the Library taken in 1891, the fitting was probably installed by Lea, Sons & Co sometime after 1892. It is illustrated in their catalogue sheet 3 fig.8530. As a library fitting it had the advantage of being movable and could be drawn down to focus light on the writing table utilising a system of weights and pulleys.

The National Trust (Cragside)

92 Pair of pendant lamps
*c.*1890
Probably supplied by Lea, Sons & Co, Shrewsbury
Brass with crackled, translucent glass shades.

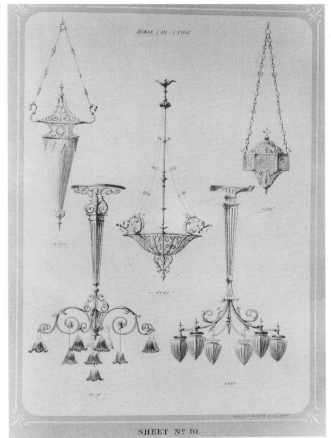

SHEET Nº 10.

LEA, SONS & Cº
ART METAL WORKERS, SHREWSBURY.

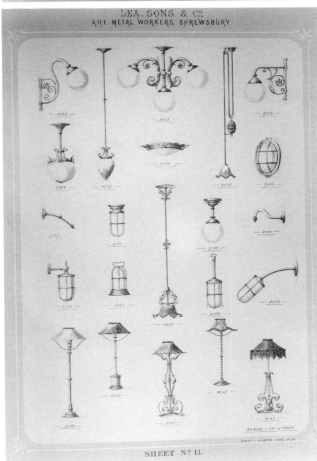

SCALE 1 IN = 1 FOOT

SHEET Nº 11.

Of sanctuary lamp form, the lampholders hang from cast brackets via a triple arrangement of coiled and wrought wire. Bands of brass support cylindrical crackled-glass shades.
H 24in (60)
PROV. Lord Armstrong, Cragside

Several of the bedrooms at Cragside have identical fittings flanking the chimneypiece or bed. They are mounted to the wall on wooden blocks and would have provided a faintly ecclesiastical source of illumination.

Lent by the National Trust (Cragside)

Furniture and Lighting

Candlestands

Portable table candlestands, often made in pairs, were used to elevate candlesticks to a convenient height. Most had a tray top and turned column threaded into a circular, lead-weighted foot; sometimes they were adjustable by means of a sliding stem. Floor standing models with a dished candle-board contrived to slide up and down a tall pole were also made between about 1740 and 1820. There is a late 18th century example at the Fitzwilliam Museum, Cambridge.

The fashion for high, richly styled candlestands origi-nated in Italy, but they were rare in England before 1650. Pairs of ebonized and gilt Venetian blackamoor stands dating from the 1660–80 period survive at Knole and Ham House (Fig.61); they were called *gueridons*, the French name for Negro pageboys, and this term came to be widely used for lavish candlestands. Pairs were often displayed alongside handsome tables or cabinets. A richly styled, silvered pair, reputedly from Ham House, the platform tops ornamented with chinoiserie landscapes, is now at Colonial Williamsburg (Figs 62 & 63). Daniel Marot illustrated four 'Grande Gueridons' in his *Nouveaux Livre d'Orfeuverie*, 1703, 1713, accompanied by patterns for column candlesticks to place on them and, in another plate, a caryatid sidetable, looking-glass and figure candlestands, one of which is surmounted by a twin branch candelabra (Elizabeth White, *Pictorial Dictionary of British 18th Century Furniture Designs*, 1990, p.302, pls 3 and 8). In 1691 there were at Kensington Palace: 'six standing Branches of Silver with foure stands in ye Galery' (information from Susan Jenkins).

Tall candlestands used in formal room settings were also known as torcheres (Cat.93) but from about 1670 many lower, simply styled stands were made to light tables (Fig.64). These frequently formed a unified suite consisting of a walnut dressing table and looking-glass flanked by a pair of tripod candlestands about 3 feet high. Although no such ensembles are recorded in the Kiveton inventory of 1727, the Duke of Leeds's other Yorkshire house, Thorp Salvin, contained several, in the bedchambers: '1 Looking Glass in a Wallnut frame/1 Inlaid table with a Drawer Do/2 old Broken stands Do' and in the Green Bedchamber '1 Looking Glass with a black frame/1 Table/2 Stands Do'. Fine intact 'triad' sets survive at Ham House, Knole and Boughton.

State rooms in many Palladian houses were provided with impressive, formally paraded candlestands. Lord Burlington's Dressing Room at Chiswick (built *c*.1725) included 'A Black Marble side Board Table inlaid with pebbles on a Carv'd Gilt frame. Two Ditto Candlestands with brass Mouldings.' When Lord Irwin was furnishing his newly created Picture Gallery at Temple Newsam in 1745/6 reputed to be 'ye handsommest apartement in England' he ordered from James Pascall a set of eight gloriously Rococo candlestands to flank two pairs of sidetables (Cat.1).

Fig.61. Ham House, one of the two 'Blackamore Stands' from the Great Dining Room, c.1675

Carver's pieces were amongst the earliest kinds of furni-ture to be infected by the spirited Rococo style and the pattern books of the period contain many extravagantly picturesque designs for candlestands. Several examples were published in Edwards & Darly *A New Book of Chinese Designs*, 1754, pl 24; Thomas Chippendale's *Director*,

Fig.62. Ham House, one of a pair of carved candlestands, silvered gesso, c.1690 (H 46in)

Fig.63. Detail of Fig.62

Fig.64. Candlestand, originally one of a pair, walnut with inlaid top, late 17th century (H 29in)

1762, pl.cxlvii and Ince & Mayhew's *Universal System*, 1762 (pls lxvii and lxix), usefully show silver candlesticks or multi-branched candelabra resting on the platform tops; other plates portray stands with candle branches sprouting directly from the central stem as in Cat.94.

Torcheres remained popular throughout the century, responding to neo-Classical ideals of taste, when the tripod form, inspired by Ancient originals, became fashionable (Cat.96). Many of Robert Adam's finest interiors were provided with sets. The pair he designed for the Tapestry Drawing Room at Osterley Park were described in 1782 as: 'Two exceeding elegant tripod stands richly carved and gilt in burnish gold with three oval Paintings. Two very elegant or Molee Vases and Pedestals which carry two lights each for the beforementioned Stands'.

Although at this time candlestands were normally restricted to reception rooms, unostentatious examples are sometimes listed in bed and dressing rooms. At Appuldurcombe in 1780 Lady Worsley's Dressing Room contained '2 high candlestands painted'; at the same date 'Two Bamboo Candlestands' stood in the Yellow Damask Bedchamber at Osterley while mahogany pairs are listed in two further dressing rooms.

Thomas Sheraton, always alert to changes in taste, offers evidence in his *Cabinet Dictionary*, 1803, of a new fashion: 'Figure lights have been much introduced of late, and which certainly produce a more noble appearance than those of the tripod kind.' Six late Regency stands made for the Great Hall at Temple Newsam illustrate an antiquarian rather than a classical version of this vogue (Cat.5).

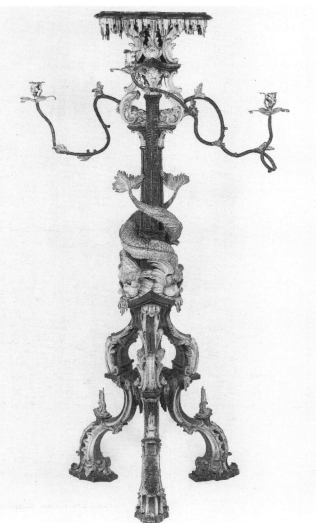

The lobed top is supported on a shaft of clustered columns entwined by a pair of dolphins and raised on an open tripod base carved with rocaille and grotto ornaments. PROV. Hagley Hall, Worcestershire

One of four candlestands from an ensemble of 'rustic' furniture made for the Gallery at Hagley Hall, Worcestershire. The form is based on plate 13 in Thomas Johnson's *150 New Designs*, 1758. Possibly associated with payments to the London cabinet-maker Edward Griffiths; however, Sir Richmond Joseph Sullivan, *A Tour Through Parts of England, Scotland and Wales in 1778*, 2nd ed., vol.2, p.18, states that the furniture and carved work in the Gallery at Hagley 'were done by an artist in the neighbourhood' (information from Lucy Wood).

Leeds City Art Galleries (Temple Newsam)

95 Pair of candlestands
*c.*1775
Pine, carved, gilt and japanned black.
H 60½in (153)
Of tripod design on a platform base; decorated in the Neo-classical style, the upper stage ornamented with eagles and entwined serpents — traditional emblems of

93 Pair of candlestands
*c.*1700–05
Gilt pine and oak
H 60½in (153)
The circular gadrooned tops are raised on richly carved triangular stems resting on open scrolled tripod bases.

These stands reflect the fashionable court taste of Louis XIV and are in the style of John Pelletier, a London craftsman of French extraction who received many Royal commissioners during the reigns of William III and Mary II. Two pairs of stands at Hampton Court can be identified as his work.

Leeds City Art Galleries (Temple Newsam)

94 Candlestand
*c.*1758
Pine, stained and painted
H 62in (158)

light and darkness. The vase-shaped holder is socketed to take a candelabrum
PROV. Uffington House, Lincolnshire

Sheraton, in his *Drawing Book*, 1793, noted that candle-stands 'are used in drawing-rooms, for the convenience of affording additional light to such parts of the room where it would be neither ornamental nor easy to introduce in any other kind. The style of finishing these for Nobelmen's drawing-rooms is exceedingly rich ...'

Leeds City Art Galleries (Temple Newsam)

95

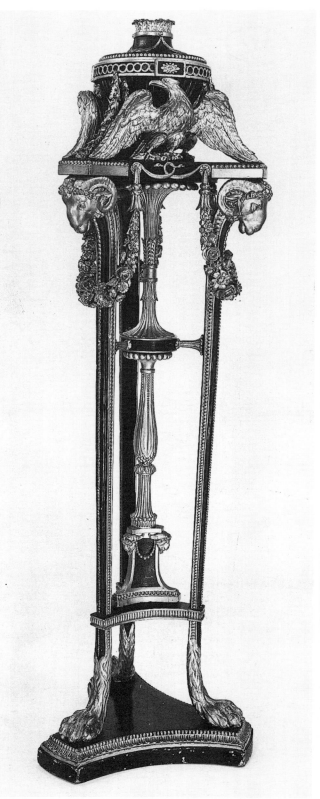

Sconces and Girandoles

The term 'sconce' was widely employed from the late Stuart period to describe a wall-light usually with candle-arms and often a reflector back plate. After about 1740, it was gradually replaced by the comprehensive word 'girandole' from the Italian *girandola*, which referred originally to small free-standing lustres or candelabra of Christmas-tree form, but came also to be applied to looking glasses with candle-branches. The 1795 Harewood House inventory recorded both types in the White Drawing Room: '2 large Circular Jerandoles with 4 Branches each/Two Glass Jerandoles upon the Chimney Piece'.

Restoration period sconces were nearly all made of metal — silver, brass or pewter — and many highly luxurious silver sets survive (Cats 6 & 7). The 1727 inventory of Kiveton Hall, Yorkshire, built and furnished by Thomas Osborne, 1st Duke of Leeds between 1694 and 1705, provides an interesting snapshot of the types of sconce in a fashionable house of that date. It yields numerous references to pairs of 'Brass Sconces Silver'd'; many rooms contained sets of 'Glass Sconces with Brass nossels' or

'Glass Arms' (like those supplied by James Moore to Erdigg in 1720); the draughty stairs and passages were lit by enclosed 'Glass Lamp Sconces' fixed to the walls.

The fire was an important source of light and served as a focal point, thus many rooms contained 'Chimney Sconces', some were 'Carved and Gilded' others had plates of looking-glass with exotic lacquered (japanned) frames. The South East Drawing Room was equipped with '6 Glass Scollopt Sconces/2 Do for the Chimney' (presumably they displayed decoratively cut edges) but the finest were in the North East Drawing Room which boasted '3 large Glass Sconces with purple and Gold Glass and frames and double brass Sockets, Silver'd/2 Chimney Sconces Do'. These magnificent status symbols may be associated with three payments totalling £239 made to John Gumley between 1700 and 1706.

The anthology of sconces and girandoles in the exhibition gives a fair idea of their variety and stylistic development. The looking-glass sconce designed by James Gibbs (Cat.97) represents a very large class, although the less grand veneered and parcel gilt example portrayed by Hogarth is perhaps more typical (Cat.99). The vast majority have now lost their candle-arms; candles were, it

Fig.65. Uppark, detail of Drawing Room in the Dolls' House showing candle sconces with smoke shades suspended from the ceiling, early 18th century

seems, only placed in the sockets when required to be lit. Several rooms in the Doll's House at Uppark are equipped with sconces, having glass smokeshades suspended from the ceiling directly above the candle-frame (Fig. 65). There are a few of these now rare survivals at Knole Park and a pair from another country house is included in the exhibition (Cat.101).

By no means all sconces had reflecting back plates; many were elaborately carved and gilt, creating a rich shimmering effect in the candle-light (Cat.98). The pair of six-light girandoles 'with hunting ornaments' carved by James Pascall for the Picture Gallery at Temple Newsam in 1745 are amongst the most spectacular examples of English Rococo furniture and make a stunning contribution to the decor of this celebrated interior during daylight hours (Cat.2).

Chippendale supplied many superb neo-Classical girandoles to Harewood House including a rare silvered pair for the Yellow Damask Sitting Room in 1775 invoiced as: '2 Exceeding neat & Rich Carved Gerandoles with ornaments and Treble Branches highly finished in burnished Silver and varnished and wrought Pans and Nossels silvered &c £40'. Although there are no grand neo-Classical girandoles in the exhibition, the small standing type is represented by a wonderful pair designed as a basket of flowers which Chippendale made for Newby Hall about 1773 (Fig.66).

Fig.67. Mirror chandelier, probably Irish, with facetted blue glass border, late 18th century

Fig.66. Newby Hall, one of a pair of carved and gilt girandoles made by Thomas Chippendale for the Tapestry Drawing Room c.1773 (H 18in)

Fig.68. Convex mirror sconce, gilt pine, a typical early 19th century design type

Towards the end of the 18th century a strikingly luxurious form of girandole believed to originate in Dublin first appeared, consisting of an elegant oval looking-glass, having a faceted border and a small chandelier either hanging in front of it or fixed to the mirror plate, so that its reflection created the effect of a complete chandelier (Fig.67). The Cecil Higgins Museum, Bedford, owns an important mirror chandelier signed by the glass manufacturer, John D. Aykboum, who had a warehouse at 15 Grafton Street, Dublin, from 1783 to 1799 (Martin Mortimer, 'The Irish Mirror Chandelier', *Country Life*, 16 December 1971, pp.1741–42). Other types of late Georgian wall light included decorative ormolu brackets, inspired by French models (Cat.100), glass branches with faceted stems and festoons of drops and, during Regency days, circular convex mirrors with flanking candle-arms and gilt frames headed by an eagle displayed, often holding in its beak two chains from which hang balls (Fig.68).

96 Pair of sconces
*c.*1705
Gilt pine
H 24in (61)

In the form of an enriched baluster with a putto head surmounted by a peacock displayed; the foliate base supports a pin-hinged candle-arm of broken-scroll design. The peacock may be an heraldic device (crest of the Dukes of Rutland).

Leeds City Art Galleries (Temple Newsam)

97

97 Sconce
*c.*1725
Designed by James Gibbs
Gilt pine
H 51in (129) W 34in (86)
The octagonal looking glass plate is set in an enriched frame with a shell cresting and fronded scrolls; the original pair of gilt metal candle-arms are ornamented with acanthus and Indian masks. The backboard chalked 'Drawing Room'.

One of the earliest recorded examples of English architect-designed furniture. James Gibbs's drawing is in the Ashmolean, Oxford.

Leeds City Art Galleries (Temple Newsam)

98 Pair of sconces
*c.*1730
Gilt lime
H 34in (86) W 22in (56)
Of imbricated scroll design, ornamented with satyr heads suspending oak festoons, lion-masks backed by shells and laurel wreaths; each is fitted with a short candle-arm and nozzle.

98

9

1

There are eight strikingly similar sconces at Grimsthorpe Castle, Lincolnshire and another of identical pattern at the MMA, New York. Possibly by James Richards, appointed Master Carver to the Crown in 1721, who in 1732 was paid for work on the Royal Barge, designed by William Kent, and was employed by Kent on other occasions.

Leeds City Art Galleries (Temple Newsam)

99 The Rake's Progress
By William Hogarth, 1735
Print 12½ x 15½in (31 x 39)
Depicts a drinking session in a bawdy-house; on the wall is a sconce with branches holding lighted candles, reflected in the broken mirror plate.

Leeds City Art Galleries

100 Pair of wall lights (from a set of four)
*c.*1775–80
Ormolu and bronze
H 33in (84)
The tapering backplate is designed with a stepped shelf supported by a bronze demi-slave figure and surmounted

by a swagged urn with lion masks; the three foliate scrolled candle branches end in fluted nozzles; pierced for electricity.
PROV. Serlby Hall, Nottinghamshire

These wall lights are probably English

Leeds City Art Galleries (Temple Newsam)

101 Two glass smoke shades
19th century, first half
Lead glass
H 9in (23)
Bell-shaped with integral suspension ring
PROV. Keir House, Stirling

Dish-shaped glass smoke shades were often suspended above candle-sconces (Fig.65); unexplained hooks in ceilings or short arms high up on walls may betray their former presence.

Old photographs sometimes show bell-shaped shades such as these suspended over the 'chimneys' of hanging colza lamps (a set is visible in an 1890s view of the Gallery at Stratfield Saye, illus, *Country Life*, 10 April 1975, p.901, fig.6). The gilt iron hook is copied from an old example.

An inventory of the stock in trade of Paul Saunders, cabinet-maker, taken in 1760 (*The Burlington Magazine*, April 1969, p.507) records several dozen 'Streight/ Crooked/Wrought Six Inch Shade Hooks' together with '26 Glass Shades'

Lent by the National Trust for Scotland

101

Reading and Music Stands

Music stands or reading desks almost always had 'Conveniences for Candlesticks' as Ince & Mayhew elegantly put it in their prefatory note to plate xxvi in the *Universal System*, 1762 (Fig.69). Conventional models were of pillar and claw design, made to rise by means of a sliding stem and rack with a horse to support the adjustable book slope. Most were originally fitted either with articulated brass arms and nozzles (Cat.102); pivotted circular brass plates or equivalent swivel candle-boards on which candlesticks were placed (Fig.70). Shearer, Hepplewhite and Loudon all illustrated examples, while a group in W.Smee's 1850 trade catalogue are portrayed with neat little candle shades.

During the Regency period, some grand libraries were furnished with large reading desks, having space for very tall volumes beneath a slope top. One such massive, three-bay book-table with elaborately scrolled candle-arms was commissioned for Woburn, possibly to the design of Henry Holland about 1800.

102 Music stand
*c.*1805–10
By Sebastian Erard, London

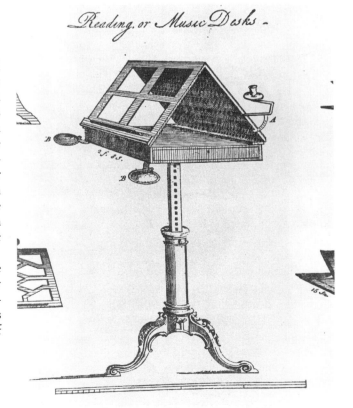

Fig.69. Ince & Mayhew, Universal System of Household Furniture, 1762

102

Satin maple, brass
H 44in (112)
The stand has a pair of adjustable brass candle-arms and
hinged folding legs; the double-sided top made to rise
with a stem and rack. A circular brass tablet on the top rail
is engraved 'ERARDS LONDON' and several members
are impressed '39' and '41'

Lent Anonymously

*Fig.70. Reading desk, mahogany with candle-boards, mid 18th
century (H 29 in, lowered)*

Library Reading Chairs

A familiar kind of reading chair, having a leather-covered
'saddle' seat and a semi-circular yoke back with padded
arm-rests which the user straddled facing towards a sliding
book-rest, became popular in gentlemen's libraries about
1720. Early examples are often fitted with a pair of small,
shallow, box-trays that swing out from under the arm-
rests, with divisions for writing accessories and all have an
adjustable desk or book-rest. Many were originally fitted
with a candle-branch at the end of each arm (Cat.103). This
novel chair continued to be made with minor variations,
until Regency days. Some mid 18th century specimens had
broad, flat wooden arm-rests with candlestick depressions
and slides beneath for pots of ink and pounce — there is
one of this pattern at Houghton Hall, Norfolk.

Sheraton's *Cabinet Dictionary*, 1803, gives a detailed
specification and devotes a plate to chairs of this type.
Ackermann's *Repository* featured designs for two library

reading chairs in September 1810, one (on the right), of
traditional form with desk, pen-draw and two candle-arms,
was said to be: 'now in great sale at the warerooms of
the inventors Messrs Morgan and Saunders, Catherine
Street, Strand' (Fig.71). A closely similar example has

PLATE 19 – LIBRARY READING CHAIRS

Fig.71. Ackermann, Repository of Arts, 1810

been recorded stamped 'W PRIEST TUDOR STREET BLACKFRIARS', a cabinet-maker who established a 'Furniture Warehouse' at this address specialising in 'Office and Library Furniture'. The second Ackermann chair was equally 'convenient and comfortable' being of rectangular mahogany framed, bergere design, the caned back and seat accommodating buttoned, square-stuffed leather cushions. The left-hand arm supports an adjustable slope, that on the right a candle-stick on an articulated swivel arm.

An advertisement issued in about 1815 by William Pocock of 26 Southampton Street for 'Improvements in Furniture & various Inventions for Invalids' illustrates an 'elegant and modern' version of Merlin's Reclining Wheel Chair equipped with a combined reading desk and candelabrum. A later number of the *Repository* (March 1813) shows Pococks' Reclining Patent Chair 'designed with classical taste in the present improved fashion of modern furniture'; it has a reading desk supporting a Greek oil lamp. Lit. G Bernard Hughes, 'The Georgian Horseman's Chair', *Country Life*, 26 March 1959.

103 Library reading chair
*c.*1730
Mahogany, upholstered in leather
H 32in (83) W 20in (53)
The stuffed-over saddle seat houses a drawer in the front rail and the solid upholstered back supports an adjustable book-rest; the padded yoke incorporating pen and ink trays that swing out, to which brass candle arms are attached — the arm on the left is a replacement.
PROV. Lanhydrock House, Cornwall

Lent by the Trustees of the Cecil Higgins Art Gallery (Temple Newsam only)

103

Card Tables

Small tables with folding tops were made for card games such as whist, loo, quadrille and faro. Some examples, dating from the late-Stuart period, have two circular dished candle-boards that swing out from slots in the frieze

(R.W.Symonds, *English Furniture from Charles II to George II*, 1929, fig.80). The tops of early-Georgian card tables, when opened for play, were generally covered with green baize or needlework, had wells for counters and circular recessed

104

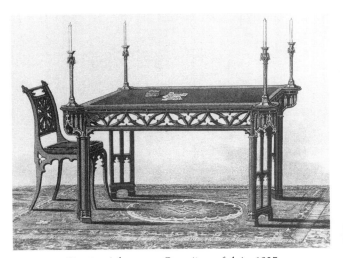

Fig.72. Ackermann, Repository of Arts, 1827

corners for candlesticks (Cat.104). towards the middle of the century many tables having square lugged corners were produced, but this design feature is seldom found on tables of the neo-Classical period. Isaac Cruickshank's caricature print *A Card Party*, published in 1794, shows a game in progress with lighted candlesticks placed at the corners of the table and a plate in Ackermann's *Repository* (July 1827) portrays a Gothic whist table with four columnar candlesticks set on lobed projections 'at the angles ... which otherwise would be in the way of the players' (Fig.72).
Lit. B.Hewitt, *The Work of Many Hands: Card Tables in Federal America 1790–1820*, Yale University Art Gallery, 1982.

104 Card table
*c.*1720
Laburnum; walnut legs
H 29in (74) W 34in (86)
Rectangular folding top with circular corners dished for candlesticks and oval counter wells

An earlier generation of round-topped card tables were fitted with either circular candle boards or slides that pulled out from slots in the frieze. There are examples of both patterns at Beningbrough Hall, Yorkshire

Leeds City Art Galleries (Temple Newsam)

Drawing Tables and Writing Desks

During the second quarter of the 18th century a type of table specially designed for gentlemen's libraries first became popular. Ince & Mayhew represented two in their *Universal System of Household Furniture*, 1762, pl. xxiv, the essential features being an adjustable hinged top usually supported on a double-rising horse and ratchet and an elaborately partitioned desk drawer that pulled forward on divided front legs. Surviving later models and versions published by Sheraton were generally simpler, but the

evident delight in ingenious contrivances was often expressed, towards the end of the century, by the inclusion of facilities for lighting. This might amount to no more than providing a plain slide or circular swivel candle-board at either one or both ends flanking the slope (Fig.73); some tables were equipped with a single tall brass standard fitted with an adjustable candle-socket on a short arm (Fig.74). Tables of this type were termed Writing and Reading tables by Ince & Mayhew; Sheraton called them Drawing

Fig.73. *Drawing table, mahogany with brass swivel candle brackets, c.1740*

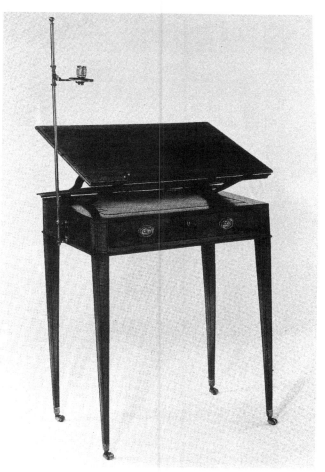

Fig.74. *Drawing table, mahogany with a sliding candle sconce on a brass pole, late 18th century (W 25in)*

Fig.75. *Lady's writing table, mahogany with candle slides, late 18th century*

Fig.77. *Bonheur-du-jour, mahogany crossbanded in satinwood with original candlearms, c.1800*

Fig.76. *Sheraton, Drawing Book, 1793*

105

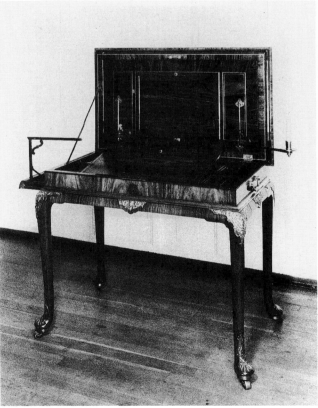

tables; they are also known today as Artists' or Architects' tables.

Various forms of writing desk and work table are related to the previous group. One of the earliest and most interesting is of rosewood with rich brass mounts and inlaid strings. The hinged top lifts to reveal a writing-slope, considered essential for good penmanship, and an interior fitted with many compartments. Two brass rods fixed to the underside of the lid have adjustable candle-arm attachments which makes this a remarkably progressive piece of furniture (Cat.105). Sheraton's *Drawing Book* illustrates several 'neat and rather elegant' Lady's Writing Tables, fitted with candle-branches, similar to the example reproduced in Fig.75. Several desks corresponding to the design on pl.xxxvii have been recorded, but most lack the candle-arms which, when pressed down, operate a spring mechanism that releases the side-boxes — an ink-drawer on the

right, a pen-tray on the left (Fig.76). The bonheur-du-jour of *c*.1800 is exceptional because its original brass candle-holders survive (Fig.77).

105 Architect's table

c.1735
Rosewood with brass mounts
H 30in (67) W 34in (78)
The top is hinged to form a slope and folds back to reveal an elaborately fitted interior with another small writing slope and a pair of adjustable brass candle-arms; two frieze drawers at the sides contain snuffers, nozzles and additional brass candle brackets
PROV. Ince Blundell Hall, Cheshire

Lent by the National Museums on Merseyside

Sideboards

Thomas Sheraton's, *The Cabinet-Maker and Upholsterer's Drawing Book*, 1793, was the first furniture pattern book to include designs for sideboards fitted with brass posts and

rails supporting candle-branches. His note to the sideboard shown on plate 26 explains that it 'has a brass rod to it, which is used to set large dishes against, and to support a couple of candle or lamp branches in the middle which, when lighted, give a very brilliant effect to the silverware ...the branches of each of them are fixed in one socket which

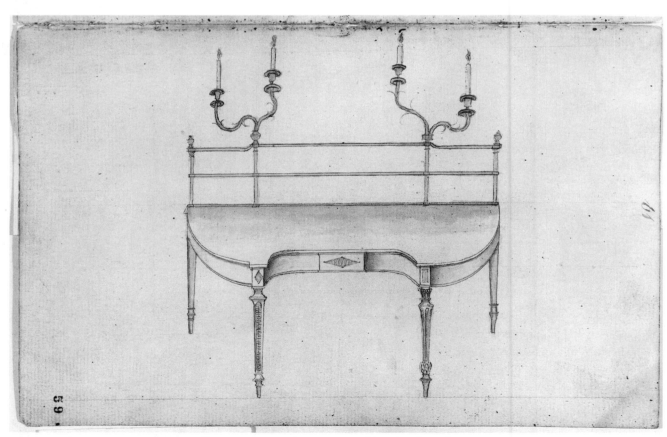

Fig.78. Gillows of Lancaster, drawing for a sideboard with candle-arms, c.1795

slides up and down on the same rod to any height and fixed anywhere by turning a screw'. Many sideboards have today lost this handsome decorative feature, its former presence being betrayed by screw or bolt holes.

A coloured sketch book amongst the Gillow records at Westminster City Libraries (735/1, p.58v and 59v & r) contain three drawings for sideboards with brass rails and candle-arms (Fig.78). Sometimes branches were attached to the corner posts (Cat.106). R.Ackermann's acquatint published in 1816 of the headmaster's room at Charter House shows a modern sideboard with scrolled brass candelabra (Fig.79). When, towards the middle of the 19th century, there was a fashion for chiffonier sideboards with towering rear structures often incorporating plates of looking-glass, several firms, such as W.Smee & Sons, published designs with candle-arms projecting from the mirror frames.

106

106 Sideboard

c.1810
Mahogany
H 59in (150) W 92in (234)
Of break-front pedestal design with four frieze drawers, two cupboards and a cubby-hole for a pot on the right hand side; decorated with reeding and ebony strings. The back supports, brass rails and posts carrying, at each end, twin candle sconces on swivel arms adjustable for height by means of a pressure spring.

Lent by Scunthorpe Museum and Art Gallery (Normanby Hall)

Dressing and Toilet Glasses

Full-length dressing-glasses, either suspended by centre screws between columns or made to be raised and lowered by means of lead weights enclosed in the uprights, in the manner of a sash window, became popular during the late 18th century. Thomas Sheraton included a design in his *Drawing Book*, 1792, for a 'Horse Dressing Glass' with brass rods fixed to the pillars, each supporting a sliding candle-arm which can be fixed at any height by turning a screw. This form of lighting attachment continued to be popular with Regency designers, although few so-called cheval dressing-glasses now retain their original brass candle-holders (Cat.107).

107

The *Cabinet-Makers' London Book of Prices*, 1793, featured a design and specification for what the compilers termed 'A Screen Dressing-Glass Frame'; the optional extras included 'Candle boards, each 6d' — presumably a simple bracket attached to the uprights, which served as a cheap alternative to adjustable brass arms.

Small dressing-table or toilet glasses as they later came to be known, usually hung between standards set on a platform base, were occasionally provided with articulated brass candle-arms (Cat.108). All recorded examples are Victorian in date. Smee & Sons published a design for one in 1850 while C.& R.Light's trade catalogue of 1881 shows examples with candle-brackets (No.1592) and arms (No.1593). Candlesticks would normally have been placed on the dressing-table itself alongside a toilet glass.

107 Cheval dressing-glass
1847
By Constantine & Co, Leeds
Mahogany
H 54in (137) W 29in (74)
The upright swing glass is suspended between reeded standards raised on splayed feet; adjustable cast brass candle-arms decorated with Indian masks and acanthus
PROV. Broughton Hall, Yorkshire

Invoiced to Sir Charles Tempest of Broughton Hall, Yorkshire on 27 July 1847: 'Large Handsome Spanish Mahogany Cheval Glass Frame with best British Silvered plate Brass Sconces and French polished all Complete £13 17s'

Lent by Roger and Henry Tempest

108 Toilet glass
Mid-19th century
Mahogany
H 24in (61) W 20in (51)
The platform base supports a swing mirror suspended between broad standards, each with an articulated brass candle-arm (sockets and pans replaced)

Leeds City Art Galleries (Temple Newsam)

Picture Lights

Although a few 18th century English picture frames are known with metal rods for curtains to protect them from daylight, none have yet been recorded which retain candle-arms to illuminate the painting at night. One of Robert Adam's drawings at the Sir John Soane's Museum, inscribed 'Picture frame for General Borgoyne — 1771' is shown with a pair of double branches mid-way up each side holding lighted candles and William Hogarth portrayed, in *The Lady's Last Stake*, a picture hanging over a chimney-piece with twin candle-branches emerging from the lower corners (Albright-Knox Art Gallery, Buffalo). Two manuscript designs of circa 1750 by John Linnell and Peter Glazier both show Rococo overmantels incorporating paintings (the latter set above a chimney-glass) each sprouting double scroll arms and nozzles (Cat.109). The chimney-breast was clearly a favoured position on the rare occasions when candles were employed to illuminate pictures. Combined with firelight, they created a focal point in the room. William Farington's letter of 18 February 1756 to his sister describing the opening of Norfolk House, St James's Square, refers to '... the Gerandoles, fix'd in the Frames of the Pictures, wch had an odd effect, & I can't think will be so good for the Paint'

(D.Fitz-Gerald, *The Norfolk House Music Room*, HMSO, 1973, p.48).

A sadly faded mid-Victorian sepia photograph shows the dining room at Methley Hall, Yorkshire, hung with very large portraits. Projecting from the wall, alongside each frame, is a short brass stanchion supporting a paraffin lamp with a reflector angled to shed a pool of light on the canvas (Cat.110). An interesting earlier arrangement is recorded in a view of the headmaster's room at Charter House, London, published by R.Ackermann in 1816 (Fig.79). It shows a panelled interior hung with pairs of full-length portraits, between each is a wall bracket on which stands a tall vestal figure holding a lamp. The room also contains a sideboard with brass rails and posts supporting two candle-arms; the sockets are empty because it was customary only to place lit candles in them. When gas and electricity arrived in country houses, picture lights started to multiply (Cat.111).

109 Design for a chimneypiece and overmantel
*c.*1750
By Peter Glazier
Pencil, pen and ink and wash
7½in x 5¼in (12 x 13.4)

This signed drawing (for a title page) shows a Rococo chimney piece and picture frame with scrolling candle-arms;

109

110

contemporary sources suggest that at this date carved overmantels quite often featured sconces.

A metal-work pattern book at the V&A contains seven plates illustrating similar Rococo sconces (N. Goodison, 'Metal-Work Pattern Books', *Furniture History*, XI (1975) pl.10).

Leeds City Art Galleries (Temple Newsam)

110 Illustration of a picture light
19th century, probably third quarter
Photograph
9in x 11in (23 x 28)

This late-Victorian photograph of the dining room at Methley Hall, Yorkshire (demolished 1956) shows three large paintings, each lit by a single paraffin lamp with glass chimney and reflector shade supported on elbowed arms set in the wall adjacent to the frame

Leeds City Art Galleries (Temple Newsam)

111 Electric picture light
*c.*1900
By Perry & Co, London
Bronzed brass, tin, mirror-plate and silk cord
L 44in (112)

111

The tubular serpentine arm bound with red cord has a metal claw at one end designed to hook over the picture rail; the other supports an adjustable tin 'bat's wing' shade lined with mirror glass and incorporating a side bulb socket; the outside of the shade originally covered with crimson, silk and braid
PROV. Fyvie Castle, Scotland, perhaps originally from Hartwell House, Buckinghamshire.

An oval tablet on another example from this set is lettered 'PERRY & CO 17 Grafton Street'. In 1900 this old-established firm of chandelier makers was trading as Electric Light Fitters. An illustration of the Great Hall at Knole published by H.Avray Tipping, *English Homes*, III, vol.1, 1929, p.237 shows identical picture lights in situ.

Lent by the National Trust for Scotland

Fig.79. Ackermann, 'The Headmaster's Room at Charter House', 1816, showing a sideboard with brass rails and candlearms (extreme left) and vestal figures holding lamps (right)

Miscellaneous Furniture

It remains to mention briefly a probably far from exhaustive anthology of furniture having 'conveniences for candles'. Many 18th century bureau cabinets were made with a pair of candle-slides inserted below mirror fronted double-doors. However, two walnut bureau cabinets of circa 1705, both bearing the trade label of John Gatehouse, London, (Cat.112) combine veneered door panels with slides which shows that they were not invariably associated with looking-glass plates. A bureau bookcase of *c.* 1800 (R.Edwards, *The Shorter Dictionary of English Furniture*, 1964, p.88, fig.56) has the unusual arrangement of a pair of candlesticks fixed to the writing bed and enclosed within the fall-front, while several of the well-known 'Week's' secretaire cabinets are headed by campana-shaped brass finials designed to hold candles (there is one in the Temple Newsam collection).

Just as music stands frequently sported candle-arms, so pianos were often made with slides to support candlesticks. Typically, a pianoforte-harpsichord signed and dated Joseph Merlin, 1780, has, above the keyboard, a frame with two forward-sliding panels designed to match the music rest (*Merlin* (Exh. Cat.), Kenwood, 1985, p.99) while a Broadwood cabinet upright grand pianoforte of 1830 is provided with quarter-round candle-slides which pull out at each end of the nameboard (Cat.113). Brass candle-nozzles designed to clip onto the edge of piano frames were also made (Cat.114).

French mantel clocks with candle-holders were not uncommon and several 'Stands for Table Clocks' published by Thomas Johnson in 1758 were designed with rather wild Rococo candle-branches but no English clocks with candle-arms were traced whilst researching this exhibition.

Many 18th century furniture pattern books contained designs for brackets, mostly 'calculated for Clocks, Busts, etc'. However, Ince & Mayhew recommended that 8 carved openwork examples (represented in their *Universal System* 1762, pl.lxxvi) as suitable for candles, while Hepplewhite's *Guide* 1794, pl.90 gives three carved and gilt wall brackets 'particularly applicable to place lights on. Some of very large dimensions (6 or 7 feet high) have been made in this manner, for placing patent lamps on in the large Subscription Room at Newmarket'. During the Regency period colza lamps were frequently placed on mural brackets: an interesting set still with their lamps survives in the Sculpture Gallery at Newby Hall, Yorkshire (Fig.80).

A trawl of published designs, cabinet-makers' bills, country house inventories and illustrated books on

furniture yields a varied haul of pieces incorporating candle-branches or lampstands. These range from a lady's elegant flax spinning-wheel, having a taper-stick, to shaving and work-tables with candle-slides; at Hutton-on-the-Forest, Cumbria, there is a little Victorian revolving bookcase with a turned wooden candle holder; Ackermann's *Repository* (July 1822) illustrates a combination flower and lampstand, while in April 1800 Thomas Chippendale the Younger charged Lady Heathcote for '2 very neat Bookcases...with 2 light branches to each and cut glass pans'. The evidence for lighting beds is ambiguous: Peter Thornton believes that some grand 17th century standing beds may have had an illumination device suspended beneath the tester, certainly many wainscot four-posters have a shelf at the bedhead which, from scorch marks, evidently held candlesticks.

112

Fig.80. Bracket for colza lamp in the sculpture gallery at Newby Hall, Yorkshire

112 Bureau cabinet
*c.*1705
By John Gatehouse, London
Walnut
H 79in (201)
Designed with a pair of candle-slides below the double doors and above the desk section
PROV. Herriard Park, Hampshire

It was common for the doors of cabinets to be faced with looking glass to reflect the candle flame, but the veneered surfaces of this cabinet are certainly original. Another labelled Gatehouse bureau also combines candle-slides and veneered doors.

Leeds City Art Galleries (Temple Newsam)

113 Cabinet upright pianoforte
*c.*1830
By John Broadwood & Sons, London
Rosewood case with brass inlay
H 74in (188) W 65in (114)
Designed with quarter-round candle-slides at each end of the name-board; when the cover is open these can be used

for candlesticks to illuminate the music
PROV. Temple Newsam, ordered by Lady Hertford for
her Chinese Drawing Room

Leeds City Art Galleries (Temple Newsam)

114 Piano clip-sconce
Early 19th century
Brass
H 5in (13)
In the form of a candle nozzle made to fit on the case of a
square piano or harpsichord near the music rest

Lent Anonymously

Sculpture and Domestic Lighting: the Golden Age

The 1559 inventory of the plate of Queen Elizabeth I lists a silver candlestick in the form of an ape with the candle holder in its hand and English-made silver candelabra with human figure stems survive from the late seventeenth century onwards. By that time the Italian fashion for figured candlestands had also reached Britain: a pair which survives at Ham House, Surrey, was recorded there in 1679. From this point only a small evolutionary step was required to combine a light holder such as a candlestick with a sculpted figure on the scale of the candlestand.

The main staircase of the Upper Belvedere in Vienna, which dates from the early 1720s, is lit by five metal lanterns, around the bases of four of which putti are clustered, apparently straining to hold them aloft. It was, no doubt, under the influence of a Continental example such as this that the architect George Dance the Elder decided to incorporate figured lights into the Mansion House in London, the interior of which he designed in the 1750s. The researches of Sally Jeffery have revealed that in 1752–53 Thomas Ady, a sculptor of some consequence with several important church monuments to his credit, supplied ten figures of Atlas, with appropriate supports, for the principal staircase. Two of them were mounted on tapering pedestals (Fig.81) and are thought to have been intended to flank the foot of the stairs on the principal floor; the other eight stood on fanciful S-shaped Rococo brackets and would have been set on the newel posts of the stairs which led up to the second floor (Fig.82). It is not clear what they were made of, but presumably it was wood or plaster; certainly the total price of £48 would have been too low for marble. All were painted a 'plain Colour' and held globes of glass, which Ady also supplied, to serve as candle shades. They have long since disappeared.

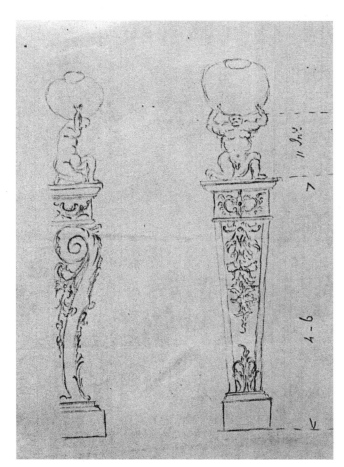

Fig.81. *Design for a lamp for the Great Staircase of the Mansion House, London, 1752*

Fig.82. *Design for a lamp for the Great Staircase of the Mansion House, 1752*

In general the role of the sculptor in connection with lighting was better developed in France than in Britain. At the Paris Salon of 1773, marble figures of *Abundance* were shown by Augustin Pajou and Félix Lecomte, both belonging to a set of four candelabra for the dining room of Madame du Barry's residence at Louveciennes, near Paris. Versions of the whole quartet had been hastily produced in plaster so as to be ready for a reception which was given at the house in September 1771. Three of them appear in a drawing of the occasion by Moreau le Jeune which reveals that the light was provided by naked candles nestling in bunches of fruit and flowers which were probably made of metal and were set within the cornucopias held by the figures.

The du Barry candelabra were certainly influential in France and it is surely more than coincidence that in the year after Pajou and Lecomte's figures were exhibited in Paris 'a statue and pedestal for a candalabrum' were put on show at the Society of Artists in London. In Britain, demand for such figures was stimulated by the prevailing enthusiasm for classical statuary. During the second half of the eighteenth century grand reception rooms in private houses were often furnished with reproductions of famous Antique figures and, with a little artistic licence, light holding versions of them could easily be produced. Nicholas Penny has plausibly suggested that this form of adaptation derived from the contemporary fashion for viewing classical statues, or casts taken from them, by candlelight or torchlight when, by the flickering gleam of a flame, the heroes and heroines of the ancient world seemed to come alive. If the figures were given their own sources of light this temporary effect could become a permanent spectacle. Reproductions of the Capitoline and Farnese Flora, adapted to hold pendant lamps, were sold from Penpont House, Brecon, in 1991 (Fig.83). Though undated, they seem to belong to the period when large figured lights were just coming into fashion but no distinctive iconography had yet been developed for them.

Whereas Madame du Barry's sculptors used plaster merely as a temporary expedient, the British resorted to it permanently because it was cheap, easy to use and, as at Penpont, it could be painted to give a convincing imitation of bronze. If a stone effect was desired that, too, could be very convincingly achieved by the use of ceramic. The exhibitor at the Society of Artists in 1774 was a manufacturer, Eleanor Coade, whose artificial stone factory at Lambeth, south London, produced light fittings which could be commissioned individually or ordered from stock. Coade Stone is indistinguishable from Portland to an untrained eye, and far more durable. It is also a great deal more attractive than plaster and required no surface disguise to make it acceptable in an upper class interior though, in fact, it was sometimes bronzed. Mrs. Coade clearly saw the commercial possibilities of figured lights and commissioned artists to make models for a great variety of them, from which products of superb quality were derived. It was she who could truly be said to have inaugurated a golden age of British sculpture in the service

Fig.83. *Bronzed plaster figures of the Capitoline Flora (left) and the Farnese Flora with pendant lamps, late 18th century, from Penpont House*

of illumination, which lasted well into the nineteenth century.

Mrs. Coade had a close business relationship with the sculptor John Bacon the Elder (1740–99) whom she employed as a designer and modeller and who superintended her factory for several years in the 1770s. 'A Statue of Urania...with a glass globe on her head, adapted for a lamp' was credited to Bacon in the handbook to the firm's new showroom, *Coade's Gallery*, published in 1799; the *Coade Etchings*, a set of illustrations of the factory's products issued *c*.1777–78, show an elegant figure in classical costume which appears to be the same object (Fig. 84). This page of the *Etchings* also shows a pair of candlesticks held by figures of Psyche and Hymen. These, too, are by Bacon (Cat.117) and are described in *Coade's Gallery* as 'elegant little statues....to be placed on chimneypieces' though *Hymen* is, in fact, illustrated on a bracket, another Coade product.

Coade stone was used often by architects, and occasionally for architect-designed furniture which thereby acquired a strong sculptural character. At West Wycombe Park in Buckinghamshire there is a set of four pedestals, each with three caryatid figures, which appear to be larger versions of 'an elegant Tripod or Pedestal for three lights' designed by James Wyatt for the Queen's Lodge at

Fig.84.   Coade Etchings, c.1777–8 showing (bottom left) John Bacon's figure of Urania, (top) Bacon's Psyche and Hymen candlesticks and (bottom right) a figure of a Vestal Virgin

Frogmore, Windsor. This was exhibited in Mrs. Coade's gallery and a model similar to the examples at West Wycombe is shown in the *Etchings* (Fig.85). Others have appeared recently on the art market; a further example was at Chicksands Priory, Bedfordshire and is now in a private collection. A variant pair, having caryatids with raised arms, was formerly at Godmersham Park, Kent, whence it was sold in 1983.

Wyatt also took a pioneering interest in the use of statues as light holders. A design by him for one end of the hall at Slane Castle, Co.Meath, dated 1775, shows a central door flanked by a pair of lamp-bearing figures on classical pedestals placed in niches. An inscription reveals that the figures were to be of artificial stone and the lamps of crystal while the pedestals were to serve as stoves. Whether this scheme was executed is uncertain but a lesser-known architect, Robert Mitchell, did make very prominent use of Coade statuary for lighting at Preston Hall, near Edinburgh (1791–92), where a maiden stands on each side of the staircase gallery. An identical arrangement existed at Silwood Park, Berkshire, another house by Mitchell (c.1796–97) which has since been rebuilt (Fig.86).

The Coade firm was willing to supply its wares in plaster, though customers were advised in *Coade's Gallery* not to choose it, ostensibly because the ceramic stone was far less likely to be 'injured and defaced', but probably also because Mrs. Coade faced very stiff commercial competition from the numerous specialist makers of plaster figures which flourished in London. These enterprises were run by sculptors, some of whom also used the more prestigious materials of marble and bronze and had considerable artistic pretensions, soliciting major commissions and exhibiting their work at the Royal Academy. Peter Chenu (b.1760) evidently decided that sculpture for lights would help him make his name. In 1789 he showed at the Academy 'a vestal for a candelabrum'; this was followed in 1794 by two figures, each 'to hold a chandelier or lamp' and in 1796 by 'a vestal designed to hold a lamp'. His speciality brought him the patronage of the Prince of Wales who in 1799 paid a total of £158 15s 4d for a variety of sculpture for The Grange at Northington, Hampshire, on which he had taken a lease. The list included a candelabra figure 'near 6ft high for the ground staircase from an approved drawing', 'four boys 4ft high holding lamps in imitation of

Fig.85. *Coade Etchings, pedestal with caryatid figures*

Fig.86. *The staircase gallery at Silwood Park, Berkshire, c.1796–7, with lampholding figures in Coade Stone, from Robert Mitchell, Plans, etc. of Buildings erected in England and Scotland..., 1801*

Fig.87. *Bill from Robert Shout to Lord Monson 1 July 1805*

bronze, made on purpose for the gallery' and two vase lamps with two burners each and shades, japanned and richly ornamented. Chenu may also have been employed to make the nine lamp-bearing term figures which lit the gallery of the Grand Staircase at the Prince's London residence, Carlton House. They were designed by the architect of the building, Henry Holland.

None of Chenu's sculpture for lighting has so far been traced. From 1798 onwards we are better informed about the work of artists in this field because of the Act of Parliament promoted by George Garrard R.A. This measure secured for a period of fourteen years the copyright of any original model or copy or cast taken from it, the right being vested in the artist or patron responsible for it, on condition that he or she 'shall cause his or her Name to be put thereon, with the Date of the Publication,

before the same shall be published and exposed to Sale'. Signatures proliferated and it becomes possible to make more connections between names recorded in documents and surviving artefacts.

Robert Shout advertised his 'Manufactory & Spacious Shew-Rooms' at 18, High Holborn, London, by a statue of Minerva over the door which also appeared on his elaborate billhead (Fig.87). The heading informed 'the Nobility & Gentry that he ha[d] ready for Inspection & Sale....a large Assortment of Figures & Tripods for holding Lamps or Candles, of various Patterns & Dimensions, fitted up in a new & fashionable Style'. Besides all this, the stock included 'several Hundreds of Figures, Busts, Vases, Medallions, etc....made to imitate real Bronze, Terra-Cota, Stone &c.' and 'Derbyshire Spar Vases & Ornaments'. Shout worked in partnership with his father Benjamin as a maker of busts and church monuments and their names appear together in street directories for the first decade of the nineteenth century. It seems that the lighting part of the business had always been Robert's domain since his name alone appears on light fittings, and also on billheads from the period 1805–06. Like Chenu, Robert Shout attracted high class patronage. In July 1805 Lord Monson paid him for 'One Pair bronz'd Vestals [with] 2 light patent fountain Lamps' and in the following year 'two bronz'd Figures of Bacchus', apparently also fitted with patent lamps, were mentioned in a bill addressed to the same person which seems to have been for goods supplied to his mother (Lincolnshire Archives Office, MON 11/55). 1806 also saw the Duke of Atholl buy a 'bronz'd 2ft. Figure of Peace, on a Marble Plinth supporting a foure light gilt Branch' and a 'pair of bronz'd Greyhounds [with] 2 light gilt Branches'. Robert continued in this line of manufacture at least up to 1818, the date on a pair of signed female figures holding three-branch candelabra at Spencer House, London. By 1823/24, however, his place at the London address had been taken by his son Charles. His date of death is unknown.

The most prolific of Shout's rivals was Humphrey Hopper (1767–1834). Like Shout, he worked in marble as well as plaster and made church monuments; in fact, he seems already to have been active in both fields by the time he entered the Royal Academy as a student in 1801. In 1808 Hopper exhibited at the Academy a figure of 'Mercury, intended to support a lamp'. He was perhaps more at ease with male subjects than female ones for there are four statues of Bacchus by him at Lancaster House, London, which are exceptionally accomplished (Fig.88). Three of them are signed 1813 and the fourth 1818. They stand in niches at either end of the oval vestibule on the ground floor of the building and two of them appear to be indicated in that position in a sectional drawing of the house which dates from c. 1843 (Museum of London). They hold urn-shaped reservoirs which must once have belonged to colza lamps and they are mounted on radiators shaped like pedestals, an interesting echo of Wyatt's Slane Castle scheme, though the heating apparatus may only date from the 1840s.

A Bacchus in the dining room at Farnley Hall, North Yorkshire, is almost identical. It is one of four plaster statues in the house designed to hold lights: the others are its companion, a Sibyl, and a pair of maidens which are now in the saloon. One of the maidens is a virtual copy of a Coade figure of a Vestal Virgin illustrated in the *Etchings* (Fig.84); the other is signed by Hopper and dated 1806. All four figures can clearly be attributed to him.

Hopper was associated with the Giannelli family of sculptors who moved from Italy to England via Copenhagen (*Journal of the History of Collections*, vol.4, no.1 (1992), pp.55, 58). Giovanni Domenico (1775–?1841) is

Fig.88. Lampholding figure of Bacchus by Humphrey Hopper, 1813, Lancaster House, London

known to have produced light fittings during the period 1805–09. The family seems to have specialised in modelled materials and Giovanni worked in terracotta as well as plaster: a Bacchus and female companion, probably Ariadne, in ebonised terracotta with gilt metal two-light branches, appeared at Sotheby's, New York, in 1990 (26 October, lot 264). The female figure is signed and dated 1807.

The versatile Francis Hardenberg (fl. 1783–1832) began his career in the Midlands as a modeller in porcelain factories but by 1800 he had established himself in London under the name 'Hardenberg and Co., Petrification Manufacturers' with premises at Mount Street, near Grosvenor Square. In the same year he invoiced the Marquess of Exeter at Burghley House for goods to the value of £136 11s 6d (Burghley House Collection 51/41/8). Most of the items were lights: 'A Vestal with Lamp and Pedestal', possibly one of the lampholding figures in the chapel (Cat.118), 'Four Graecian Lamps festoond With Chains', two 'Duble Cupit[s] with Three Light Graecian Lamp[s]' and a further pair of 'three Light Graecian Lamp[s]'. The entrance hall at Heaton Hall, Manchester, contains four female lampholding figures two of which represent Comedy and Tragedy and the others Vestal Virgins, one signed and dated 1805. Hardenberg's subsequent activities included dealing in foreign china and, in partnership with Federico Nicoli, carving marble busts and monuments. He is no longer listed at the Mount Street address in 1835 and nothing is known of him thereafter.

Shout's billhead specifically mentions halls and staircases as suitable places for his lamp-bearing figures and tripods. Very few of the large figured lights which he and his contemporaries supplied have survived in the locations for which they were originally intended but it is clear that in country houses they were confined to the grand public spaces. The Bacchus in the dining room at Farnley Hall appears in its present position in a watercolour by J.M.W.Turner painted c.1818; the ten figures at Burghley House have lit the chapel at least since 1815 and were almost certainly ordered for that purpose. It would be interesting to know how far the choice of a particular figure was determined by the function of the room for which it was acquired. Bacchus would obviously have been suited to a dining room but he would also have fitted the welcoming function of an entrance hall, as at Lancaster House. Vestal Virgins, such as those in the Burghley chapel, represent the servants of the cult of Vesta who tended the eternal flame at her temple in ancient Rome. This made them highly suitable as bearers of illumination but scarcely appropriate to a place of Christian worship unless they were also supposed to be seen as the Ten Wise and Foolish Virgins of the New Testament parable.

The other main factors which influenced the iconography of these light-holders were the forms and function of the lights themselves, the supporting role of the figures and stylistic considerations. John Bacon's *Urania* who appears in the *Coade Etchings* was the classical Muse of Astronomy and the globe which contained the light on her head was one of her standard attributes. The figure of *Peace* which Robert Shout supplied to the Duke of Atholl harks back to a tradition in Renaissance and Baroque art in which she is seen with a flaming torch setting fire to a pile of weapons. The statues of Atlas on the Mansion House staircase would have been easily recognisable as representations of the Titan of Greek mythology who was condemned to bear the heavens on his head and hands. Likewise, the tradition of using terms as load-bearing elements in architectural decoration made them readily adaptable as pedestals for lights, as at Carlton House and Temple Newsam (see Cat.5).

Once it had taken hold, the fashion for figured lights came to be associated with the taste for chinoiserie and the Egyptian Revival as well as the more prevalent neo-Classical style. On 25 August 1807 Giovanni Domenico Giannelli published two pairs of statues of a Chinese man and woman, about two-thirds life size, each holding a handkerchief in one hand and a light in the other (Christie's, London, 11 November 1971, lot 105; Christie's Wateringbury Place, 31 May 1978, lot 204). One pair has nodding heads, following a chinoiserie fashion of the time. Neither seems to have been intended to represent any particular person or symbolic figure; more likely they were conceived purely as decorative objects for rooms fitted out

in a compatible style. The kind of effect they would have produced can be seen in Thomas Sheraton's engravings of the Chinese Room at Carlton House, published in 1793, which show three pairs of figured table candelabra matching the décor.

The Egyptian Revival, which gained a new impetus after Napoleon's campaigns of 1798–1801, appears at its most extravagant in Gaetano Landi's *Architectural Decorations*, a pattern book published in London in 1810. One of the plates shows a chimneypiece with a male and a female figure standing on the mantleshelf, each holding two-branch candelabra (Fig.89). Whether anyone had the audacity to put this idea into practice is not clear but the style was adopted by Giannelli for a priestess figure, dated 1805, which was on the London art market c.1967 and seems to have been designed to hold a hanging lamp, or pair of lamps (repr. *Victoria and Albert Museum Bulletin*, vol.4, no.1, January 1968, p.15, fig.8). A pair of winged figures in the dining room at Corsham Court, Wiltshire, now wired for electricity, are believed to represent Nut, the mother of Osiris. They are signed and dated 1803 by 'L Gahagan', possibly the Lucius Gahagan who had been paid three years previously for making the wax model from which a silver table centrepiece at Castle Howard was cast, to a design by C.H.Tatham.

The contemporary Gothic taste seems to have been eschewed by the plaster workshops as a style for figured

Fig.89. Design for a chimneypiece in the Egyptian taste, from Gaetano Landi, Architectural Decorations, 1810

lights, though it was on occasions adopted by the Coade factory. In 1810 Coade and Sealy (as the firm was known by this time) supplied a set of ten candelabra for Thomas Hopper's Gothic conservatory at Carlton House, together with models for the lamps which were cast in brass, each one having six burners. The style complemented the architecture of the room and the candelabra were conceived largely in architectural terms, as columns with bases and capitals, the middle of each shaft being articulated by blind arcading with lancets. The capitals were decorated with monkeys in relief, the lancets were adorned with heads of kings, bishops and other men, and pygmy craftsmen entwined with dragons clustered around the tops of the bases. In 1817 the art patron and collector Sir George Beaumont bought from William Croggon, the manager of the Coade factory, a pair of 'rich Gothic candlesticks' by John de Vaere (1755–1830), a Flemish-born sculptor who had spent most of his career in England and had worked for Wedgwood.

William Beckford showed his reverence for the social customs of the Middle Ages when he recreated the custom of employing human torch-bearers at banquets, in the setting of his fantastic Gothick residence, Fonthill Abbey in Wiltshire. *The Gentleman's Magazine* reported that when Lord Nelson and Lady Hamilton were entertained there in 1801 'the staircase was lighted by certain mysterious living figures at different intervals, dressed in hooded gowns, and standing with large wax-torches in their hands'.

As well as grand projects, sculptors undertook smaller commissions such as John Bacon's *Psyche* and *Hymen* candlesticks mentioned above, and Shout's figure of *Peace* for the Duke of Atholl. The Vestal Virgins which Shout sold to Lord Monson cannot have been very large as they were evidently intended as wall lights, to be supported on bronzed brackets which the artist also supplied. His Bacchus figures, which seem to have been destined for the Dowager Lady Monson, only cost five guineas and this likewise suggests a diminutive scale. Both Hopper and Giannelli made pairs of ladies reclining on couches, derived in miniature from Antonio Canova's marble portrait of *Princess Pauline Borghese as Venus Victrix* (Galleria Borghese,

Fig.90. Antique marble figure of a chimera in low relief, from C.H.Tatham, Etchings... of Ancient Ornamental Architecture..., 1799–1800

Fig.91. Candlestick signed B.VULLIAMY & SON.... 1809. One of a pair

Rome). They serve as candlesticks or candelabra and were almost certainly meant to stand on chimneypieces. In 1794 Chenu exhibited two figures for chandeliers at the Royal Academy and a gilt plaster group of a man and a woman with a putto flying overhead formed the central feature of a giltwood chandelier sold by Sotheby's in 1983 (London, 8 April, lot 121). One artist, James Deville (1776–1846), seems to have made all his sculpture for lighting on a very modest scale. His work in this vein is well exemplified by a two-light candelabrum with figures of Bacchus and Venus, dated 1803, in the Victoria and Albert Museum (W.12–1947). He is also known to have designed the plaster bases for a pair of oil lamps (Cat.65), and perhaps the lamps themselves.

Small figured candlesticks and candelabra competed in the marketplace with similar articles in pottery, porcelain, bronze and silver, some of which were made from models by distinguished artists. One of them was Bacon; another was John Flaxman the Younger who did this type of work for Wedgwood and the goldsmiths Rundell, Bridge and Rundell. Design work and model-making for manufacturers had a low status for sculptors, who generally preferred to be known as the authors of marble portrait busts and monuments or, better still, of ideal works of sculpture which were all the more prestigious because they served no practical purpose. Those who were employed by factories

were not always keen to advertise the fact, nor did their employers necessarily give them credit where it was due. Mrs Coade exhibited models by Bacon under her own name; only in the year of his death, when *Coade's Gallery* was published, did she acknowledge that they were in fact his. The result is that much anonymous creative work lies hidden behind engraved or stamped labels which may be those of manufacturers or retailers rather than designers or modellers. Even when the original author of an object can be identified it is difficult to use this knowledge as a basis for attributions since plagiarism was rife; it seems to have been quite easy to circumvent the 1798 copyright act by introducing small changes in detail. A pair of four-light table candelabra in the Royal Collection have stems in the form of three addorsed semi-nude female figures who are represented shielding their eyes from the light (*Carlton House*, Queen's Gallery, Buckingham Palace 1991–2, no.151). They are signed and dated 1811 by Benjamin

Fig.93. Engraving by Marcantonio Raimondi of a perfume burner designed by Raphael

Fig.92. Colza oil lamp, bronze, c.1835

Lewis Vulliamy but research has revealed that the figures were modelled five years earlier by an assistant of Flaxman's, James Smith (1775–1815), whose chief claim to fame is the cenotaph to Lord Nelson in the City of London Guildhall. Vulliamy's name also appears on two magnificent pairs of candlesticks copied, with varying degrees of fidelity, from a picture of an Antique marble chimera in C.H.Tatham's *Etchings... of Ancient Ornamental Architecture...*, 1799–1800 (Fig.90). One bears the same date as the Smith/Vulliamy candelabra; the other, shown here, is dated 1809 (Fig.91). Both may be partly Smith's work.

The publication of G.B.Piranesi's *Vasi, Candelabri, Cippi, Sarcofagi...* in 1778 revealed to an international readership the ingenuity which the ancient Romans had displayed in the design of small oil lamps. Several of the plates include still-life compositions of these objects which took an amazing variety of sculptural forms : a duck, a foot, a cow's head, a blackamoor head, even a chariot drawn by two bulls with a winged charioteer. A wealth of classical adaptations followed. The firm of Thomas Messenger and Sons, which had premises in Birmingham and London, produced colza-burning table lamps with reservoirs and cisterns based on a Roman funeral monument illustrated in the *Vasi...* (Cat.121). One double-burner colza light combines a reservoir in the form of an Antique vase with a pedestal incorporating a group of the Three Graces: the latter derives from an engraving of a perfume burner designed by Raphael and ultimately from ancient statuary (Figs 92 and 93).

New personalities continued to emerge. William Bullock advertised himself in the Liverpool press of 1801 as a 'Silversmith, Jeweller, Toyman and Statue Figure Manufacturer'. Four years later, in the late spring or early summer of 1805, he opened a 'New Egyptian Hall' at his 'Museum and Bronze Figure Manufactory' in Church Street, offering for sale 'a great variety of Bronze, Egyptian and Grecian Figures, Vases, Brackets, Tripods, Branches, Candleabra, Antique Lamps, &c. for supporting Lights'. This new venture provided an occasion for him to publish, on 1 July, a Black Basaltes vase, an example of which is now in the British Museum. On the strength of the design and decorative details several items of bronze lighting equipment can be securely attributed to him, including the candelabra in this exhibition (Cat.119).

Bullock had a rival in his younger brother George, now better known as a cabinet maker, who was then trading from the same street in Liverpool with a partner named William Stoakes. In May 1805 the firm invoiced Stephen Tempest of Broughton Hall, near Skipton, for a pair of 'Bronz'd French figures', each fitted with a lamp, and a three-branch candelabrum with a pair of putti (Broughton Hall, Tempest papers XV/36). Attempts to identify these items with objects now at Broughton have so far proved unconvincing. It would be interesting to know if the 'French figures' were genuine foreign articles or simply in a French style. The latter seems more likely as the word 'bronzed' suggests the characteristically English

material of plaster rather than real metal. Supported in this way, the lamps would have been in keeping with the only comparable objects by Bullock which have so far been recognised, a pair of candlesticks held aloft by female figures in gilt plaster which are signed and dated 1804 (Birmingham Museum and Art Gallery, inv. no. 1986 M70 1&2).

In London the process of adapting ancient source material to the new technology was carried forward by James Smethurst. In 1802 he registered a patent (no.2654) for 'certain improvements applicable to lamps and reflectors', giving his address as St. Margaret's Hill, Southwark, but he later moved to New Bond Street. A two-light colza lamp bearing his name was sold by Christie's in 1990 (South Kensington, 3 October, lot 172). It has a pedestal with a pair of cranes supporting a circular socle, a combination of features derived from a candelabrum which Piranesi had composed from Antique fragments found at Hadrian's Villa at Tivoli and had published in the *Vasi...* (Fig.94). The birds recur on lamps at Chatsworth which may be by the same manufacturer (Cat.120).

We do not know who did Smethurst's design work. Both Flaxman and Sir Francis Chantrey are said to have worked for Messenger's but proof is lacking. There are also major gaps in our knowledge about some of the manufacturers and retailers. Who, for example, ran the richly-stocked emporium at 446 The Strand, London, in the early nineteenth century? A mutilated copy of its advertisement

Fig.94. Candelabrum assembled by G.B.Piranesi, 1769–75, from the Vasi..., 1778

survives lacking the proprietor's name on the heading. A long list of articles is given beginning with 'bronze statues and figures' available in various sizes ranging from nine inches to six feet and representing historical, mythological and allegorical subjects, including 'Roman Vestals'. The whole range was 'principally mounted with Patent Lamps on the new principle or Gilt Branches for Candles, and rich cut Glass Lusters, adapted for every purpose, both Ornamented and useful' (Lincolnshire Archives Office, Monson 11/26/49). A Richard Clark, sometimes trading under the name of Richard Clark and Co., is listed as a lamp maker and wax chandler with premises at 447 The Strand in directories from 1844 to 1854: he or his predecessor in the business might be the person in question.

The production of cheap British-made metalwork hastened the decline of the plaster workshops. They had already suffered a loss of business at the end of the Napoleonic Wars when trade with the Continent revived and the demand for imitation bronze shrank as the genuine article became available once more. A trade card produced by Messenger's *c.*1835 (Fig.95) hints at the change which had taken place by that date. 'Lamps of every description in bronze and or-molu' were offered for sale and one held by a standing maiden appears on the far right of the engraving, exactly the kind of object which Hopper, Shout, Hardenberg or Giannelli had been producing twenty years earlier. However, the fashion for the statue rather than the figurine as a lightholder was on the wane by

Fig.95. Trade card of Thomas Messenger and Sons, c.1835

this time. The advent of gas lighting must have played some part in the decline for it would have been difficult to introduce the necessary piping into a plaster cast which was not designed to take it. Furthermore, most of the sculptors who had used the material were simply not there any more to confront the challenge of incorporating the new technology into their work. Adaptation did take place with the term figures in the Great Hall at Temple Newsam but they are of wood and holes for the pipes were bored in them with a hot iron (Cat.5).

For those willing to invest in new statuary for their gaslights the way forward had been shown in Rudolph Ackermann's *Repository of Arts* for 1813: his premises in The Strand were entirely lit by this method and the library was provided with a figure of a young woman, gas lamp in hand, standing above the fireplace (Fig.46). Over half a century later, in 1864, the third Duke of Buckingham and Chandos built a gas works in the grounds of Stowe House, his palatial country seat. The arrival of this new source of power gave him an opportunity partly to refurnish the Marble Saloon which had been denuded of its statuary in the 1848 sale occasioned by the bankruptcy of his father. Marble figures of Bacchus, Ariadne, Diana and Actaeon(?) were commissioned from Tito Angelini, a sculptor working in Naples who was already known to the Duke. They suffered the indignity of being pierced for gas piping and were installed in the middle niches of the quadrants of the oval room, each one fitted with a ground glass shade (Huntingdon Library, California, Stowe Mss., STG Accounts, Box 163; *The Stowe Miscellany*, May 1973, pp.8–9). In 1922 the figures were sold; lacking their light fittings, they are now at Cottesbrooke Hall, Northamptonshire.

As the nineteenth century progressed and more and more people made use of new lighting technology, the candle acquired a romantic appeal for its aesthetic qualities and historic associations. The Drawing Room of Balmoral Castle was equipped with six pairs of four-light candelabra supplied by Herbert Minton and Co. in 1854 (Fig.96); each takes the form of a gilt metal hunting trophy, incorporating a stag's head, to which bugle-shaped candle arms are attached, the whole being supported on a lance held by a figure of a Highlander with a dog seated by his side. The Parian Ware figures (and perhaps the metalwork) were designed by Sir Edwin Landseer who was a sculptor as well as a painter. The easy naturalism of the ceramic groups is typical of its time but the general design has an anachronistic character which befits the archaic technology and derives directly from the classical figures which lit Georgian and Regency interiors.

Conservatism slowed the pace of change in some country houses; in others owners were willing to introduce new methods of lighting but not to throw away the more attractive parts of the old equipment. Lamps were converted, sometimes more than once. At Burton Constable two pairs of torcheres were ingeniously turned into paraffin lights by matching the decorative forms of the new metal to those of the old wood (Cat.122).

Fig.96. Candelabrum, 1854, Balmoral Castle, Aberdeenshire

115 Triton candlestick

c.1773
Wedgwood factory
Black Basaltes
H 11in (27.9)
Marks: WEDGWOOD (impressed twice) and double scroll

A nude figure of a Triton kneeling on a rock and clasping a candleholder in the form of a whorled shell. Plants are growing on the rock and seaweed rises between the Triton's legs.

LIT. Wolf Mankowitz, *Wedgwood* (1953), pp.109–10, 256, pls 54, 75; Timothy Clifford, ''Mr. Stuart's Tripod' and a Candelabrum', *The Burlington Magazine*, vol.114 (1972), p.874; Nicholas Goodison, *Ormolu: the work of Matthew Boulton* (1974), pp.53, 58, 102–03; review by Timothy Clifford of Nicholas Goodison's *Ormolu* (cited above), *The Burlington Magazine*, vol.116 (1974), p.764; *ibid.*, 'John Bacon and the Manufacturers', *Apollo*, vol.122 (1985), pp.294, 298, 304, appendix II, no.8; Robin Reilly,

Wedgwood (1989), vol.1, pp.463, 637–9, colour plate 174, vol.2, pp.380, 754–55.

Candlesticks of this type normally occur in mirror-imaged pairs. The candle nozzle, which was set into the mouth of the shell, is missing.

The 1773 Wedgwood catalogue lists Triton figures in this size and it appears from a letter written by Josiah Wedgwood on 19 November 1769 that the factory was supplied with a carved model of one of them, probably in wood. The catalogue also states that the Tritons were 'from Michael Angelo'; however, the design was taken from a seventeenth century Roman bronze of which there is an example in the Art Institute of Chicago. Wedgwood's own example was lent to him by the architect William Chambers and was later in the Torlonia Collection, Rome. Some difficulty was experienced in making a second model as a pair to the first. According to Mankowitz both the models used in production were executed by John Flaxman the Younger. On 4 June 1770 Wedgwood wrote to his partner Thomas Bentley about the possibility of making a companion piece to the large version of these candlesticks (see below), suggesting that the sculptor John Bacon the Elder be employed to model the design in clay and suggesting that 'they wo.[d] with metal branches make a most superb p.[r] of Candelabrias'. A design for just such an object, with twin branches for candles, appears in Matthew Boulton and John Fothergill's Pattern Book no.1, p.19, and their sale of 1771 included a 'tryton in dark bronz, holding branches for two candles in or moulu, on a bassment of the same neatly ornamented'.

Wedgwood also produced Triton candlesticks in blue and white Jasper, in 'straw' colour and in bronzed Basaltes, with variations in design. A larger version of one of the figures was recorded in the 1773 catalogue. New models went into production in 1863 with multicoloured glazes, and Triton candlesticks were also made at the Derby factory. A sketch for the Wedgwood figures is in the firm's London Pattern Book at the Wedgwood Museum, Barlaston (p.102; repr. Goodison, *op.cit.*, pl.12). A pair of clay master models used by the factory also survives (Wedgwood Museum; repr. Clifford/Bacon, pl.11).

Leeds City Art Galleries (Temple Newsam)

116 'Michelangelo' lamp
*c.*1780–85
Wedgwood factory
Black Basaltes
H 14in (35.5)
Mark WEDGWOOD impressed
A vase-shaped reservoir with a gadrooned lid, supported in the centre by a column and by three figures of slaves on a triangular pedestal with concave sides. Three spouts protrude from shallow dishes above the upper rim of the reservoir whose cover has a finial in the form of a palm trunk around which are seated figures of Sibyls.
LIT Jennifer Montagu, 'A Renaissance work copied by Wedgwood', *Journal of the Warburg and Courtauld Institutes*, vol.17 (1954), pp.380–81; Nicholas Goodison, 'Mr. Stuart's Tripod', *The Burlington Magazine*, vol.114 (1972), pp.695–704; Nicholas Goodison, *Ormolu: the work of Matthew Boulton* (1974), pp.58, 108–9, 161–3; Robin Reilly, *Wedgwood*, (1991), vol.1, p.472, nos 678, 679, 679A, colour plate 184.

This vase form has traditionally been known as the Michelangelo lamp but the bowl was copied from a Hellenistic bronze lamp dating to about 400 BC while the slave figures supporting the lamp were adapted from a silver-gilt crucifix by Antonio Gentile da Faenza presented to St. Peter's, Rome in 1582. It is possible that Gentile copied models by Michelangelo. Of the four figures on the crucifix only three were used by Wedgwood; two of these were illustrated by William Chambers in his *Treatise on Civil Architecture*, 1759, under the heading 'Persians and Caryatides' where he describes them as being 'copied from candelabres'.

Prior to the production of the lamp, the bowl form had appeared on a number of ormolu tripod perfume burners the design of which can firmly be attributed to the architect James Stuart. Wedgwood may have acquired a model directly from Stuart or via a common source, and he used it on many of his tripods.

The same figure supports were used by Matthew Boulton for his ormolu 'Geographical' clock case, completed in 1772, and on his 'Persian' candle vase, one of a pair supplied to Sir Lawrence Dundas in the same year.

11

Boulton's models were obtained as casts from John Flaxman the Elder to whom he paid 2 guineas for a 'group of Hercules and Atlas' on 5 December 1770. Josiah Wedgwood may have used the same source.

The Wedgwood lamp is illustrated as Shape no.180 in the *Vase Shape Drawing Book*. It is listed as 13 inches high, made in Black Basaltes or Jasper at 8 guineas. Several versions of this lamp form are known, including a pair in Black Basaltes at Saltram, where John Parker, 1st Lord Boringdon, paid 14 guineas to 'Wedgewood [sic] for Black Staffordshire Ware' on 27 March 1772.

Lent by the Trustees of the Wedgwood Museum

117 Pair of candlesticks: Psyche and Hymen
1795
Modelled by John Bacon the Elder for the Coade factory
Coade Stone, bronzed
H 18½in (47)
Impressed *COADE* Lambeth on *Hymen*, COADE LONDON 1795 on *Psyche*
Both candlesticks are held by figures in classical costume mounted on shaped rectangular bases.
LIT. *A Descriptive Catalogue of Coade's Artificial Stone Manufactory.......with Prices Affixed* (London, 1784), p.4, nos 46 & 47; *Coade's Gallery or Exhibition in Artificial Stone* (London, 1799), p.33, nos 101, 102; *The Fashionable Fireplace*, Temple Newsam House, Leeds 1985, no.73;

17

Timothy Clifford, 'John Bacon and the Manufacturers', *Apollo*, vol.122 (1985), pp.293, 303; Alison Kelly, 'Coade Stone Interiors', *The Antique Collector*, July 1986, p.52; ibid., *Mrs Coade's Stone* (Upton-upon-Severn, 1990), pp.186–87, 360.

In 1777 Eleanor Coade exhibited under her own name 'Hymen and Psyche; two Figures for Candelabrums' at the Society of Artists (No.183). The *Descriptive Catalogue* of 1784 lists the figures in two versions, a plain one, priced at four guineas per object, and another 'fitted with Spring Tubes for lights', at five guineas. In *Coade's Gallery* of 1799 similar candlesticks were described as 'from models...by the late Mr BACON for Mr LOCKE, to be placed on chimney-pieces.' William Locke was a well-known connoisseur who lived at Norbury Park, Surrey. A pair is illustrated in the *Coade Etchings* (Fig.84) but Hymen is shown holding a candlestick in the form of a torch, rather than one with a straight-sided shaft, as here.

Psyche and Hymen are separately connected with lighting in ancient mythology. In the story told by Apuleius in *The Golden Ass*, Psyche is forbidden to look at Cupid but cannot resist holding a lamp over him to do so. He is woken by a drop of hot oil which falls from the vessel, causing her to search the world for him. Hymen is the Greek and Roman god of marriage, usually represented carrying a torch (*cf*. the *Coade Etchings*).

The figure of Hymen seems to have been inspired by an Antique lamp illustrated in Piranesi's *Vasi...* Some of the

plates in this book were circulated individually prior to its publication in 1778. For further discussion, see p. 132.

Lent by Manchester City Art Galleries (Heaton Hall)

118

An identical pair of statues, from Stratfield Saye, has been attributed to Humphrey Hopper (*Connoisseur*, vol.154 (1963), no. 622, back cover). For the iconography of the figures, see p. 136.

Lent from the Burghley House Collection

119 Pair of candelabra
*c.*1805
Attributed to the workshop of William Bullock
Bronze, partly gilt
H 14in (35.6)
The stem takes the form of a Grecian figure with crossed arms, owl finial and scrolled candle branches with grape and vine decoration. The tripod base has concave sides and lobed flanges, each side with an applied gilt mask, supported on anthemion scrolls and claw feet.
LIT. Timothy Clifford, 'William Bullock — fine fellow', *Christie's International Magazine*, July 1991, pp.14–15

The attribution is founded on a Black Basaltes urn, signed and dated 1805, now in the British Museum, which has a very similar base. Other apparently identical bases and similar stems have been noted on colza lamps, candlesticks, candelabra, a clock and a table centrepiece, some with a known country house provenance (Rossie Priory and Elveden Hall).

It appears that Bullock had a range of components which he assembled in various combinations to create objects of varying type and character. Some of these components he may have commissioned or designed himself; others may simply have been bought in. The somewhat incoherent appearance of these candelabra may be explained by such a process.

Lent by Mr. and Mrs. Timothy Clifford

118 Lampholding statue of a Vestal Virgin
1800(?)
Attributed to Francis Hardenberg (*fl.*1783–1832)
Bronzed plaster, metal, glass
H 82in (208)
A figure of a young woman in Roman costume holding a lamp with an urn-shaped reservoir. The pedestal takes the form of a Roman altar, with rams' heads, festoons, ribbons and rosettes.
LIT. Anon., *A Guide to Burghley House, Northamptonshire, the Seat of the Marquis of Exeter...* (Stamford, 1815), pp.30–31; Dorothy Stroud, *Capability Brown* (London, 1975), p.76; Alison Kelly, *Mrs Coade's Stone*, (Upton-upon-Severn, 1990), pp.97, 105 n.21, 127, 131, 142 n.3, 365.
PROV. Burghley House, Stamford

One of a set of ten identical lampholding statues from the chapel at Burghley House, first recorded in that room in the 1815 guidebook. Formerly thought to be of artificial stone and supplied by the Coade factory, the set is now associated with an invoice submitted by Hardenberg on 6 November 1800 (see p. 135). The first item is 'A Vestal with Lamp and Pedestal', charged at 8 guineas; this may have been one which was ordered as a trial before the full set was acquired. The glass lampshades and mounts are later in date. The lamps originally burned oil: the earliest known picture of the chapel, an engraving of the christening of Lady Victoria Cecil in 1844, shows several of the statues with straight glass chimneys. They have since been wired for electricity.

119

20

120 Lamps (two from a set of four)
c.1835
Ormolu and cut glass
H 26in (66)
Each lamp has an urn-shaped reservoir on a cylindrical pedestal to which are attached two angled branches, ornamented with acanthus leaves, and ending in argand burners. The whole is supported by three addorsed cranes standing on a circular plinth.
LIT. Gere, pp.214–15
PROV. Probably Devonshire House, London; Chatsworth House, Derbyshire

Objects of identical design are shown in a watercolour of the Saloon of Devonshire House, London, painted by William Henry Hunt in 1822 (Devonshire Collection, Chatsworth). The house was demolished in 1924–5 when these lamps were probably removed to Chatsworth. For further discussion see p. 139.

Lent by the Trustees of the Chatsworth Settlement

121 Pair of lamps
1838
Thomas Messenger and Sons, Birmingham
Ormolu and opaque glass
H 16½in (42)
Each engraved on the top of the reservoir with a ducal coronet over the letter N and stamped in six places with the numerals 1 (one lamp) and 3 (the other).

The lamps are in the form of an Antique rhyton with a boar's head spout and an integral handle, resting on a rectangular base with four feet. The detachable reservoir incorporates the regulating lever and is ornamented with egg and dart and fluting.The shades are of acid-etched glass with wheel-cut Greek key ornament.
LIT. *The Fashionable Fireplace*, Temple Newsam House, Leeds, 1985, no. 76; Lomax (1986); *ibid.*, 'The Continuing Thread', *The Antique Dealer and Collector's Guide*, March 1988, p.63.
PROV. The 4th Duke of Newcastle, probably at Clumber Park, Notts; John Tillotson, The Albany, London; sold by his executors at Christie's, London, 29 November 1984, lot 91, where acquired.

In August 1838 the Duke of Newcastle visited Birmingham and in the following month he bought from Messengers three pairs of lamps of which this is presumed to be one (Newcastle Archives, Nottingham University, Ne C 7299). The design of the rhyton is derived from G.B.Piranesi's illustration of the sepulchral monument to Augustus Urbanus on the Appian Way in Rome, published in his *Vasi, Candelabri, Cippi, Sarcofagi.....* of 1778. The plate was dedicated to the Duke's uncle, Henry, Earl of Lincoln, so the Duke himself almost certainly knew of it and he may have suggested that it be used. The stamped numerals indicate that this pair was part of a set or factory batch comprising at least four lamps.

Numerous other lamps of very similar design are known: some, like these, are gilt but most are in plain bronze. A pair stamped with the name of Messenger is now in Birmingham Museum and Art Gallery; others have

121

appeared in recent sales, including a pair with the label of Bright & Co. of Bruton Street, who may in this case have acted as retailers. An interesting variant of the design with dolphin's head rhytons appeared at Phillips, London, on 16 June 1992 (lot 157).

The shades are not original to the lamps but may be contemporary.

Leeds City Art Galleries (Temple Newsam)

122 Torchere and paraffin lamp (one of a pair)
19th century
Torchere probably Italian
Torchere of gilt pine, partly burnished; lamp cast brass with opal glass flambeau
H 68in (172.7)
Circular plinth supporting figure of ?an American Indian whose head supports a circular tray edged with fruit originally intended to hold a candelabrum. Converted into a paraffin lamp by the addition of cast metal fruit and leaves concealing the cylindrical paraffin reservoir. The burner has a pierced gallery which once supported the chimney and shade. Later converted to electricity.
PROV. Burton Constable

The torchere may have been acquired by Clifford Constable on his Grand Tour in Italy during the second decade of the 19th century. The conversion into a paraffin lamp may have been part of the refurnishing work done by Richardson's of Hull in 1869–71. A similar, larger, pair of torcheres, with paraffin lamps added, survives on the first landing of the staircase, at the entrance to the King's Suite.

Lent by Leeds City Art Galleries and the Burton Constable Foundation

12

Acknowledgements

Colin Anson, Patrick Aubrey-Fletcher, David Beevers, Gaye Blake-Roberts, Roy Boardman, James Broadbent, Paul Brompton, George Clarke, Matthew Clinton-Williams, Nicola Colby, Annette Cook, Jonathan Cook, Belinda Cousens, Jon Culverhouse, John Davis, Peter Day, Roger Dodsworth, Gregory Eades, Giles Ellwood, Kate Fielden, Micheal Finlay, Geoffrey Fisher, Jim Fox, the Earl and Countess of St Germans, Lucy Glaister, Philippa Glanville, Halina Graham, Tessa Gudgeon, Robin Harcourt-Williams, Christopher Hartley, the late Gerald Heath, Keith Holt, Susan Hopkinson, Nicholas Horton-Fawkes, Hotspur Ltd., Lord Martin Fitzalan Howard, Ralph Hoyle, Sally Jeffery, Susan Jenkins, Simon Jervis, Keeper of the Records of Scotland, Alison Kelly, Cherry Knott, George Lane-Fox, Myra Lawson, David Learmont, Allan McKay, Mrs Maxwell Scott, Phyllida Melling, Sarah Medlam, Mitzi Mina, Tessa Murdoch, Patricia Paleologina, Nicholas Penny, Jerome Phillips, Victoria Pommery, Charles Pugh, Eddie Richards, Hugh Roberts, Tom Robinson, Alan Rubin, Tony Sale, Elizabeth Sprenger, Nigel Sturt, George Thompson, Michael Turner and the Department of the Environment, Clive Wainwright, Beth Carver Wees, Lavinia Wellicome, Roger Whitworth, Alan Wilson, Lucy Wood, Elizabeth Wright.

Photographic acknowledgements Anon, Cats 17, 23; HC Baxter and Sons, Fig.77; Trustees of the Bedford Estate, Cats 18, 42, 43, 44, 67; Royal Pavilion, Art Gallery and Museum, Brighton, Figs 14–20, Cat.45; Burton Constable Foundation, Figs 35, 38, Cats 28, 56, 68, 69; Christie's, Figs 83, 91, 92, Cat.121; Timothy Clifford Esq, title page; Mr and Mrs Robin Compton, Figs 66, 80; English Heritage, Fig.88; the Earl of St Germans, Figs 2–4; Cats 76–80; East Sussex Record Office, Fig.21; Guildhall Library, Figs 84, 85; John Halsey and Victor Chinnery, Fig.64; David Hambly, Figs 2–4, Cats 76–80; Christopher Hutchinson, Cats 9, 11, 13, 36; Jeremy Ltd, Fig.67; Brotherton Library, University of Leeds, Fig.32; Lincolnshire Archives, Fig.87; Corporation of London Record Office, Figs 81, 82; Manchester Central Reference Library, back cover, Fig.46; Manchester City Art Gallery, Cats 16, 30, 36, 37, 117; Martin Mortimer, Figs 26–29; The National Monuments Record of Scotland, Fig.86; The National Trust, Fig.65; Oldham Art Gallery, Cat.10; Partridge Fine Art PLC, Figs 23, 30, 73; Phillips, London, Fig 68; Phillips of Hitchin, Fig.70; The Royal Collection, St. James's Palace © Her Majesty The Queen, Fig.96; the Museum of Science and Industry in Manchester, Fig.57, Cat.86; Ruth Macklin Smith, Fig.75; Trustees of Sir John Soane's Museum, Fig.89; Spinks, Cat.6; E Swonnell Ltd, Cat.46; Trustees of the Tate Gallery, front cover; Trustees of the Victoria and Albert Museum, Figs 1, 39, 40, 42, 43, 61, back of title page; Trustees of the Wedgwood Museum, Cat.116; Westminster City Library, Fig.78; Colonial Williamsburg, Figs 22, 62, 63.

Objects from Burton Constable have been lent by courtesy of the Trustees.